Contents

Note on spelling and dates

The reader will find various inconsistencies in the following text. Some of these are to do with spelling, which until the seventeenth century was often extremely variable, even in regard to proper names. This was very largely due to the fact that until the printing press imposed a degree of uniformity there was no method of spelling which did not admit of occasional variations, so that the same word can occasionally be spelt differently even within one document. The inevitable errors of careless scribes have also to be taken into account.

I myself have assumed the responsibility of deciding whether or not a pre-seventeenth century text was to be modernised or not, acting on the premise that, as this work is not primarily intended for the linguistically sophisticated, but for a more general class of reader, those extracts which present considerable difficulties of comprehension have been modernised, whilst others less intractable are left in the original. Some letters too have had to be pruned of the less tolerable orthographic and grammatical excesses of their writers.

Dating presents its problems too. During much of the seventeenth century two reckonings of the calendar were in use in Europe. Most countries had adopted the revised calendar of Gregory XIII (1562), but until the middle of the eighteenth century Britain, with not unusual eccentricity, adhered to the old Julian version. What was January 1st in Britain, therefore, was January 11th in Europe, and the new year here was taken to start on Lady Day, March 25th. It is therefore possible for two year dates to be given for the period between January 1st and March 25.

1. Introduction

Christianity provided the art of the western world with a stimulus of a far-reaching kind. It opened up new sources of imagery of a richness and complexity which neither the limited iconography of the classical world, nor the regionalised 'pagan' cults of the barbarians could emulate. The Old and New Testaments, and the imagery which they generated were not only visually stimulating, but because they were immediately recognisable by people of differing social and regional backgrounds joined together in a common faith (whatever its minor local variations) provided them with an expression of their hopes and fears which could never have been so universally satisfied by the restricted cults of classical mythology or tribal religions. Even more remarkable was the extent to which Christianity was able to absorb within its own theological structure many of the beliefs of the past. Jupiter merged from time to time with God the Father, and even in twentieth-century Italy, churches still bear over their portals the inscription *Deo Optimo Maximo* which used to adorn the temples of ancient Rome. In a local context too, the hunger for regional cult figures became blended with devotion to the saints, whose lives, in any case supplied a rich store of anecdotal imagery. Tribal heroes, primitive deities and similar charismatic figures were transformed into saints such as Christopher and George, whilst the goddesses who watched over streams, wells and fountains became virgin martyrs, presiding over healing waters.

But more important than the new wealth of iconography which Christianity provided was its underlying ideology which demanded from the faithful a far greater degree of religious conformity than had been known before. It was not only necessary to believe, but also to believe correctly. Partly this was achieved by the spoken word, by services and sermons, but more potently even, by the use of imagery in every conceivable medium. Statues and murals, ranging from the most unsophisticated to the most complex, proliferated in churches and public places with a profusion motivated by the combined desire to instruct and to proselytise. They stimulated religious fervour, and though, in theological theory, they were supposed to represent the stories or characters they portrayed, it is more than doubtful whether the mass of the faithful was fully aware of such doctrinal niceties, and miracle-performing statues, or even pictures, rapidly became part of the mythology of Christian Europe. Churches became more essential for corporate worship than the temples or shrines of pre-Christian religions, centres of community life, and, as recurring waves of invaders from the east or the north swept across Europe and into the British Isles, centres of comparative security as the round towers of the Celtic monasteries or the rugged churches of Northumbria so strikingly demonstrate. Tangible embodiments of belief, sources of local pride, symbols of community identity, they attracted the donations of the rich and the freely-given labours of the poor. The development from the fourth century onwards of a hierarchical structure of church government common to the whole of the west, and derived originally from the pattern of the Roman *imperium*, fostered the growth of cathedrals from which bishops ruled their dioceses, first as spiritual, and then as temporal overlords. By the eighth century it had become an accepted practice, as is shown at Durham and York, and later at Canterbury, that the more important ones should contain the relics of some local saint, which converted them into centres of pilgrimage, thus enormously enhancing their wealth by attracting the donations of kings and nobles, no less than the offerings of the poor. The mere fact that these great shrines were visited by the faithful in huge numbers, enlarged the visual experiences of those who visited them and stimulated the dissemination of architectural techniques and artistic styles. Village churches aped the splendours that their incumbent or parishioners had seen at some great cathedral pilgrimage centre.

If the beliefs of Christianity stimulated painting, sculpture and architecture, its liturgy provided a hitherto unrivalled impetus to what a later age would describe as the 'decorative arts'. A whole range of services of increasing elaboration varying from the eight or so a day which would be held in a cathedral or monastic church, to the two or three in a simple chapel, demanded a complex supply of vessels, garments and cult objects. Chalices for mass, ciboria for giving communion, monstrances for displaying the host, thuribles for incense, candlesticks and more elaborate forms of candelabra, processional crosses, sanctuary lamps, episcopal rings and croziers; the list is endless. And it was considered not only desirable, but even essential that these should be made in precious metals, adorned with precious stones and made in as elaborate and skilful a manner as could be obtained. Cathedrals and abbeys such as Canterbury, Westminster, Winchester or Gloucester were virtual Aladdin's caves of magnificent objects, some idea of the splendour of which can be derived from the inventories drawn up by the agents of Henry VIII after the passing of the Act of Supremacy in 1534. It should not however be forgotten that in small, poor parishes none of this splendour could be found, and the reports of episcopal visitations frequently complain about the use of wooden chalices and the like. These cult objects were themselves sacred; not to be touched by laymen. Christianity had introduced into western consciousness that cult of the precious object, which still lies at the foundation of our modern attitudes to works of art, explaining both the enormous sums paid for them, their preservation in museums and art galleries where we go virtually to worship them, and the exaggerated importance we attach to whether or not an artefact has actually been touched by the hand of its supposed creator.

In addition to liturgical vessels, there was a demand for vestments, which in their design and complexity of workmanship grew increasingly elaborate as time went by, stimulating the creation of textiles and embroidery of great beauty, the latter produced in England, and known as *opus Anglicanum* achieving an international reputation. In an abbey, a cathedral or a large church, there was a need for copes, chasubles, dalmatics, stoles, altar fronts and mitres, as well as more simple vestments such as surplices and albs. Although these vestments, as well as the liturgical vessels, were sacred objects, they fed the eyes of congregations with visions of splendour which sharpened their aesthetic sensibilities, and stimulated the wealthy to imitate them in a more personal and domestic environment. There was in fact a constant intercourse between the sacred and the profane. Kings and nobles gave coronets, rings, jewels and other personal valuables to be converted into religious objects. Merchants bequeathed their silk and velvet gowns to be made into chasubles or copes, their richly embroidered coverlets to be transformed into altar-frontals for a favourite church; women left their sheets for altar-cloths, and their necklaces to be inset into chalices. The medieval church was intended for the worship of God, but it was the creation of the community, whose aspirations it represented, and whose pride it enshrined. Religion was not so much an occasional activity, as a way of life.

Christianity was above all else the religion of the book, and the word of God took many different forms, their reproduction facilitated by the technical improvements which took place in the first centuries of the Christian era, when vellum took the place of papyrus, and the book with separate pages supplanted the scroll. The new format was ideal not only for transcribing the Bible and other religious texts, but even more so for providing the books of the liturgy; the missal which contained the words of the mass for every day in the year and the breviary (or its abbreviated version, the Book of Hours) which contained the prayers and psalms sung or recited at the Divine Office, which divided the day into matins, prime, terse, nones, vespers and compline. Here again the distinction between the sanctity of the significance of an object and the actual intrinsic sanctity of the object itself became confused. Vehicles of the word of God, books came to be venerated in themselves; after reading the gospel for instance, the deacon at mass brought the book to the celebrant who kissed it. Inevitably therefore, partly to enhance their splendour, partly to emphasise the significance of their content, books were produced wiith immense care and skill and adorned with pictures, either incorporated into, or supplementing the text. These manuscript books, comparatively easily transportable, became virtually pattern-books, for they were carried frequently from one abbey or cathedral to another, by missionaries and peripatetic monks. Ceolfrith, abbot of Wearmouth and Jarrow at the end of the seventh century, took books from his scriptorium to present to the Pope; the Bangor Antiphonary ended up in Milan, and Anglo-Saxon manuscripts are to be found in Basel, Würzburg, St Gall, Niederaltaich, and Maeseyck. Journeyings were often even more complex. Two manuscripts from the cathedral of Würzburg seem to have been written in Italy, brought to England, and then exported to Germany; one had missing pages replaced in Northumberland, and the other has the signature of an abbess associated with Worcester in the eighth century. What used to be thought of as the first signed English manuscript, an eleventh-century copy of St Jerome's commentary on the Book of Isaiah, has a picture of the artist Hugh Pictor. The book comes from Exeter Cathedral, but Hugh was a monk at Jumièges, in Normandy, and the monks of Exeter, as well as those of Durham, both of which had Norman bishops, bought books from Normandy. Lanfranc, archbishop of Canterbury bought a copy of Gratian's *Decretals* from his own abbey at Bec, and gave it to the monks of Canterbury, with the inscription that it should not be removed from there under pain of eternal damnation. (Significantly, it is now in Trinity College,

Cambridge, cf. Christopher de Hamel *A History of Illuminated Manuscripts*, Phaidon, 1986 p. 94).

Books were invaluable propagators of style, but as part of Christendom, Britain was far less insulated in the Middle Ages than we are apt to think. The early Anglo-Saxon kingdom of Northumbria, for instance, as early as the seventh century was flooded with both Mediterranean and Irish Celtic influences, often conditioned by trading patterns as well as by the need of the Romanising to impose their own form of Christianity on the native Celtic version. Benedict Biscop, according to Bede, brought builders and glaziers from Gaul to build the church of St Peter at Wearmouth in the seventh century, and at the same time Wilfrid was building at Hexham 'a church such as had never existed on this side of the Alps' with masons from Rome. When Aldhelm came back from Rome to Malmesbury at the beginning of the eighth century, he brought with him 'an altar of shining white marble', which seems to have been a relic of Graeco-Roman antiquity, and in the eleventh century that redoubtable warrior, bishop and politician Henry of Blois, the younger brother of King Stephen, imported into Winchester statues excavated in the Roman Campagna by the soldiers of Robert Guiscard, and sported on his person a cameo bearing the image of the Emperor Augustus. When, in 1104, the body of St Cuthbert, who had died in 687 was transferred to a new resting place in Durham Cathedral, it was discovered that he was wrapped in garments, subsequently shown to have come from Byzantium, with inscriptions in Kufic script, in a coffin showing signs of Syrian, Celtic and Merovingian influences, containing a pectoral cross made by Saxon craftsmen in Northumbria, and an ivory comb of Eastern Mediterranean workmanship. Nor was the traffic one-way. By the thirteenth century English embroidery of the type known as *Opus Anglicanum*, the decorative patterns of which were related to East Anglian manuscript illumination, was exported to France, Spain, Portugal, Germany, Switzerland and Italy. The Vatican inventories of 1295 recorded 100 references to such work, and the popes donated vestments of English manufacture to the cathedrals of Ascoli, Piceno and Pienza, where they may still be seen. At about the same time, Nottingham was becoming the centre of an international trade in the export of altar-pieces and statues, for both private and public use, made out of the local alabaster, examples turning up in Seville, Santiago de Compostela, Hólar in Iceland, Rome, and elsewhere. Indeed it has recently been estimated (cf. F. W. Cheetham, *Medieval English Alabaster Carvings in the Castle*

Museum, Nottingham, Nottingham 1962) that there are still no less than three thousand examples of this English work still surviving on the continent.

If Christianity provided an incentive to the production of works of art and craft, and an ideology which ensured their constant production and dissemination, all this might have been otiose, had it not been for one other major innovation. The priesthoods of earlier religions had been largely inchoate, inspirational rather than professional, attached loosely to shrines or temples, divided by language and cult. The Christian clergy were entirely different. Sharing in Latin a common language, owing obedience to a single head, the Pope, hierarchically organised, participating in a, more or less, unified liturgy, they were not so much a body of devotees, as an entirely new class in society. Largely exempt from the necessity of earning a living in the usual manner, free from those feudal duties which had become incumbent on the rest of the population, they might rather loosely be described as the first body of professional 'intellectuals' that the west had known. Usually educated above the level of their contemporaries, dedicated, in varying degrees to the study of learning as well as to the cultivation of virtue, their profession impelled them, by its very nature, to become both patrons and producers of the arts and crafts. It was their responsibility, their duty, to ensure the building of churches, cathedrals and abbeys; to stock them with those objects necessary not only for the conduct of services, but also for promoting the piety of the laity; to produce, commission or buy not only service books, but also others of a more general nature designed for their own education and that of their successors. And to achieve all this the faithful, prompted in varying degrees by fear of the hereafter, ostentation and simple piety, gave with astonishing generosity.

The catalysing role of the clergy in the promotion of art persisted throughout, and indeed in Catholic countries, beyond the Middle Ages, the period between about 650 and 1200 was dominated by the outstanding role of the monastic orders. Right from the beginning, in the period when the Celtic monks of Ireland and later Scotland and Northern England were producing those marvels of intricate calligraphy exemplified by the Book of Kells and the Lindisfarne Gospels, the creative output of these virtually tribal communities had been as remarkable for its extent as for the enthusiasm which engendered it. Some notion of the atmosphere in which these Celtic manuscripts were produced can be gleaned from the story of St Columba's 'Cathach', or 'The Fighting One', as the Old Irish word can be roughly translated. In the middle of the sixth century the monk Columba borrowed from the monk Finnian a manuscript, which he copied illegally, staying up at night to finish the job, during which time his fingers shone like candles, illuminating his whole cell. Finnian sent a messenger to reclaim the book, but his eyes were pecked out by Columba's pet crane. The two monks appealed to the local king, who gave a verdict in favour of Finnian, on the grounds 'to every cow her calf, and to every manuscript its copy'. Columba stirred up the unfortunate king's enemies against him, and they defeated him at the battle of Cul Drehme in 561. Presumably Columba kept both the book and its copy, but one of them was always carried into battle by its possessor, in a special shrine or *cumdach*. There are few more striking examples of the power of the written word.

But the rather erratic monasticism of the early Celtic and Middle-Eastern monks was supplanted by a more regulated version at the beginning of the sixth century when Benedict of Nursia created a system which was to dominate Europe. The Benedictines (later to be followed by variants such as those of the Cistercians and the Carthusians) were governed by a rule which imposed on them obligations of celibacy and obedience, and the duties of assiduous performance of the Divine Office, manual labour, the education of the young, and the copying and dissemination of manuscripts. These tightly organised communities became for most of the Middle Ages power houses of intellectual and creative activity. It was mostly the monks themselves who built their monasteries and churches, and the activities of ambitious abbots such as John and William at St Albans in the twelfth century were duplicated all over the country, and created that heritage of monastic architecture, which was not only a glory in itself, but an exemplar for secular and military architecture. By the thirteenth century, for instance, the monks at Canterbury had an elaborate and technically advanced domestic water supply and a waste-disposal system. The colleges, which by the next century were being built at Oxford and Cambridge, were modelled on monastic patterns, and continued to be so until the eighteenth century. Creative centres, linked by the monastic system with their counterparts throughout Christendom, the great abbeys stimulated the flow of artistic as well as intellectual ideas. The pointed arch was first introduced from Burgundy by the early Cistercians, whose reforming zeal inclined them originally to prefer an austere style, and when William of Sens was engaged to build the choir at

Canterbury, he adopted the style with which he was familiar in his home town, and the same style, with its monastic connotations, was adopted by all the builders of the great churches, notably at Lincoln and Wells. Not all new ideas came from abroad, and one of the glories of medieval architecture, the octagon tower at Ely, was the work of Alan of Walsingham, the sacristan, and is unique of its kind. Actual names such as his occur with surprising frequency. We know the names of the scribes who produced some of the earliest British manuscripts – Eadfrith, Wigbald, Cadmug, Mac Regol, and many others who signed their work. We know of Gundulf, bishop of Rochester, who himself is said to have been skilful and efficient in the skills of a *cementarius* or mason, of patrons such as Rannulf Flambard who was responsible for fine building work in each of the three churches – St Martin's Dover, Christ Church in Hampshire and Durham Cathedral, with which he was connected, of Geoffrey de Noiers, described as *fabricae constructor*, who was employed by St Hugh of Lincoln (who himself is said to have worked as a labourer carrying hods of stone and mortar in the rebuilding of the cathedral there in the late twelfth century). This example of episcopal craftsmanship was not unique. St Osmund, the Norman bishop of Salisbury not only encouraged the production of manuscripts for his cathedral, but wrote and bound some himself. St Dunstan had been a musician, illuminator, designer and bell-maker, and amongst the treasures of the abbey at Abingdon were various objects, including an organ and a precious retable of gold and silver attributed to Ethelwold, one of his disciples. A monk of Bury St Edmunds, with the unmonastic name of Spearhavoc was a skilled goldsmith, who made a crown for the Emperor Henry IV in 1053, and later became Abbot of Abingdon. Mannig, Abbot of Evesham who was also a scribe and musician, executed commissions for Canterbury and Coventry and carved the shrine of St Egwin in his own monastery.

Usually monasteries provided their own illuminators and scribes, who, according to a gloss in a late twelfth-century *Exodus*, produced about twelve pages of unadorned script a week. Between 1131 and 1147 Cirencester Abbey was especially active in producing manuscripts, most of which were transcribed by members of the community, including Adam, who later became prior, Deodatus, Jocelin, Simon of Cornwall, Walter, Alexander the Cantor, and Fluco, who also became prior, and who had no less than six books to his credit. But they also employed a professional scribe Ralph de Pulleham, possibly to give technical advice. By this time the professionalisation of artistic activity was becoming more wide-spread. Faricius, who was abbot of Abingdon during the first quarter of the century, engaged six *scriptores* to copy patristic texts, though the monks still reserved to themselves the task of producing liturgical books. Sometimes an assembly-line technique would be adopted, with a professional drawing the pictures, and a less skilful worker filling in the colours. These professionals, whose work can be detected in the productions of the Winchester School (cf. Sir Walter Oakeshot *The Artists of the Winchester Bible*, London 1945) were often peripatetic. A mid-twelfth century version of the Epistles of St Paul, with glosses, which originated in Winchester, migrated to Exeter, and is now in the Bodleian, was the work of a scribe who wrote and illuminated a chronicle at St Michel in Normandy, which is now at Avranches. The illuminator of the Lambeth Bible, which probably originated in Canterbury, seems to have originated from Canterbury *c.*1150 but it bears strong resemblances to a gospel book which was written at Liesses Abbey in Hainault in 1146. A professional scribe, who worked at St Albans in the 1170s also produced books for Worcester Cathedral, Bonport Abbey in Normandy and Troyes in eastern France. But the most remarkable example of the cosmopolitanism of medieval art, and the interrelationship of its different forms is the relationship, first pointed out by Oakeshott in his *Sigena, Romanesque Paintings in Spain, and the Winchester Bible* (London 1972), between the wall paintings in the chapter house of the monastery of Sigena in northern Spain, and the work of two of the illuminators of the Winchester Bible.

A change was taking place; art and its related activities were increasingly becoming secularised, and though monasteries continued for some considerable time to be nurseries of art, in that it was often from them that men emerged who who were to be patrons of art and architecture, by the end of the twelfth century they no longer held the dominant position which had been theirs in the preceding centuries. Society was becoming more secularised, and although the need to satisfy ecclesiastical needs persisted, and although the Christian ideology still dominated men's minds and aspirations, other factors were at work which were altering standards of taste and changing the nature of society. The state, in the person of the king was acquiring new powers, and a new significance, and to help establish this it was beginning to take over many of those opinion-forming devices inherent in the fine and applied arts. The activities in this area of a monarch such as Henry III were extensive. He had a deep and detailed interest in architecture and in the interior decoration of his residences. The kingship was still partly peripatetic, and the building of royal palaces – Henry possessed some thirteen – stimulated technical progress and provided objects of emulation for the nobility, whilst almost constant warfare promoted the growth of military architecture in response to the needs of containing the Welsh and the Scots, as well as defending the south coast against the French. Cathedrals and abbey churches were no longer the dominant forms of building, and increasing attention was given to the needs and the luxuries of ordinary living. It had been in castles that the chimney had first evolved, and its slow but constant extension to private dwellings was one of the many factors which were gradually enhancing the actual quality of life. In a smoke-free home more attention could be given to such things as wall-hangings and to creative activities of different sorts.

The growth of royal power had other effects. It produced a new type of patron in the creation of a bureaucracy which grew up to serve it, even though it was largely recruited from an ecclesiastical background. Becket, whose conflict with Henry II epitomised the changing order of things, was not able to reconcile his two roles as both God's servant and the king's, but there were many after him who could, and they played an important part in the development of art. Typical of these was William of Wykeham, bishop of Winchester, Keeper of the Privy Seal and Lord Chancellor, who died in 1404 at the age of eighty. Reputedly the son of a serf, and educated at Winchester, he entered the service of Edward III in the 1350s, and was engaged on a miscellany of jobs; keeping the king's dogs, and selling his horses at Windsor. Then he was appointed surveyor of the king's works at Windsor – a castle for which Edward had a special affection – where his duties consisted in liasing with the builders and craftsmen, engaging workmen, paying them, purchasing materials, and generally supervising the enlargement of the castle, to serve both as a royal residence and the headquarters of the newly formed Order of the Garter. It was his activities at Windsor which led directly to the royal favour, and prompted Wyclif's later gibe that the bench of bishops included 'a cleric wise in building castles'. In 1366, when he was appointed bishop of Winchester, William was archdeacon of Lincoln, the holder of eleven canonries and a rectory in Cornwall. These, and the emoluments, and no doubt bribes, which he derived from his offices of state made him a very wealthy man; the very epitome

of the new type of patron. Between 1380 and 1386
endowed 'Seinte Marie College of Wynchestr
(which was to become famous as New College),
colleges which the adolescent university poss
accommodation for seventy scholars and fellows
he stipulated had to be skilled in astronomy. I
1394 he built Winchester College intended to serve as a nursery for
his Oxford foundation. It was by far the largest institution of its
kind housing ninety-six scholars, choristers and commoners: its
status as a self-governing independent body was far superior to that
of any similar body, creating an architectural and educational pre-
cedent for Henry VI's foundations at Eton and Cambridge.

It was significant that when men such as William of Wykeham
(and he was unique only in the scale of his benefactions) decided
to spend money in ways which involved the arts, it was on cre-
ations, which despite their ecclesiastical tincture, were basically
secular. The emergence of the universities of Oxford and Cambridge
again accented the arrival on the scene of a new cultural class,
similar in some ways to monks, but more pragmatic in their
outlook, less blinkered by liturgical precedents. The colleges which
were built, though monastic in basic design, were more secular
and educational in function, thus stimulating architectural attitudes
which were applicable to domestic purposes. The new aims of this
type of building encouraged an exuberance which would have been
out of place in the austerity of those Cluniac buildings which
epitomised monastic and clerical ideals. New elements were
creeping into imagery. There was an increasing emphasis on the
more raunchy episodes from the Old Testament. As a consequence
of the growth of humanistic studies, fostered at the universities,
themes and motifs from the Graeco-Roman tradition began to
appear with increasing frequency in books and in tapestry
especially, even though they were expressed with an engaging
naiveté. The retreat from the comparatively austere ornamental
idiom of earlier centuries was stimulated not only by the Crusades,
which brought Britain into contact with a Muslim culture, which
was nourished by elements coming from as far away as India and
China, but by the ever-increasing passion for pilgrimages –
especially to Compostela and the Holy Land, which brought quite
ordinary people into contact with different cultures and new experiences. In the early fifteenth century, for instance, at the age of
about forty, Margery Kempe, having borne fourteen children,
decided to make a pilgrimage to the Holy Land to expiate an early

Travelling on her own initiative via Venice, sometimes actually alone, sometimes joining other groups of pilgrims, constantly getting involved in scrapes of one kind or another, she wrote a vivid description of her experiences (cf. Louise Collis *Memoirs of a Medieval Woman*, New York 1983). What she was able to express must have been an experience shared by countless others, who brought back to their life in England a new sense of visual experience, an enlarging of the boundaries of taste. Pilgrimages were the package tours of the High Middle Ages, and their influence must have been as potent as that of their latter-day counterparts.

The growth in international trade, and the increasing sophistication of business methods stimulated by the invention of double-entry bookkeeping and the adaptation of the Arabic numbering system, brought to England an ever growing number of foreign merchants and foreign luxury goods. By the reign of Edward I communities of foreign merchants, established under royal protection, had come to play an important part in English affairs. Men such as Luke of Lucca, or dynasties such as the Frescobaldi of Florence maintained a steady flow of commerce in both goods and ideas between Britain and Italy. In exchange, first for the wool and then for the cloth for which England had become famous, there came from the areas of Mediterranean spices and drugs of various kinds, oriental silks, sweet wine, cotton, velvet, sugar, the alum of Folglia, which came from Asia Minor, pigments, velvets and satins, gold and silver articles, precious stones as well as fine armour, ecclesiastical vestments, books and paper. The Genoese brought woad, which English dyers used to produce green and violet cloth as well as blue. The Venetians exported glass as well as wines, making Southampton their main port. It is possible that actual works of art were also imported, in the same way that Florentine paintings were smuggled into Avignon in bales of cloth.

As towns grew in importance and England became a less predominantly rural society changes took place in the creation and distribution of works of art and craft. Architects and builders had always been a largely self-contained, and peripatetic profession, with groups travelling throughout Europe, bound together by oaths of loyalty and pledges into a kind of occupational unity, which tended to make for the creation of standards, the dissemination, and to a certain extent the imposition on 'clients' of styles and fashions, and so the emergence of a form of taste. They were now also beginning much like other craftsmen to settle in one place. Typical of this new type of 'static' architect was William de Malton, who in the fourteenth century supervised the completion of the nave of Beverley Minster, and in his will left to the Austin Friars of Haltemprice a builder's yard containing, amongst other things, 'wainscots, pumice, tiles, a clock with spindles and iron wheels and a quantity of stone'. Towns stimulated the growth of retail trading, and people who wanted to buy precious objects now had a far greater opportunity of making a choice, with all that this implied in the creation of style and fashion, those impenetrably ambiguous concepts. By the end of the fifteenth century a Venetian visitor commenting on the wealth of London noted that 'in one single street, named the Strand, leading to St Paul's, there are fifty-two goldsmiths' shops, so rich and so full of silver vessels great and small, that in all the shops in Milan, Rome, Venice and Florence put together I do not think there would be found so many of that magnificence'[1] He also indicated that there was no lack of customers for such wares, 'There is no small innkeeper, however poor and humble he may be, who does not serve his table with silver dishes and drinking cups, and no one who has not in his house silver plate to the value of at least £100 which is equivalent to 500 golden crowns with us, is considered to be a person of any consequence.' Clearly he was exaggerating, but it is equally clear that a new kind of patron, the affluent merchant, was becoming more prominent, and more likely to exert an influence on the market for luxury objects.

London, as the main centre of an ever more elaborate government, was becoming the *arbiter elegantiae*, and as early as 1380, when the north-country magnate Sir John de Nevill decided to endow Durham Cathedral with a new reredos, and an addition to St Cuthbert's tomb, he had the work carried out in London, 'and then packed in crates and transferred by sea to Newcastle, when the prior of Durham had it carried by land to the cathedral'.

---

1. There seems to be some confusion in the naming of the street (cf. J. D. Mackie, *The Earlier Tudors*, Oxford 1972, p. 31). Part of the Strand was outside the city of London, and in any case it cannot be said to lead to St Paul's. The traditional goldsmiths' quarter was Cheapside, where in 1491 Thomas Wood, a goldsmith who was sheriff of London built Goldsmiths' Row, described by Stow in 1598 as 'the most beautiful frame of fair houses and shops that can be within the walls of London or elsewhere in England containing ten fair dwelling houses and fourteen shops, all in one frame uniformly builded four stories high, beautified towards the street with the Goldsmiths' Arms and the likenesses of woodmen riding on monstrous beasts, all of which is cast in lead, richly painted over and gilt'.

Government, at both local and central levels was indeed coming to have a greater say in determining certain aesthetic choices. Town planning had made its appearance in the planning of Winchelsea and Berwick. Local authorities, especially in the City of London, were beginning to make the most detailed regulations about housing, specifying heights, materials used, and even the colours (usually white) to be used on the outside. From the fourteenth century onwards an increasinge flow of royal proclamations regulated, in immense detail though without great success, the nature of the clothes to be worn by various classes of society, giving specific details about the materials, ornaments and accoutrements allowed. These reached their highest point of proliferation in the reign of Elizabeth I, when proclamations also controlled the nature of popular portraiture, limiting the production of pictures of the queen to certain approved prototypes, and forbidding, for instance the hawking of portraits of people such as the popular Earl of Essex. (cf. pp. 124–5). Various regulations, especially where works initiated by the king were concerned, controlled the supply of labour. Workers in the building industry were subject to impressment by the crown until the end of the sixteenth century. The arrangements made by Edward III to conscript labour on a large scale for the rebuilding of Windsor Castle show that the system did not always work smoothly. In 1360 thirteen sheriffs were ordered to send 568 masons to Windsor, where they were to be housed in specially constructed lodgings, but it appears, from the Wardrobe accounts, that no more than 300 were ever employed in one year. The desire of building workers to earn wages higher than those prescribed for royal works led the sheriff of York, always an area with a great density of builders, to supply the men he impressed with red caps and jackets 'lest they should escape from the custody of the conductor'. (cf. Knoop and Jones 'The Impressment of Masons for Windsor Castle, 1360–63' *Economic History*, iii, 1937, pp. 350–61.)

Freemasons (who were so called because they worked in free-stone as opposed to rubble) organised themselves in lodges, but in virtually all the other callings associated with the arts and crafts, guilds had become established, and were constantly increasing their control over the recruitment of members, the application of closed-shop principles, the demarcation of functions, the quality of work, and the control of competition, especially from foreigners, even indeed from craftsmen who came from another town or part of the country. Painters, who worked on wood or stone; stainers, who worked on cloth and other materials (there was an ever increasing demand for stained wall-hangings for smaller domestic interiors) tapestry-makers, goldsmiths, pewterers, carpenters, joiners, all had become formed into guilds which, amongst other things, also specified certain standards of excellence both in workmanship and materials, and, by rigorous application of apprenticeship regulations, created a rudimentary form of art education. Stalls or shops had now become the accepted channel of buying and selling most works of art and design, though there still persisted a tradition of peripatetic artists and craftsmen, who must have been largely responsible for the often elaborate mural paintings which still adorned even small churches, and for providing the smaller rural home with things such as stained hangings, tableware and religious imagery of one kind or another.

The fact that by the fifteenth century castles were being built of brick rather than of stone suggested the new domestication of architecture; an Englishman's castle had become his home, and its design was now dictated rather by the need for comfort than for defence. Eton was one of the outstanding examples of the new fashion for brick, and between between 1442 and 1452 William Veyse, a Fleming who was brickmaker to the king, provided some two and a half million bricks for its construction. The houses of city merchants had started to take on more impressive proportions and qualities, especially in cities such as London, Norwich and Bristol, where they were also usually places of business as well. In 1405 the Dean and Chapter of St Paul's entered into a contract with John Dobson, citizen and carpenter of London for the erection of shop premises in Ducklesbury, they supplying the wood, cartage and nails, he being paid £46 13s. 4d., and 'all the chips and bits of wood under a foot in length'.

A great shop 22 ft 4 in by 18 feet with a display room 10 ft by 18 ft and a gate and alley leading to the back premises. Over these shall be two stories, the first jutting back and front, the second jutting only towards the street with a garret above; the first storey to be 11 ft high, and to have two bay windows for a chamber and a parlour. The second, nine ft high shall have two chambers with handsomely lintelled windows. Behind over the great cellar, he shall build a warehouse 9 ft high, and over it a hall 33 feet by 20, and 16 feet high to the wallplate, with an open roof, having a bay window and two others. A gallery full of windows shall lead from the hall into the first floor rooms above the shop, above this shall be a small chamber leading into the second floor of the house.

Above the west end of the hall and the small chamber shall be a principal chamber, 20 ft by 11 ft with a flat battlemented roof. At the east end of the hall he shall make steps and an oriel, giving access to the hall and light to the buttery and pantry, which are to be built, with the kitchen over a coal-shed, a wood-shed and a latrine. Above the kitchen and pantry is to be a chamber with a garret over it, and over the east end of the hall and part of the kitchen is to be another chamber.

(Quoted in L. F. Salzman's *Building in England*, Oxford 1952, Appendix B No. 49, p 478)

It is significant that the builder of this edifice was a carpenter, for in these less bellicose times, wood with its immense decorative potentialities, and its adaptability had become a favourite building material, and was to remain so until well into the seventeenth century. Hammerbeam roofs proliferated, and timber-frame houses became the rule rather than the exception. This led to the multiplicity of windows – there is heavy emphasis on them in Dobson's contract – and glass was being produced and imported in comparatively massive quantities. The best was imported from the Hanseatic merchants of Germany, who provided the material for the York glass-painters, shipping it through Hull. Good quality glass also came from Caen, and other towns in Normandy, as well as Flanders and Lorraine. Usually it was plain, but it could be bought either coloured or already 'powdered', that is covered with painted flowers or other ornaments. In England inferior white glass was made in Chiddingfold, Rugeley in Staffordshire, in Shropshire and in parts of Kent. Glaziers such as John Prudde, in the middle of the fifteenth century were able to produce stained glass by the foot for a wide variety of purposes, both ecclesiastical and domestic. Glass 'powdered' with figures of prophets was 8½d. a foot; that 'florished with roses and lilies and certain arms' 10d. a foot, while windows depicting a religious or secular happening were 1s. 2d. a foot.

If styles in building, in carving and in sculpture were tending to become standardised, especially on a regional scale, partly because of the degree of organisation implicit in the masonic lodges and the craft guilds, there was pressure in the same direction from the fact that occupations, at all levels of late medieval society, tended to be hereditary. There was a Massingham dynasty of carpenters, carvers and painters, the earlier generations of the family being merely carpenters, but by the beginning of the fifteenth century a John of the third generation in the family made the wooden patten for the effigy of Richard Beauchamp, Earl of Warwick, to be cast in bronze for the chapel of St Mary's Collegiate church, and was one of the first sculptors to introduce into England those new naturalistic standards which were already established in European cities such as Paris, Florence and Augsburg. (cf. John Harvey, *English Medieval Architects*, London 1954, p. 183). The fourth John of the family, who died in 1478, was also a painter, who coloured the stone statue of the Virgin and Child over the outer gate of Winchester College.

The quest for naturalism had become almost universal throughout Europe by the end of the fifteenth century, an almost unconscious reaction to that greater belief in the individual which had been created by improvements in the quality of life, the revival of learning, the growth of a religious spirit which placed an emphasis on the direct relation between man and God, rather than between man and the institutions of the church and all that group of changes which is conveniently lumped together as the Renaissance. Society was being secularised; society was becoming individualised. There was a great increase in the number of sepulchral monuments of a realistic kind, and these were no longer confined to the great of the land. The demand for craftsmen of all kinds who could perpetuate the actual appearance of a man or woman was growing all the time, and the Wilton diptych is one of the few survivors of that interest in portraiture, which over the centuries was to become recognised as one of the characteristics of English painting. Another feature was becoming apparent too; a dependence on foreign artists. Although by the early sixteenth century there were English carvers and sculptors of great distinction, men such as Lawrence Imber and the Drawswerd family of York, when something spectacular was needed recourse was had to Italy, Germany or Flanders. Pietro Torrigiano was brought over from Florence to execute the tombs both of the Lady Margaret and of Henry VII, and was commissioned to build the altar to the west of the king's tomb, which was in effect completed by Benedetto di Rovezzano. Wolsey employed a number of Italians on the construction of his dream palace at Hampton Court, which sported Renaissance details with something of the indiscriminate enthusiasm which might have been expected of a butcher's son turned Chancellor and cardinal. Optimistically, but futilely as it turned out, he commissioned Antonio Cavallari to design his tomb and the king himself (as well as Somerset the Lord Protector after him) employed John of Padua as 'deviser of His Majesty's buildings'.

It was in painting generally, and in portraiture especially, that foreign influence made itself felt. English attitudes to painting were still medieval, and the position and status of the appropriately-titled Sergeant-Painter to the king, admirable though he may have been in adorning the poops of barges, or the décor for the Field of the Cloth of Gold, were vastly inferior to those of Leonardo at the court of Francis I, or of Raphael in the power corridors of the Vatican. Spanish artists such as Miguel Zittoz, court painter to Isabella of Spain, Flemings such as the Hornebolts from Ghent and Johannes Corvus from Bruges, and above all of course the German Hans Holbein, who from 1536 till his death in 1543 was a member of the royal household, were the men who recorded the men and women of Tudor England. And the tradition persisted throughout the century. In the year that Holbein died, Antonio Toto, who had come to England with Torrigiano, was made Sergeant-Painter. Gullim Stretes from Amsterdam painted Edward VI; the most famous portrait of Queen Mary is by Anthonis Mor, and her cousin Cardinal Reginald Pole sat to Titian. Of the many portraits of Queen Elizabeth I recorded by Roy Strong (*Gloriana*, London 1987) most of them are by foreigners, and the major artists of the reign were Flemings such as Marcus Gheeraerts, Paul van Somer and Daniel Mytens. Native artists were mostly confined to the art of miniature, though even here the two most famous, Nicholas Hilliard and Isaac Oliver, were of foreign descent. Gresham's Royal Exchange, one of the major public works of the period, was designed by Henri de Pas the architect of the Hanseatic Hall at Antwerp; the sculptors and tomb-makers, who mostly worked in Southwark, were predominantly German or Flemish, and the burgeoning art of engraving for books was largely dominated by the Doroeshout brothers from Brussels. Prints of foreign origin too, especially views of famous cities of the past and present, formed the bulk of the stock in the numerous print shops which proliferated around Blackfriars and the Strand. In the following century, when James I and Charles I set about, not unsuccessfully revivifying the tapestry industry in England, once again it was to Flanders that they looked for organisers and staff, even passing regulations to facilitate their nationalisation here.

In the long run the most important, indeed in some ways the most catastrophic event, which influenced many of the arts and crafts, and how people regarded them in England, was the Henrician reformation. In the past there had always been some degree of control over images and the like, exercised mostly by the church. In 1306, for instance, a German carver named Tidemann had been hauled before the consistory court of Ralph Baldock, bishop of London, for producing a 'certain carved crucifix with a cross-beam which docs not represent the true form of the cross'. But the changes in belief, dogma and liturgy which Henry initiated represented a total ideology, which removed one of the most important sources of patronage and inspiration which had effectively operated for the best part of a millenium. There was an almost complete cessation of church building between 1534 and the end of the seventeenth century, between Henry VII's chapel at Westminster and Wren's St Paul's. This happened too at a time when in the Catholic countries of the continent ecclesiastical architecture was achieving some of its greatest triumphs. Not only was there a complete cessation of the demand for images, in two or three dimensions, but the iconology which had inspired them was taboo. There was no longer any call for those richly embroidered vestments which had produced *opus Anglicanum*; or for the elaborate wealth of liturgical vessels, reliquaries and the like which had created testing grounds for design and technique in a whole range of crafts. The dissolution of the religious orders had no very great effect; for some time monasteries had stopped being effective patrons and promoters of art, and to a certain extent some of their functions had been taken over by the two universities. What was tragic however was the wave of iconoclasm which destroyed an immense amount of the legacy of the past, and which in the following century, at the time of the Commonwealth, was followed by another of equal violence. Statues, tombs, rood-lofts, altars, stained-glass windows, the whole apparatus of medieval religious life was attacked with a vehemence which equalled in intensity the respect and devotion which once had been lavished on them. Motivated by fanatacism, or by greed (monastic and capitular treasures were looted on a Goeringesque scale), enthusiasts wrecked havoc with the treasures of the past. Clearly it was not a passion shared by the whole mass of the population; people accepted easily enough the short-lived reversal of the process which took place under Queen Mary, and there are frequent stories of priests and churchwardens hiding away statues and other liturgical objects from the eyes of Henrician or Parliamentarian inquisitors. But those who did participate in what might almost be called an 'anti-art' movement were actuated by the strongest possible feelings, originating usually from the notion that the objects which they were destroying were the tangible symbols of ideas and principles which they both hated and feared (the Church of Rome was seen as the very epitome of political as well as religious menace), though occasionally there were undercurrents of a more generalised hatred of imagery as such. When, as Protector, Oliver Cromwell took over the palaces of Charles I and continued to live in them, an unknown female correspondent wrote to him begging him to demolish the bronze statues of Venus and Cleopatra and the marble ones of Adonis and Apollo, in which, she said, there was much evil, for 'as long as the groves and altars of the idols remained untaken away, the wrath of God continued against Israel'. (*Original Letters and Papers of State Addressed to Oliver Cromwell*, edited by John Nickolls, London 1743, p. 115.)

There were, however, more indirect effects on art resulting from the dissolution of the monasteries and the reformation of the liturgy. Vast sums were involved. A selection of the actual objects which changed hands reveals that Henry VIII acquired a great cross of emeralds from Winchester, three caskets of jewels from Chichester, and from the richest source of all, the shrine of St Thomas at Canterbury, two great chests of jewels 'such as six or eight strong men could do no more than convey one of them' and some twenty-four wagons of assorted treasures beside, according to Nicholas Sander the Catholic historian, who became papal legate to Ireland, and spent much of his latter life trying to engineer the overthrow of Elizabeth. Such wealth as this found its way easily into the Privy Purse, but the vast monastic estates were used in a way which did much to alter the state of society, and the nature of the economy. By and large Henry used them to tie to his dynasty by links of economic dependence a whole new class of nobility and landowners, whose attitudes to the papacy were determined by the fact that its restoration would mean ruin for them. Peers such as Essex, Norfolk, Rutland, Suffolk, Shrewsbury, Sussex and Howard all got lands worth more than £2,000; courtiers and royal servants did well – Sir Ralph Sadler, the king's secretary being especially favoured in this respect. Henry was shrewd enough to spread monastic wealth amongst others too; the bulk of the lands went to grantees, usually described as knights or esquires, who often had family contacts with the foundation whose estates they were acquiring, whilst quite considerable grants of land were acquired by lawyers, merchants, physicians and other representatives of the expanding middle classes. (Cf. J. D. Mackie, *The Earlier Tudors*, Oxford 1985, pp. 399 *et seq.*)

This new influx of wealth, and it was compounded by a whole

host of other economic factors, made possible an increase in ex
ture on activities such as building, and with it the demand
more luxurious ways of living. Mansions and houses sprang
over Elizabethan England which were intended at least in part, to
express the newly acquired wealth, the new social status of their
owners, in a style which, combining a basic Gothic traditionalism
with odds and ends of Italianate classicism, is both engaging and
impressive. Great houses such as Hardwick, Hatfield and Burghley
echoed on a less grand scale, and with more of a domestic
emphasis, the splendid aspirations which had led Wolsey to create
Hampton Court, whilst others such as the Martyns at Athel-
hampton, or the Sackvilles at Knole added new extensions or
interiors, modelled often enough on Flemish pattern-books.

The new wealth had created a new social mobility, as we call
it in the late twentieth century, which, as ever, stimulated a passion
for competitive ostentation. Inside the home wainscotting and
tapestry appeared on the walls, modelled plaster on the ceilings;
oak, which had once been confined to churches and palaces, was
to be found everywhere; carpets, often imported from the Middle
East, took the place of rushes; enormous bedsteads of wood,
constructed with great elaboration of carpentry, took the place of
straw pallets; drinking glasses were imported in large quantities; the
cheaper varieties from Normandy, the more expensive from
Venice. Eating instruments, some of them newly designed, were
to be found on tables adorned with silver and gold plate for the
very wealthy, and pewter for the less so. Dress reached new heights
of ostentation and luxury, and this perhaps is the cause for the
constant flow of regulations about it which was characteristic of the
Elizabethan age. *Fare la bella figura* was as important in London as
it was thought to be in those Italian cities whence contemporary
moralists claimed all social evils originated. According to Ben
Jonson, to become a fine gentleman it was necessary to go to the
city 'where at your first appearance it were good you turned four
or five hundred acres of your best land into two or three trunks
of apparel'. With breeches costing from £7 to £70, silk stockings
around £1, shirts at £2 and boots from £4 to £10, this was no
exaggeration. Nor was the emphasis on 'the city' misplaced; with
a population which numbered a tenth of that of the whole of the
British Isles, London was the most populous city in Europe, and
it was there that taste and fashion were determined.

But in the search for gentility and social assurance it was not
only the outer man that counted. Books of manners and behaviour

began to appear, often based on Italian prototypes (cf. p. 170). Considerable emphasis was placed on the ability to draw and paint, as well as to appreciate the great works of the past and the present. Foreign travel, as Bacon indicated, was coming to be thought of as a social rather than a religious necessity; guide books and travellers' tales proliferated, and the tendency was exaggerated by a variety of factors. Roads were improving, so too were other means of transport; the diplomatic system was expanding, and becoming more intricate, with alert British representatives at the courts of all European nations, usually prepared to provide their friends and patrons at home with works of art, and a host of foreign luxuries; silks, spices, glassware and the like. The religious troubles of the sixteenth century and the constitutional ones of the seventeenth, unleashed on Europe a whole host of English refugees, who often maintained close contact with their connexions at home, or returned here when circumstances became more propitious. English society had become more consciously cosmopolitan, and the first great achievement of what might justifiably be described as classical Renaissance architecture here, the Banqueting Hall, was designed by Inigo Jones, whose visit to Italy had introduced him to the architecture of Palladio. Jones was also significant in another way; he was more highly educated, more of a 'gentleman' than most of his professional predecessors had been, and it was becoming obvious, even before Christopher Wren epitomised the whole process, that the social status of the artist, and even of some craftsmen, had improved considerably.

By the time of James I the collecting of pictures and works of art had become an acceptable, and even desirable occupation for anyone with pretensions to gentility, and it even possessed political undercurrents. One of the most enthusiastic collectors of the early Stuart period was the comparative parvenu George Francis Villiers, Duke of Buckingham, whose agents in Europe larded their letters to him with constant references to the fact that the acquisition of whatever work of art they were trying to sell him would make others envious, and himself supereminent. And whereas earlier collectors such as the Lumleys of Lumley Castle had mostly acquired portraits, either of members of their family or of kings of England, the Caesars and the like (cf. *A Lumley Inventory of 1609*, Walpole Society, 1918), by the time he was assassinated Buckingham had acquired, amongst other things, 19 paintings by Titian, 17 by Tintoretto, 15 by Veronese, 6 by Holbein, 4 by Andrea del Sarto, 2 by Raphael, and 30 by Rubens. But Buckingham was a mere tyro in comparison with Thomas Howard, Earl of Arundel, probably the most interesting collector England has known. A moderately successful soldier, an unhappy politician, who reluctantly presided at the trial of Stafford, Arundel was an enthusiast, who was little concerned with the status his possessions conferred on him – as Earl Marshal and member of an ancient family he had little need to be – and was, for instance, so besotted with a painting he owned by Dürer, that he carried it about with him in his coach wherever he went. His agents ransacked Europe and the Middle East to provide him with paintings and classical sculptures, the remnants of which can be seen in the Ashmolean Museum at Oxford. As Peacham said in his *Compleat Gentleman* of 1621 (p. 3)

> And here I cannot but mention the every way Right Honourable Thomas Howard, Lord High Marshall of England, as great for his noble Patronage of Arts and ancient learning, as for his birth and place. To whose liberall charges and magnificence this angle of the world oweth the first sight of Greek and Romane statues, with whose admired presence he began to honour the Gardens and Galleries of Arundel House about twentie yeares ago and hath ever since continued to transplant old Greece into England.

Arundel is usually considered to have been the mentor in art of Henry Prince of Wales, the first of the Stuarts to manifest an informed interest in artistic matters, and who started the collection of works of art which was built up by his brother into the most important collection of its kind that had hitherto been known. Amongst Charles' major purchases were that of the entire collection of the Dukes of Mantua, for which he paid £80,000 in 1627, and the statues and bas-reliefs from the Temple of Apollo at Delphi which Sir Kenelm Digby obtained for him for £17,989. Indeed the money Charles spent on art may well have contributed to the outbreak of the Civil War, so heavy was the burden it placed on his resources.

Charles, like many of his contemporaries, was taught drawing and painting, so too were his children. His sister Elizabeth of Bohemia was, according to the mildly sycophantic Evelyn, a gifted artist, and her two daughters certainly were. Her son, Rupert of the Rhine, was not only a dashing cavalry commander, and admiral of some note, but an engraver of distinction, examples of whose works are to be found at Windsor and in the British Museum. He was partly responsible for the invention of the process of engraving known as mezzotint, and was certainly responsible for popularising

23

it in England. He also invented a brass-type alloy which was used for door-furniture until the end of the eighteenth century. Nor was amateur art, or the collection of prints and pictures confined to the upper classes, as Pepys' *Diary* so convincingly proves. The houses of most of those above the poverty level had some kind of pictorial adornment, the favourite themes being portraiture or topography, with a sprinkling of religious subjects. The art trade, in the shape of picture shops selling works produced in England or imported from abroad, was flourishing, despite the strictures of the Puritans. The sale of the main part of the king's collection between 1645 and 1653 created an interest which resulted, after the Restoration, in the inauguration of art auctions. Cromwell himself was not unduly austere as far as the arts were concerned, retaining for his own use those of the royal pictures which had not been sold, and we have already seen how his retention of the sculptures from Delphi brought down on his head the ire of one of his more devout followers. The actual influence of the Puritans and their associates on art and taste was, in fact comparatively negligible. In the first place their tenure of power was of short duration; in the long run the nature of art and taste was still determined by the well-to-do whose status, and often whose power, were little affected by the constitutional changes which had taken place. Despite occasional appearances to the contrary, the Civil War had never been a social one.

What was really happening in seventeenth century England was that the Middle Ages had at last come to an end, and a kind of belated, native Renaissance was taking place, exemplified at its finest by the buildings of Wren, that truly Renaissance man. Indeed the Royal Society could well be seen as a tardy version of those academies which had adorned the courts of Italy more than a century earlier. Echoing Augustus, James I is reputed to have said that he found London sticks, and left it bricks, and a series of regulations issued by him and by Charles stipulated that new houses should only be built in the city where there were already existing foundations, that their outer walls should be of brick or stone, a brick and a half thick, and that each story should be 10 ft high. This did not prevent the Great Fire, but that, in the long run, was one of the best things that happened to English architecture, giving a new impetus to the tentative urban planning which had been going on, and ensuring that as the landed gentry who owned parts of London began to realise the advantages of venturing into property development, that it would be undertaken with at least a modicum of visual decency.

The arts had acquired a new kind of respectability; knighthoods were conferred on Rubens, Van Dyck, Lely and Wren, but it was not until 1720 that an English painter would receive one. Gentlemen painted, drew and became architects, some, like Sir Nathaniel Bacon, the painter, and Sir Roger Pratt, who was to play an important role in the rebuilding of London after the Great Fire achieving professional status. There was an increasing degree of sophistication in taste. Britain's ever expanding commercial interests introduced exotic strains. The import of tea and coffee stimulated a demand for porcelain, which was imitated here, as well as being collected as a form of virtù. By the 1670s in addition to a heavy import of textiles from the east, calico was being manufactured in London with oriental patterns, the production being based on Indian techniques. Oriental screens and wallpapers were becoming popular. Chinese elements of decoration were appearing in the work of gold and silversmiths, and a chain pump based on Chinese prototypes was in use during the reign of Charles II. Purcell, who was not slow to latch on to any new fashion set the fifth act of *The Fairy Queen* in 'a transparent prospect of a Chinese garden, the architecture, the trees, the plants, the fruit, the birds, the beasts quite different to what we have in this part of the world'.

The choice of a garden was itself significant of a new aspect of the increasing importance of the pleasure principle as an influence on the creation of taste. 'I do believe', wrote John Aubrey in *The Natural History of Wiltshire*, 'that there is now, in 1691, ten times as much gardening about London as there was in 1660. In the time of Charles II gardening was much improved, and became common.' Although it was the French influence which predominated in garden design (as indeed it tended to in the decorative arts generally) there was still something specifically English about such splendid examples of the art as those to be found at Woburn, designed by the celebrated John Field, Sir Henry Capel's garden at Kew, and that laid out by Moses Cook at Cassiobury. The horticultural wonder of the age, of course, was George London's hydraulic landscaping at Chatsworth. It is an indication of the increased importance attached to the garden that the Antwerp-born Jan Sieberecht built up a considerable reputation as a portrayer of gardens, for, as John Rea commented in his *Flora Ceres et Pomona* (1665), 'Fair houses are more frequent than fine gardens; the first effected by artificers only, the latter requiring more skill in their owner.'

By the end of the seventeenth century the secular reformation created by the Renaissance had become firmly established at last in England. A variety of causes, chief amongst them the invention of printing with moveable type, had divided the culture of Europe into two main sections: that of the literate and that of the illiterate; that of the well-to-do and that of the impoverished; almost, one could go as far as to say, that of the town and that of the country. Whereas in the Middle Ages there was no very great difference between the aesthetic tastes of one class and another, now there was such a thing as 'taste', such a thing as 'fashion'. Both, for it is very difficult to find a satisfying definition of the fluctuating boundaries in difference of meaning between the two, had become a divisive element in society, a means of dividing the sheep from the goats, 'them' from 'us'.

2. A Christian art

The impact of religion

2.1 The image of our Lord on a board

In AD 597 Augustine and a group of monks arrived in England to spread Roman Christianity. Arriving at the island of Thanet, they met Ethelbert, king of Kent, and immediately established that link between visual imagery and Christianity which was to be one of the characteristics of medieval life. Bede recounts the incident in his *Ecclesiastical History of the English Nation* (c. 720).

Some days later the king came into the island, and sitting in the open air, ordered Augustine and his companions to be brought into his presence. For he had taken precaution that they should not come to him inside any kind of building, lest, according to an ancient superstition, they might practise magical arts, and so get the better of him. But they came armed with Divine and not magical powers, bearing a silver cross in front of them, and an image of Our Lord painted on a board, and singing a litany. . . . Accordingly he permitted them to reside in the city of Canterbury, which was the centre of all his dominions, and besides allowing them sustenance, gave them liberty to preach. It is said that as they drew near the city, after their manner, with the holy cross and the image of our sovereign Lord and King, Jesus Christ, they in concert sang the litany. There was on the east side of the city, a church dedicated to St Martin, built whilst the Romans were still on this island, wherein the Queen who was a Christian used to pray. In this they first began to meet, sing, pray, celebrate mass and preach, until the king was converted to Christianity, when he allowed them to preach openly, and build or repair churches in different places.

2.2 The making of the Lindisfarne Gospels

Although written into the book in the tenth century, some two hundred years later, the account in the Lindisfarne Gospels of its creation is remarkably explicit.

Eadfrith, bishop of the church at Lindisfarne originally wrote this book jointly for God and St Cuthbert, and for all the saints whose relics are on this island. And Ethilwald, bishop of the Lindisfarne islanders embellished it on the outside, and added the covers, as well he knew how to. And Bilfrith the anchorite, forged the ornaments which are on the binding, and adorned it with gold, and with gems and also with silver-gilt, pure metal. And Aldred, unworthy and most miserable priest, glossed it in English between the lines. Eadfrith, Ethilwald, Aldred, all of them either made or adorned this Gospel Book for God and Cuthbert.

2.3 Culture in the north

An awareness of the cultural history of the British past was more widespread than we are sometimes apt to believe, and in the early twelfth century William of Malmesbury was able, in his *Chronicle* to attribute to the monks of Northumbria, and in particular Benedict Biscop (628–690) recognition for their role in introducing architectural and other ideas from abroad. (Benedict himself had been a monk at Lerins, accompanied Theodore of Tarsus from Rome to Canterbury, and after being abbot of St Peter's in that city established his monastery on the Wear in 674.)

Britain indeed, though by some it is called another world, as it is entirely surrounded by the ocean, and is not well known to geographers, possesses in its remotest region, bordering on Scotland the birthplace of the Venerable Bede. This region which was once redolent with the gracious odour of monasticism, and which once boasted many cities built by the Romans, but subsequently destroyed by the Danes and then by the Normans, is now not an attractive place. It is dominated by the river Wear, of considerable breadth, and with a rapid tide, which, running into the sea, receives ships, borne by gentle breezes into the calm bosom of its harbour. Both its banks have been made famous by one Benedict, who built there churches and monasteries, one dedicated to St Peter, the other to St Paul, both united in the bonds of brotherly love and monastic discipline. The industry and patience of these monks and their abbots anyone will admire who reads the works of the Venerable Bede. It was Benedict who brought there a great wealth of books and he was the first person who introduced into England builders of stone edifices, as well as makers of glass windows. The love of his country and his passion for beauty assuages the hard labour of

introducing to his fellow countrymen things of novelty and orig-
inality, for never before the time of Benedict had buildings of this
style been seen in England, and never before had the rays of the
sun penetrated transparent glass.

2.4 Art from Gaul and Rome

The conversion of England to the Roman rite involved the acquisition of liturgical objects to correspond with the needs of that rite.
In his *Vitae Sanctorum Abbatum* (*c.* 700) the Venerable Bede
recounted in greater detail how Benedict Biscop built and furnished
the abbey church of St Peter at the mouth of the Wear. The
emphasis on pictures as a form of instruction for the illiterate was
to persist through the Middle Ages.

After the interval of a year, Benedict crossed the sea into Gaul, and
no sooner asked than he obtained, and carried back with him some
masons to build him a church in the Roman style, which he had
always admired. So much zeal did he show in his love for St Peter,
in whose honour he was building it, that within a year from the
laying of the foundation stone, you might have seen the roof on,
and the solemnity of the mass celebrated therein. When the work
was drawing to an end, he sent messengers to Gaul to fetch
glaziers, or rather craftsmen in glass, who were at this time
unknown in Britain, that they might glaze the windows of his
church, the cloister and the monastic rooms. This was done, and
they came and not only finished the work, but taught the English
people their craft and skills, which were well suited for enclosing
the lanterns of the church, and also for making glass vessels for
various uses. Benedict also took special pains to procure all things
necessary for the service of the church, such as vessels and sacred
vestments from foreign parts because they could not be obtained
in England.

Some decorative objects and other like things could not even be
obtained in Gaul, and these the pious founder decided to get from
Rome itself, and he returned laden with even more religious objects
than before, after his fourth visit to that city. In the first place he
brought back a large quantity of books of all kinds; secondly a great
number of relics of Christ's apostles and martyrs, all likely to bring
a blessing on many an English church; thirdly he introduced the
Roman mode of chanting, singing and ministering in the church,
by obtaining permission from Pope Agathus to take back with him

John, the precentor of the church of St Peter, and abbot of the monastery of St Martin, to teach the English. This John, when he arrived in England, not only communicated instruction by teaching personally, but left behind him numerous writings, which are still preserved in the library of the said monastery. In the fourth place Benedict brought with him a thing by no means to be despised, namely a letter of privilege from Pope Agathus, by which the monastery was to be forever free from any intrusion on its rights. Fifthly he brought with him pictures of devout subjects to adorn the church of St Peter which he had built; namely a likeness of the Virgin Mary and of the twelve apostles, with which he intended to adorn the central nave on panels of wood, stretching from one end of the wall to the other, also some figures from church history for the south wall, and others from the Apocalypse of St John for the north wall, so that everyone who entered the church, even if he could not read, wherever they turned their eyes, might have before them the benevolent face of Christ and his saints, though it were but in a picture, and with watchful minds might meditate on the benefits of Our Lord's incarnation, and having in front of their minds the perils of the Last Judgement, might the more strictly examine their consciences on that score.

2.5 An altar from Rome, *c.* 700

A relative of Ine, King of the West Saxons, who when he himself abdicated in 726, went to live in Rome, Aldhelm had established over south-east England the kind of ecclesiastical dominance which his cousin had established in the political sphere. An assiduous builder of churches, he seized every opportunity to embellish them.

When Aldhelm came back from Rome, he brought with him an altar of shining white marble, six feet in thickness, four feet in length, and three palms in breadth, with a lip projecting from the stone it seems to have been some relic of classical antiquity, and beautifully carved around the outside. A camel, it is said, carried it as far as the Alps – for what animal of our country could carry such a burden? The altar and the camel's back were both broken in the process, and both were miraculously mended by the saint, though the break in the marble is still visible. He gave the altar to King Ine, who placed it in a royal villa called Briwetune [Bruton] for the service of the mother of God. It is still there today [*c.* 1125], a living proof, so to speak, of the sanctity of Aldhelm. There is also another larger church dedicated to St Peter [at Malmesbury] which tradition asserts, not without some justification, was built and consecrated by this holy man. The east front of this has lately been enlarged and remodelled in accord with more modern taste.

(William of Malmesbury, *Gesta Pontificum Anglorum*)

2.6 The pride of Rome

The idea of Rome as the centre of artistic excellence had haunted mens' minds since the eighth century, a fact which is reflected in William of Malmesbury's *Gesta Pontificum Anglorum* (*c.* 1125) when he describes the building activities of Wilfrid, bishop of York (634–709) who made several journeys to Rome.

It is amazing how many buildings Wilfrid brought to perfection, with walls of imposing height, and which contained many winding corridors. Many of these buildings were planned by himself, but others were the work of masons, drawn there from Rome by the hope of liberal reward. It was then commonly said by people, and even recorded in writing, that such a building had never existed on this side of the Alps like the church he had built at Hexham. Even those who come from Rome themselves have said the same thing, and those who see the church could swear that the splendour of Rome had been created there, so little have the ravages of time and war robbed the buildings of their beauty.

Wilfrid, as William relates, rebuilt the cathedral at York.

The church originally built at York by King Edwin, on the advice of Paulinus, lacked a roof; its walls were in a bad state of repair, verging on utter ruin, and useful only as a place for birds to build their nests. The bishop Wilfrid moved by grief at this deplorable state of affairs, strengthened the masonry, elevated the roof, and once that had been done protected it from damage from storm and rain with leaden sheets. In the windows light came through linen cloths or sheets of transparent alabaster. Age and the impact of the weather had dirtied the stonework of the building, so he had it whitewashed with shining lime. Ripon also benefited from the activities of the bishop, a new church being built there right from the foundations, with marvellous curved arches, finely laid stones and wondrous porches.

2.7 The gifts of Athelstan

When St Cuthbert's body was at Chester-le-Street in the course of its wanderings between Lindisfarne and Durham, it attracted much attention as a pilgrimage centre. It received much royal patronage. King Guthfrith, for instance granted lands to the saint; Alfred presented the shrine with a golden censer, and in 934 Athelstan 'going with a large army into Scotland, came to the shrine of St Cuthbert, and commending his army to the protection of the saint, bestowed on him many gifts' (*Historia Regum*). The nature of these gifts, which are recorded in the *Historia Sanct Cuthberti* (Rolls Series, vol. 1) is suggestive of the richness and diversity of Anglo-Saxon artefacts.

I Athelstan, King, gave to St Cuthbert this copy of the Gospels, two chasubles, one alb, one stole with a maniple, one girdle, three altar cloths, one chalice of silver, two pattens; the one made of gold, the other of Grecian workmanship, one censer of silver, one cross skilfully wrought of gold and ivory, one royal cap woven with gold, screens or tablets (possibly icons) wrought in gold and silver, one missal, two copies of the gospels, ornamented in silver and gold, a life of St Cuthbert written in verse and prose [possibly now in Corpus Christi College, Cambridge, MS 183], seven robes, three curtains, three pieces of tapestry, two cups of silver with lids, three great bells, two horns, and two golden armlets; two banners and one lance.

2.8 The relics of St Cuthbert

On 29 August 1104, the body of St Cuthbert, who had died in 687, was translated into a more splendid shrine in Durham Cathedral, where it had become an object of pilgrimage. Reginald of Durham's account of the saint's robes gives some idea of the richness and sophistication of materials imported in the seventh century.

Concerning his episcopal robes; how precious they were, and of what colour, beauty and elegance, and how admirable their texture.

Next he was clad, like other Christian bishops, in the tunic and dalmatic, and the quality of both of them was most impressive and elegant, by reason of the rich purple colour, and elaborate weaving. The dalmatic, indeed, which is the outer of these two vestments, and the more easily seen, shows a reddish purple colour quite unknown today, even to men of wide knowledge and experience.

It still retains throughout the same comely beauty which it must have had when it was originally made, and when touched, it gives out a crackling sound, because of the richness of the workmanship and the substantial quality of the material. It is finely embroidered, and images of flowers and small animals are woven into it the stitches, and the intervals between them being extremely small. And for greater beauty its appearance is diversified by strands of different colours mingled with it – a yellowish colour which is supposed to come from the lime tree. This pleasing variation is repeated all over the purple background of the cloth, producing new and constantly varying patterns by the mixture of patches of differing colours. You can see that there is a yellowish colour dyed into the cloth, sprinkled uniformly over the whole, and as a consequence the reddish purple colour is given greater luminosity. A golden border, like an orfray, completely encircles the outer edges of this dalmatic, and because of the gold which is woven into the fabric, it is not easy to fold it back, and when it does do so, it makes a crackling sound. It is possible to roll the material back, but because of its thickness, it automatically rolls back to its original state. The border is as wide as the palm of a man's hand, and its workmanship is very painstaking and skilful. There was a similar border at the end of both sleeves, from which the arms and hands of the blessed bishop emerge. Round the neck of the garment, where the head emerges, there is a broader gold border, and it is even more elaborate in its workmanship than the other borders. This covers the greater part of the shoulders, both at the back and in front, because in both directions it is broader by the width of nearly a palm and a half. His hands, lying alongside the upper parts of his stomach, can be seen to lift up the fingers, as though stretching them up to heaven to seek the Lord's mercy on his faithful people. The chasuble, which was removed from him eleven years after his death, was never subsequently replaced. On his feet he wears his episcopal shoes, which are commonly called sandals. Their upper parts are seen to be pierced by countless tiny holes, the careful workmanship of which seems to suggest that they were made like this deliberately. For the rest, no one knows whether underneath he wore some softer garment, or a monastic cowl, for nobody had the temerity to touch or examine what lay nearest the flesh. Therefore all is doubtful about his other garments, whether linen or woollen, since nobody has been allowed to make a clear investigation of these matters. Above the amice belonging to the dalmatic there are other coverings of the holy body, made of silk or precious cloth the exact nature of which is not fully understood. And over all this there was wrapped a sheet, measuring nearly nine cubits in length, and extending to three cubits in width. This enclosed all the holy relics. This sheet had fringes of linen thread on either side measuring about a finger in length. Moreover all round the edges of this sheet, there is a border worked by the same skilful hand of the weaver, and it is found to be as broad as a thumb is long. On this material is embossed a very fine embroidery, which is found to represent figures of birds and beasts interwoven in the border. Always however, between two birds or beasts, appears a woven image of a tree, which divides and separates their shapes, thus making them distinct from each other. The shapely image of the tree thus displayed, is seen to spread out its leaves, tiny though they are, on both sides. And immediately underneath them, in similar fashion, embroidered pictures of animals are to be seen. Both of these features are clearly to be seen as a raised pattern around the edges of the sheet. This cloth was removed from the holy body at the time of its translation, and was for long preserved as a covering for the sacred relics when they are daily exhibited to the faithful. Above this sheet there was placed another thicker cloth, which is said to be of three-ply material, and it served to veil the whole expanse of the sheet itself and the collection of relics underneath it. Then there could be seen over this another cloth, impregnated with wax, which surrounded and covered the coffin of the holy body within and all the relics pertaining to it. This cloth clearly had not touched the holy relics, but is supposed to have been a later addition to protect them from the dust. So then these three cloths were removed from the body of the holy bishop, and instead of them, others more beautiful and more costly were laid over it. The first of these, which was put on top of the aforementioned vestments, was of silk, very fine and delicate; the second was a purple covering of inestimable value, while the third was of the finest linen, and this was the outermost covering of the holy body. He had also with him in the sepulchre a silver altar, a chalice of gold with a patten, and scissors, still retaining the beauty they had when they were new, and with which apparently his hair was shorn. These are placed at his head, on a kind of shelf, fixed across the sepulchre where they are still safely kept together with his ivory comb, which is pierced in the middle, in such a way that nearly three fingers could be inserted in it, and whose proportions are such that the width is the same as its length, except that in the matter of ornamentation, the one differs somewhat from the other. By reason of its age it is overspread with a reddish colour, and the character of the glossy white bone which nature had meant it to be, is changed by the suffusion of the red due to the passage of time.

Concerning his coffin, and how it was constructed and carved in a marvellous diversified way.

At this point we have come to the end of our account of the manner in which Christ's glorious bishop Cuthbert was laid at rest in his tomb.

Now however we shall explain what his inner coffin was like. He was first placed in this coffin in Lindisfarne, when he was taken out from the grave wherein he had been buried, and in it from that day onwards his incorruptible body has been preserved. The coffin is rectangular, like a chest, and has small doors which do not rise higher than the sides, and can be unfastened and lifted up as a whole, and in it two circular rings are inserted, one of which is fixed midway near the feet, and the other near the head. By means of these rings the board is lifted or lowered, for there is no other way of closing and locking the coffin. The whole is constructed of black oak, but it is doubtful whether the black colour is a consequence of age, by some artificial process, or by reason of its own nature. The whole of the exterior is covered with the most wonderful engraving which is so minute and finely executed that it seems a matter for pure amazement that a mere craftsman could produce such a thing. The single panels are indeed very narrow, and on them pictures of animals and flowers and images of men are inlaid, carved or engraved. This chest is enclosed within a larger one, which is entirely covered with leather and is strongly bound and fastened together with iron nails, and with clasps of the same material. There is however a third chest in addition, which is placed over the former and this is studded all round with gold and gems. It is joined together by the toothed tenons of the boards which come from both sides to meet each other by long iron nails. This chest therefore cannot be separated from the other by any means whatsoever, for the nails cannot be extracted from the chest without breaking it.

Note

St Cuthbert, whose shrine at Durham became the north-country equivalent of that of St Thomas at Canterbury, was originally buried at Lindisfarne, where he ended his life as abbot. After many wanderings it was moved some three centuries later in 998, and came to rest in the primitive church built on the site of what was to be the city of Durham. Later when the great cathedral was in the process of being built the body was transferred to a shrine behind the high altar. This was the occasion which is described by Reginald, a monk of Durham who had a considerable reputation as a historian, and who, from the minutely accurate account of the materials and objects found in the tomb, seems to have had the qualities of a natural archaeologist. The account is taken from his *Libellus admirandis Beati Cuthberti Virtutibus*, written *c.* 1160 at the instigation of St Ailred of Riveaux. Not all the items described are of the seventh century, but all of them offer evidence of the remarkable cosmopolitanism of Anglo-Saxon art. The coffin itself bears resemblances to that of St Paulinus in Trèves with signs of Celtic, Syrian monastic and Merovingian influences. The pectoral cross seems to be a seventh-century product of a northern Saxon workshop, working for Northumbrian court circles; the comb may have come from the Eastern Mediterranean (according to Bede, Pope Boniface V made a present of one to Queen Ethelburga of Kent at about the time of Cuthbert's death). The stole and the maniple were made in the tenth century, and their style originated in Byzantium, and was later developed by the Winchester school of illumination and the textiles, which bear pseudo-Kufic inscriptions (used for decorative purposes), were produced in some part of Western Asia under Byzantine dominance. (Cf. *The Relics of St Cuthbert*, ed. C. F. Battiscombe, Oxford 1956.)

2.9 Books for St Albans, c. 1080

The *Gesta Abbatum Monasterii Sancti Albani* records the acquisition of some illuminated manuscripts shortly after the Conquest in a manner which throws light both on the existence of cultured knights, and the way in which styles migrated from one centre, in this case Canterbury, to another.

When Abbot Paul held office (1077–1093) a certain warlike Norman knight bestowed on the abbey, thanks to the persuasive talents of the Abbot himself, two thirds of the tithes of his estate at Hatfield, which he had received from the King at the time of the distribution of the lands of the Saxons. At the Abbot's wish he assigned these tithes to the provision of books for the Abbey, for the Knight himself was a literate and intelligent man, as well as a great lover of the scriptures. There were also assigned to the same purpose certain tithes in Redbourne, and the Abbot decreed that certain allowances should be given to the scribes from the charity of the community and of the cellarer, since such gifts of food would be already cooked, and so no time should be wasted. The Abbot caused these noble volumes to be written by scribes whom he sought from far and near, and to show his gratitude he gave to the Knight, Sir Robert, for use in his chapel at Hatfield, two sets of vestments, a silver chalice, a missal and other liturgical books. The rest of the books which were produced by the scribes, and were based in their style on examples lent to him by Archbishop Lanfranc, were kept for the Abbey.

2.10 Edward's church

The acquisition of spiritual prestige was as potent an incentive to create or acquire what we would call works of art as is that of social prestige in our own time. It is significant that in one of the *Lives of Edward the Confessor* (Rolls Series, ed. H. R. Luard, 1858) which appeared shortly after his death as part of a kind of hagiographical propaganda campaign, emphasis was placed on the building of the abbey church of St Peter at Westminster, on the site of an earlier church, which he undertook as a substitute for a vow to make a pilgrimage to Rome. It was consecrated on 28 December 1065, only ten days before his own death.

Now Edward laid the foundations of the church,
With large square blocks of grey stone;
Its foundations are deep;
That part which faces the east he makes round;
The stones are very strong and hard;
In the centre rises a tower,
And two at the western front,
And fine and large bells he hangs there.
The pillars and entablature
Are rich outside and inside;
At the bases and the capitals
The decorations are fine and royal.
Sculptured are the stones, and storied are the windows;
All are made with the skill
Of good and loyal workmanship.
And when he finished the work,
With lead the whole of the roof he covers.
He made there a cloister, a chapter house in front,
Towards the east, vaulted and round,

A refectory and a dormitory,
And round them all the necessary offices.

2.11 Mishaps

Medieval building was not perhaps as robust or fault-free as we would like to think. Chronicles and histories are replete with stories not only of natural calamities such as storms and lightning destroying churches and the like, but of towers and other parts of such edifices collapsing because of human frailties. Here are some examples.

At Ramsey c. 985

One day when the monks rose in the morning they were dismayed to see what looked like a huge fissure in the wall of the great tower, gaping from top to bottom, which seemed to threaten the destruction of the whole church. This disastrous fault may have been due to the hurry with which the work had been done, or to faulty foundations, but it was certainly due to the masons. The spectacle of the leaning tower struck fear into the hearts of all who saw it, and the monks sought the advice of masons. They asserted that it was because the foundations of the tower were inadequate, and that to remedy this it would be necessary to take down the whole tower. Hiring workmen therefore, the brethren set about this task, a certain stubborn pride adding strength to their efforts, and they demolished it completely. Examining the cause of the disaster, they excavated the earth to a greater depth and saw how faulty the foundations were. They remade them, filling the cavity with great stones, firmly compacted, and pounded with rams, the whole held together with tough mortar.

(*Chronicon Abbatiae Ramesiensis*)

At Gloucester c. 1170

When Roger, bishop of Worcester was celebrating mass at the high altar on the abbey of St Peter at Gloucester the great high tower of the church suddenly came crashing down, just as the mass was finishing. The whole church was filled with such a mass of dust from the shattered stones and the mortar that for some time nobody was able to see anything or even open their eyes. Yet from this catastrophe nobody was injured, for the tower was at the west end of the church, and when it happened all the congregation had gone close to the high altar to receive the bishop's blessing, given at the end of mass.

(Giraldus Cambrensis, *Opera*, vii 64)

At St Albans, 1323

In the same year on the feast of St Paulinus, Bishop, after the celebration of the mass of the Blessed Virgin an accident occurred, so terrible that previous disasters might be considered to have been considered as naught compared with its magnitude. For, when there was a great crowd of people in the church to pray or to hear mass, suddenly two great pillars on the south side of the church suddenly collapsed at their base, and fell in turn to the ground with a terrible noise and crash. Monks and laity gazed with terror at this appalling sight, and then, scarcely an hour later, the whole wooden roof and the entire aisle on the south side of the church also collapsed.

(*Gesta Abbatum S. Albani*, ii 129)

2.12 The rebuilding of the choir of Canterbury

In 1174 the cathedral at Canterbury was largely destroyed by fire. Gervase of Canterbury (*c.* 1188), one of the most prolific historians of his own time, wrote an account of its rebuilding, and conveys a sense of the magnificence of what the recent murder of Thomas à Becket was to transform into one of the great shrines of Christendom.

So the brethren remained in grief and sorrow for five years in the nave of the church, divided from the congregation merely by a low wall. They sought in vain for a means whereby the church might be rebuilt, but without success, because, apart from anything else, the pillars had been considerably weakened by the fire, and were scaling away, so that even the wisest were scared out of their wits. French and English craftsmen were consulted, but they differed in the advice they gave. However amongst those workmen who did come was William of Sens, a most active and enterprising man, who was skilled in working both wood and stone. Him therefore they retained on account of his good reputation, and dismissed the rest. After carefully surveying the pillars both in their upper and lower storeys, he ventured to confess to the brothers that the pillars, rent with fire, and all they supported would have to be pulled down if they wished to have a safe and excellent building. At length they consented, resignedly rather than willingly, to the total destruction of the old choir. And then he addressed himself to procuring stone from beyond the sea. He designed ingenious machines for loading and unloading ships, and for lifting masonry and stone. He gave the sculptors whom he had got together moulds or patterns to follow, and diligently prepared other things of the same kind. The choir was pulled down, and nothing else done in that year.

But as the new building is completely different from its predecessor, it may be a good thing to describe the old one, and then the new . . . I will first decribe the work of Lanfranc, beginning from the great tower, not because the whole of this older church has been destroyed, but because it has been greatly altered. The tower, raised upon great pillars, is placed in the midst of the church, like the centre point of a circle, and has a gilt angel at its apex. On the west of the tower is the nave of the church, supported on either side by eight pillars. Two lofty towers with gilded pinnacles are at the end of the nave, over the west door. A gilded chandelier hangs in the middle of the church. A screen with a loft separates the tower section from the nave, and had in the middle, on the nave side, the altar of the Holy Cross. Above the loft, and going straight across the church was the beam, which bore a great cross, two angels, and the figures of the Blessed Virgin and St John. The great tower had two transepts, one to the north, the other to the south, each of which had in its middle a stout pillar, which sustained a vault which sprang from the wall on three of its sides, the plan of each transept being identical. The south transept bore the organ on its vault, and beneath was an apse, extending to the east . . . The pillar which stood in this north transept, as well as the vault, which rested on it, was taken down, so that the altar built on the place where St Thomas had been slain could be seen by pilgrims from a greater distance. Around, and at the height of the said vault a passage was constructed, from which hangings and curtains might be hung. From the transept to the tower, and from the tower to the choir there were several flights of steps. There was a descent from the tower area to the nave through a double door.

Now that the choir of Conrad has been so miserably consumed by fire, my pen shall attempt its description . . . Let us begin therefore at the area of the aforesaid great tower, which is in the centre of the church, and then proceed eastwards. The eastern pillars of the tower projected as a solid wall, and were each formed into a round half-pillar. Hence, in line and order, were nine pillars on each side of the choir, nearly equidistant from each other; after these, six in a sequence were arranged in a circle, that is from the ninth on the south side to the ninth on the north, of which the two end joined by an arch. Upon these pillars, arches were built, connecting them, above these the wall was set with small blank windows. This wall on either side, bounding the choir, met the corresponding one at the head of the church in that circuit of pillars. Above the wall was the passage called a *triforium*, and the upper windows. This was the upper termination of the interior wall. Upon it rested a ceiling decorated with excellent paintings and the roof. At the base of the pillars was a wall built of marble slabs, which, surrounding the choir and the presbytery, divided the body of the church from the surrounding aisles. This wall enclosed the monks' choir, the presbytery, the high altar dedicated in the name of Jesus Christ, the altar of St Dunstan, and the altar of St Elfege. Above the wall, in the circuit behind and opposite to the altar was the patriarchal throne, formed out of a single stone, in which the archbishops sat during the solemnity of the mass until the moment of the consecration, when they descended to the high altar by eight steps.

From the choir to the presbytery were three steps; from the pavement of the presbytery to the altar three steps, but to the patriarchal throne eight steps. At the eastern corner of the altar were two wooden columns, gracefully ornamented with gold and silver, carrying a transverse beam which was decorated in gold, and supported a figure of Christ in majesty, with statues of St Dunstan and St Elphege, as well as seven chests, covered in gold and silver, which contained the relics of various saints. Between the columns stood a gilt cross, surrounded by a circle of sixty transparent crystals. In the crypt, under the high altar stood the altar of the Blessed Virgin Mary. This crypt occupied the same area as the choir above it and hanging in its centre was a gilded chandelier with twenty four candles . . .

Master William of Sens, as I have already said, began to prepare all things necessary for the new work, and to destroy the old. This took up all the time till the feast of St Bertin [5 Sept] 1175 when, before the onset of winter, he erected four pillars; that is two on either side, and then two more to make three on either side, upon which and upon the exterior walls of the arches he placed elegant arches, and a vault, that is three key-stones on either side. With these works the second year was completed.

In the third year he placed two arches on either side, the two end ones being supported by marble pillars, and because at that point the choir and the transepts were to meet, he made these the chief pillars. Having added the keystone and vault he sprang the lower *triforium* from the central tower to these pillars with a number of marble columns.

In the summer of the fourth year, starting at the crossing, he built ten pillars, five on either side. Of these the first two were adorned with marble pillars, matching the two principal ones. On top of these were arches and vaults. Having completed the triforia and upper windows on each side, at the beginning of the fifth year, he was just in the act of preparing with machines for the turning of the great vault, when suddenly the beams broke under his feet and he fell to the ground, with stones and timber falling all round him some fifty feet. Thus sorely bruised he became incapable of continuing the work.

He had to stay in bed for some considerable time, but even so his condition did not improve, and as winter was approaching, and it was necessary to complete the upper vault, he entrusted the overseeing of the work to a certain clever and industrious monk, who was in charge of the masons, an appointment which aroused a good deal of envy and malice, as it made this young man seem more competent than those superior to him in monastic rank. But the master, from his bed, commanded all the things which had to be carried out and arranged a timetable for them.

The master, realising that he had not benefited from the doctors, gave up the work and returned to his home in France. Another succeeded him, one William, an Englishman, small in height, but in his workmanship acute and thorough. He, in the end of the fifth year finished the ciborium over the high altar, and laid the foundation for the extension of the church at the east end, wherein the body of St Thomas was to be buried. To do this he had to dig up an old cemetery where many holy monks had been buried. These were carefully collected, and buried in a large trench in the corner between the chapel and the south side of the infirmary . . .

In the beginning of the sixth year, when the work was resumed, the monks were seized with a great passion to have the choir finished by the coming Easter, and the master set himself manfully to try and fulfil this wish. He constructed with all diligence the wall which surrounds the choir and presbytery. He built three altars in the presbytery, and carefully prepared tombs for St Dunstan and St Elphege. A wooden wall was set up with three glass windows in it between the pillars, and so the monks were able to return from the nave into their own choir on April 19th 1180, Holy Saturday, 5 years, 7 months and 13 days after they had left it . . .

The differences between the old and the new work may now be explained. The pillars of both are alike in form and thickness, but different in length, for the new ones were extended by at least twelve feet. In the old capitals the work was plain, in the new it is exquisitely carved. In the old there was a circuit of 22 pillars; in the new 28. There the arches and everything else were either plain, or sculpted with an axe and not a chisel; now there is beautiful carving everywhere. Then there were no marble pillars, now they are everywhere. In the old building in the circuit around the choir the vaults were plain, in the new they are ribbed, and have keystones. There a wall set upon pillars divided the transepts from the nave choir, but here they are separated from the choir by no such partition, and converge together on one keystone, which is placed in the middle of the great vault, which rests on the four principal pillars. Then there was a wooden ceiling, decorated with fine paintings, but now the roof is made of the most beautifully fashioned stone.

2.13 Rules for houses

As early as 1189 regulations were beginning to determine the design and construction of private dwelling houses. The London Assizes of 1189 included the following rules.

When two neighbours have decided to build between themselves a wall of stone, each shall concede a foot and a half of land, and so they shall construct at their joint cost a stone wall three feet thick and thirteen feet in height. And if they agree, they shall make a gutter between them, to carry off the water from their houses, as they may consider most convenient. But if they do not agree, either of them may make a gutter to carry the water dripping from his house onto his own land, provided that he can carry it into the main street.

And if anyone shall have windows looking towards the land of a neighbour, and although he and his predecessors have long possessed a view through the aforesaid windows, nevertheless his neighbour may lawfully obstruct the view through these windows by building opposite them on his own ground, according to his choice, unless he who has the windows can show by any document that his neighbour may not obstruct the view from these windows.

Let it be remembered that in former times a great deal of the city was built of wood, and the roofs were made of straw, reeds and other such things, so that when any house caught fire a great deal of the city was destroyed by that fire, as happened in the first year of the reign of King Stephen [1135]. For it is written in the chronicles that in a fire which started at London Bridge, St Paul's was burnt down, and the fire went on from there, burning all the houses and buildings as far as St Clement Danes. Therefore many citizens to avoid such danger built, according to their means, on the land they owned, stone houses covered and protected by thick tiles against the fury of the fire, whereby it often happened that when a fire broke out in the city and burnt many buildings, and reached such a house and not being able to ignite it the fire would die down and not reach other peoples' houses . . .

Therefore the citizens' council ordains that all the cook shops on the Thames should be whitewashed and plastered both inside and out, and that all inner partitions be removed.

Whosoever wishes to build, let him take care, as he loveth himself and his goods, that he make not roofs of reed or rush or any manner of litter, but with tiles or shingle, or wood, or if possible with lead within the city. Also all houses which till now have been roofed with reed or rush which can be plastered, let them be plastered within eight days, and let those which are not so plastered be pulled down by the city council.

All wooden houses, which are near to stone houses on Cheap and so may be a source of danger, shall be made secure against fire, and if not, pulled down, no matter to whom they belong. And let old houses in which brewing or baking is done be whitewashed and plastered within and without, that they may be safe against fire.

2.14 Activities at St Albans

In the thirteenth century the monastic community of St Albans, under its various abbots was involved in a number of architectural and artistic activities, not all of them successful, due to a combination of mischance, ineptitude and the weaknesses of human character. All these are recorded in the *Gesta Abbatum sancti Albani* (Rolls Series, vol. 28).

Abbot John (1195–1214) relying on the hundred marks which had been left by his predecessor Abbot Warin, decided to rebuild the abbey church. He had the facade of the old church, which was made of tiles and mortar demolished, and began to accumulate stocks of stone, wood and other materials. When he had assembled the masons, who were under the control of Master Hugh Godcliff, a deceitful and untruthful man, though an excellent architect, and the trench had been dug, he discovered that he had spent a good deal more than 100 marks, and the wall had not even reached the level of its foundation. Worse still, after that, before the wall had risen to the height of an ordinary house Master Hugh added carvings and figures which were both inappropriate and insignificant, which added greatly to the expense. The Abbot got fed up with the whole thing, the project languished, and since the walls lay exposed to the weather, they began to disintegrate, the pillars and capitals fell down, to the derision of those who saw them; the workmen departed, and they weren't even paid . . .

After the years had passed by fruitlessly, as far as the building of the new church was concerned, Brother Gilbert of Sisseverne was put in charge of the work, but thirty years passed without him doing more than add another two feet.

Abbot John therefore decided to turn his attention to other projects. He had the old refectory demolished, and a new one built, much more elegant than the old one, which had been dark and decayed, and this was accomplished in his own lifetime so that he was able to eat there with his monks. Encouraged by this success, he had the old dormitory, which was in a dilapidated condition and collapsing with age completely pulled down, and a handsome new one built in its place and finished absolutely to perfection. For the construction of these two buildings the monastery allocated its wine revenue for the whole of fifteen years.

Also to the honour of Abbot John should be adduced what the monks themselves did during his tenure of office. In the time of Abbot John, by the industry and the righteous labours of Prior Raymond, the brother of Roger of Park, the Cellarer, there was made a great frontal, partly of metal, partly of wood, executed with the greatest artistry, which is now in front of the High Altar in our church. He also had made two bas-reliefs in silver-gilt, on one of which is the Crucifixion, with the Blessed Virgin and St John; on the other God in majesty, with the four evangelists, both of them cut in the most elegant carving by the skilled labours of Brother Walter of Colchester who, through the persuasion and prompting of Brother Gubiun took the religious habit on our monastery – a happy event.

Walter's brother William painted before the altar of the Blessed Virgin a panel with a reredos beautifully carved, and surmounted by a cross, all finely made. He was also responsible for the frontals on the side altars, namely those of St John, St Benedict, St Stephen and St Amphibalus. His pupil and brother Master Simon, the painter, did those on the altars of St Peter and St Michael. Brother Richard, who was the nephew of William and the son of Master Simon, did the frontal of St Thomas' chapel. These and many other works of art, some of them not in the time of Abbot John, but later, were made for the honour and the decoration of the House of God.

We are of the opinion that these things should be committed to writing for perpetuity so that we may continue to bless the memory of those who by their zealous labour bequeathed to us a monastic church so finely adorned.

Abbot William [1214–35] finished the dormitory most suitably by providing oak beds, and all the community were able to sleep there. Moreover in his time the two transepts of the church were strengthened in the roof. with large oak beams, well joined together, and these were supported by smaller ones. The old ones which they replaced had rotted away with the damp and worms, and admitted an abundance of rain. The spire of the tower which rises like a great scaffold, was constructed out of the best material, well-joined together, and raised much higher than the old one which was threatened with destruction. And the new spire was entirely covered in lead. The work was carried out through the diligence and industry of Richard of Thidenhanger, one of our laybrothers, who was also the monastic chamberlain, a duty which he diligently carried out at the same time. Due credit however should be attributed to Abbot William, without whose authority this work could not have been carried out.

Indeed when Brother Richard died, the abbot had the spire uncovered again, because the lead had been badly fixed, and it was reroofed properly and durably. Decorations were added on the sides, namely, eight rectilinear pilasters extending from the tip of the spire to the wall of the church, so that the octagonal shape of the tower was more clearly defined, all this was done at his own expense by the persuasion and instigation of Lord Matthew, who was then bailiff and keeper of the seal of Cambridge. These lines, which are commonly called aristae wonderfully strengthened the tower and added pleasant decoration to it too, as well as helping to keep out the rain. Now the tower, the shape of which had been previously undefined clearly showed its shape, as opposed to what it was before, plain and meagre, harmonising badly with the rest of the building.

Abbot William also decided to restart the work on the front of the church, which had suffered such dilapidation, and attempts to improve which had been dragging on for such a long time. In a short time he had constructed a new facade, with a roof of fine material, with timbers and beams and with glass windows perfectly constructed. This was joined to the earlier part of the building and covered with lead.

He also repaired the stonework and the glass of those windows which are in the wall above the place where the great missal is kept, and where the lesser clerics sing matins and the other liturgical hours. Moreover he did the same for many other windows in the church, making good both the tracery and the glass. So the church, now newly lit by these fine windows seemed entirely new.

Also in his time, when Dom Walter of Colchester, an incomparable painter and sculptor who was also sacristan, had completed a rood-loft in the middle of the church, with its great cross, figures of the Virgin and St John, as well as other fine carvings and decorations, at the expense of the sacristy, but with his own effort, Abbot William solemnly removed the shrine with the relics of St Alphibalus and his companions from the shrine where it had previously been kept (behind the High Altar, and next to the shrine of St Alban) towards the north of the church in the area which is enclosed by iron lattice-work, and built there a beautiful altar with a richly painted frontal.

Moreover to add to the fame of the said Abbot William it must be recorded that he added a number of fine additions to the high altar, including especially a beam on which was painted in surpassing artistry the story of St Alban. This was magnificently carried out by Dom Walter of Chichester, to whom we have already referred with praise, but the Abbot of course was responsible for providing the funds.

2.15 Royal building

The *Liberate Rolls*, orders issued for commissioning or paying for undertakings on the king's behalf, during the reign of Henry III (1207–72) show the immense amount of building work going on way and beyond those major works which have attracted most notice.

21st. We command that you cause to be made at Kennington on the spot where our chapel roofed with thatch is situated, a small church with a staircase of plaster, which will be thirty feet long and twelve feet wide; in such a manner that in the upper part there be made a chapel for the use of our Queen, so that she may enter it from her chamber; and in the lower part let there be a chapel for the use of our household.

22nd. Walter de Burgh is commanded to wainscote both the upper and the lower chapel of the Queen at Kennington, and to raise the flue of the King's chimney there, and to do other small necessary building works.

23rd. And cause a map of the world to be painted in our said Hall at Winchester, and cause the chamber of the Queen to be wainscoted, and painted with a history.

24th. *June 14th 1240*. The Queen's chamber (in the Tower of London) to be panelled, and entirely whitewashed inside, and newly painted with roses; a partition wall of wooden panelling to be made between that chamber, and its garderobe, and the whole to be tiled outside. Our great chamber to be whitewashed and repainted, and its shutters to be remade with new wood, new catches and hinges and newly barred with iron. Our coat of arms to be painted on the shutters. Also all the glass windows in the chapel of John the Baptist be repaired, and also the windows in the great chamber which overlooks the Thames. In the corner of the same chamber towards the east, to make a great round tower to be built in such a way, that at its lowest level it goes down into the Thames. Also a louver to be made over the top of the kitchen of the keep.

28th. Edward Fitzotho is commanded to cause to be built a certain great porch which the King has commanded to be made at Westminster, and which is to be such as may be becoming to so great a palace, to be made between the lavatory in front of the King's kitchen, and the door entering into the smaller hall, so that the King may dismount from his palfrey in it, at a handsome front, and walk under it between the aforesaid door and the lavatory aforesaid, and also from the King's kitchen and the chamber of the knights, and he is to cover it with lead.

28th. You must cause to be made in the hall at Geddington two windows with columns, like the other windows, and in the window which is in the gable of the hall make a white glass window with an image of a king in the centre.

28th. The bailiffs of Woodstock are also to cause the Queen's chapel in our palace there to be lengthened by twenty feet towards the east, and create vaulting above and beneath.

30th. *March 14th 1246*. A fireplace of plaster to be made in the Queen's chamber; to repair the glass windows in the king's chamber and chapel, and in the queen's chapel; to cover the chamber of the king and queen with shingles and to repair the walls.

31st. Also to make in the hall of the king's castle at Rochester in the northern gable, two glass windows, one having the shield of the king, and the other the shield of the late Count of Provence, and also to make two small glass windows on each side of the same hall, and in each of them the figure of a king.

32nd. To make a new mantel at the King's castle at Clarendon, on which mantel he is to cause to be painted the Wheel of Fortune and Jesse, and to cover the King's pictures in the said chamber with canvas less they should be injured. And to cause the history of Antioch and the combat of King Richard to be painted in the same chamber, and to paint that wainscot of a green colour with golden stars.

34th. *August 24th 1250*. Odo, the goldsmith of Westminster without delay to put aside the picture which was begun to be painted in the king's great chamber at Westminster, beneath the large history painting in the said chamber, with the scrolls containing the figures and representations of lions, birds and other beasts, and to paint it green after the manner of a curtain, so that the effect of the great history be not diminished or impaired.

34th. *9th October 1250*. A baptistery is to be made in the chapel of all Saints at our palace at Clarendon, and to be put on the chapel a bell turret with two bells, to make a crucifix with two images on either side of wood, and an image of the Blessed Mary with her Child. The queen's chamber to be decently paved, and in her hall let there be made a window towards the garden, well barred with iron; and there are to be two windows in the Queen's chapel, one on each side of the altar, which are to be divided down the middle, so that they can be opened or shut at will. And a bench to be made around the garden, and the wall above it to be whitewashed.

37th. *April 1253*. An image of the Blessed Virgin with her Child [a statue?] to be made on the front of the chapel of St Thomas in the palace at Winchester; the queen's wardrobe to be painted with green paint and golden stars; to paint an angel on the other side of the chapel, and the figures of the prophets round the chapel; to paint in the glass window of the chapel St Edward with his ring; to pave the chamber of Edward, the king's son with flat tiles; to put benches round the king's chamber; to put glass windows in the chapel of St Catherine, at the top of the castle, and to panel it; to make mats for the king's chapel; to make a house for the chaplain dwelling in the castle in a fitting place. Also to make in the king's upper wardrobe, where his clothes are kept, two cupboards on either side of the fireplace with two arches, and a wooden partition across the wardrobe.

44th.   To repair the gutters of the chamber of the chaplains at Winchester castle, and build a pillar in the oriol towards the Queen's chapel. The sheriff of Southampton is directed to build on oriol between the new chamber and the Queen's chapel in the same place, of the width of the said chamber, and a passage to the oriol of the aforesaid chapel, with four glass windows, and other small openings of glass, and a fireplace in the said oriol to heat the Queen's victuals, and to build under the aforesaid oriol two walls from the same chamber to the chapel aforesaid.

44th.   That they be paid for that which they expended on the king's order in repairing the king's chimney at Westminster, which threatened to fall, and in making a certain conduit through which is carried underground to the King's lavatory, and to other places there; and in making a certain conduit through which the refuse from the King's kitchens at Westminster flows into the Thames; which conduit the King ordered to be made on account of the stink of the dirty water which was carried through his halls, which was wont to affect the health of the people frequenting the same halls.

2.16   A week of wages at Westminster

The continuing work carried on at Westminster Abbey in the year 1253 is recorded in a roll of payments in the Public Record Office, and an example of one week, the second after Easter in that year, gives some indication of the ongoing expenditure on wages and purchases which work on the Abbey entailed. The Feast of St John *Ante Portam Latinam* was one of those days on which workmen had to give their labour free to the king, as part of the feudal contract.

Second week after Easter, containing the feast of St John *Ante Portam Latinam* which belongs to the King.

To wages of 49 cutters of white stone, 15 marblers, 26 stonelayers, 32 carpenters, with John and his partner at St Albans, two painters with an assistant, 13 polishers, 19 smiths, 14 glaziers with four plumbers; 15li. 10s. 1d.

To wages of 176 workmen, with overseers and clerks and two two-horse carts, daily 9li. 7s. 2d.

Sum of wages; 25li. 17s. 2d.

EMPTIONS; To Master Albericus for arrears of form-pieces, 66s.;53 feet of parpents 4d. per foot; 59 feet of voussoirs with fillets, at 3d. per foot; 1221 feet at 3d. a foot; 50 assises at 5d. each assise . . . and seven steps cut by taskwork, 7li. 13s. 1d.

Item; for nine capitals, 68 feet of escus.

Item; for 25 hundred and a half quartern of chalk for the vaults, 8li. 7s.

Item; for 22 hundred and three quarters of freestone, 6li. 16s. 6d. To Roger of Reygate for eight hundred and a quartern of free-stone 53li. 7½d. To Richard the limeburner for 3 hundred of lime, 15s.

To Agnes for two hundred and a half of lime, 12s. 6d. To Richard of Eastcheap for dozen hurdles or crates with poles (for scaffolding) 9s. 7d. To Richard Oggel for 5 dozen hurdles with poles, 12s. 6d. To Henry of the Bridge for iron nails and whetstones, 19s. 8d. To Benedict for carriage, porterage and weighing of twenty cartloads of lead, 9s. 4d.

Sum total of emptions, 27li. 12s. 10½d.

Sum total of the week, 53li. and 1½d.

2.17 An English scribe abroad

There was a constant interchange of craftsmen and scribes between different countries, and the documents of the Cistercian abbey of Dunes near Dunkirk (*Codex Dunensis* ed. Kervyn de Lettenhove, Brussels 1876) contains the following agreement, drawn up *c.* 1260, with remarkable precision and formidable sanctions.

To all those who read these letters, the Archbishop of Orleans conveys health in the Lord.

Be it known that, in our presence Robert of Normandy, an English scribe, has solemnly promised by his troth to write, continue and finish, according to his ability, for Dom W. de Lion, cleric, the commentary of Pope Innocent on the *Decretals*, in the same style which he has adopted in the second volume of that work, and in equally good letters, for which he shall be paid the sum of four pounds of Paris money, to be paid by the said cleric to the said Robert, on the same scale that he would receive as a free-lance scribe. Moreover the said scribe has solemnly promised that he will undertake no other work until this commission is completed. The same Robert has also sworn that if he should stop writing, continuing and finishing the said work, he shall be kept in prison in chains within the house of the said cleric, and shall not be released until the work is finished. And if he fails in these undertakings, he has agreed that our Provost or one of our servants, may seize him and commit him to imprisonment as detailed above, and he has sworn that he will in no way contravene any of these provisions. And for the keeping of the aforesaid provisions, the same Robert has pledged to the aforesaid Dom W. his own person and his heirs, and all his goods, whether moveable or immoveable, present or future, renouncing on oath all exemption through canon or civil law, all privilege of crusade, granted or to be granted, and any other way of escaping from the responsibilities inherent in this contract, submitting himself in this matter to the jurisdiction of our Court in Orleans.

3. Knights and burghers

A secular art appears

3.1 Artists' materials, 1284

The sale of artists' materials was an accepted trade and on 17 June 1284 the following debt was recorded in the Letter Book of the City of London. Hugh Motun was also the City Chamberlain. The mention of canvas is interesting.

On Friday, the eve of St Botolph in the twelfth year of the reign of King Edward 1st Nicholas Bacun, painter, acknowledged that he was bound to Hugh Motun in the sum of 20 shillings, for cinople [a green colour much used in heraldry], vermilion and canvas, varnish and verdigris; the same to be paid to the said Hugh or his certain attorney, 10 shillings at the feast of St Bartholemew (August 24th) and 10 shillings at the feast of St Michael (September 29th) without further delay.

3.2 Censoring images

The church held very strong views about the style and form of images, endeavouring to petrify them into rigid prototypes. On 2 August 1306 Ralph Baldock, bishop of London, author of a history of England, and later Lord Chancellor, addressed the following letter to the prior of Holy Trinity, Aldgate. (Published in *Proceedings of the Canterbury and York Society*, 1911.)

We have heard on trustworthy authority that one Tidemann of Germany has sold, some time ago to Geoffrey, Rector of St Mary's in the Poultry, a certain carved crucifix, with a cross-beam which does not represent the true form of the cross, and that the Rector has placed this in his church, and that the foolish faithful have flocked to see it in large numbers, even though it is not a true image of the cross, and as we realised, it might chance that their souls would be imperilled. By reason of this cross therefore we summoned the said Tidemann and Geoffrey to our presence, and having made diligent inquistion of both of them, we have ordained the following, less by continuance of this error worse things should befall. That the aforesaid Tidemann should take, as indeed he subsequently has, an oath on the Gospels that he should never henceforth make, or allow to be offered for sale within our city or diocese a cross such as this, or crosses with arms contrary to the accustomed style, under pain of excommunication for disobedience. And because the said Tidemann is an alien, and a simple man, who might probably in all innocence been ignorant of the traditional mysteries of the crucifix and the figure attached to it, therefore we have graciously granted to him the following remit. That he, having returned to us the invoice for twenty three pounds sterling, which he had from the Rector, shall be given back the crucifix which had been confiscated, and placed in your keeping, for the avoidance of peril to men's souls, by the discreet Master Richard of Newport, who was then our Vicar-General. Wherefore we enjoin and command you that, having received the invoice from the said Tidemann, which you will faithfully return to us, you will straightway give him the image, provided always that it be taken to some place outside our diocese from your monastery, either early in the morning, or late at night, when it can be done most secretly, and with least scandal, and that you will appoint someone to see that this has been done, and report back to us certifying this openly and plainly to us. Given at our palace of Fulham, August 2nd 1306.

3.3 Private possessions

The ordinary well-to-do person possessed by the fourteenth century many things which involved at some point in their production a high degree of design and craftsmanship. Typical of such belongings are those left to Johanna le Blund by her father Walter, in 1301 (Riley H. T., *Memorials of London and London Life*, 1868, p. 44).

These are the goods left by will to Johanna, daughter of Walter le Blund, now wife of Stephen de Abyndone, and delivered to the said Stephen on Thursday the eve of St Andrew the Apostle [November 30th] in the 29th year of the reign of King Edward, in presence of Elias Russel, then Mayor of London, Geoffrey de Norton, William de Leyre, and other Aldermen, namely: One silver cup with a foot; two cups of mazer, with silver feet; one cup of stone; six silver spoons; one silk purse; three needle-pieces of silk; one gilded girdle, trimmed with silver; two crepines [hair-nets] of silk, one garlanded with pearls; one gressoir [shawl] of silk; two kerchiefs and three barbettes [a kind of wimple]; four ear-pillows [cushions] two of which are of silk and two of pall [embroidered cloth]; six sheets, three counterpanes of wool; one counterpane of Reyns [fine linen from Rennes]; one gilded coverlet; one counterpane of gris [grey fur]; two women's chemises; one woman's rochet; three table-cloths; twelve towels in six pieces; one banker [a cushion for a bench] three feather beds, and three head-bolsters; one large chest. All the things aforesaid had been in the keeping of Hugh Pourte.

3.4 A house for a pelterer

A fourteenth century contract between a 'carpenter' and William Haningtone, a pelterer, or furrier is illuminating about the type of house such a man would have, and is also interesting for the payment, partly in cash, partly in kind.

Simon de Canterbury, carpenter, came before the Mayor and Aldermen of the City of London on the Saturday after the feast of St Martin the Bishop in the second year of King Edward, son of King Edward [November 11th 1308] and acknowledged that he would make at his own expense, down to the locks, for William Haningtone, pelterer, before the feast of Easter coming, a hall and a room with a chimney and one larder between the said hall and room and one sollar over the room and larder, also one oriole at the end of the hall, above the high bench, and one step with an oriole from the ground to the door of the aforementioned hall. But on the outside of it; and two enclosures as cellars, opposite to each other, beneath the hall, and one enclosure for a sewer, with two pipes leading to the said sewer, and one stable between the said hall and the old kitchen twelve feet in width, with a sollar above the said stable, and a garrett above the said sollar, and at one end of this sollar there is to be a kitchen with a chimney, and also an oriole between the said hall and the old chamber eight feet in width. And the said William Haningtone acknowledged that he was bound to pay to Simon, aforementioned, for all this work the sum of £9 5s. 4d., half a hundred of Eastern marten skins, fur for a

woman's hood worth 5s. and fur for a robe for him, the said
Simon.

3.5 Fake brass pots

On 24 February 1316 the Potters (the word refers to those who
made metal pots) of London came before the Mayor with a
complaint about faking which sounds not unfamiliar to twentieth-
century ears.

Be it remembered that on the Monday after the Feast of St Mathias
in the ninth year of the reign of King Edward, son of King Edward,
came the good folk of the trade of potters of London, and to the
Aldermen, that many persons who busy themselves both with
buying and selling pots of brass, and more especially one Aleyn le
Sopere, buy in divers places pots of bad metal, and then put them
on the fire, so as to make them resemble pots that have been used,
and are of old brass; and then they expose them for sale in
Westchepe on Sundays and other festival days, to the deception of
all who buy such pots, for the moment they are put on the fire,
and exposed to great heat, they come to nothing, and melt. By
which roguery and falsehood the people are deceived, and the trade
aforesaid is badly put in slander. Wherefore they pray that the
Mayor and Aldermen will ordain some remedy against the knavery
before-mentioned.

By reason whereof, the said Mayor and Aldermen commanded
that the aforesaid good folks of the trade should chose four dealers
and four founders of their trade, the most trustworthy and the most
knowing, for making a certain assay what alloy of lead belongs to
the hundredweight of brass, of whatsoever quality such lead may
be; that so all workmen in the trade might from henceforth work
according to such standard.

Whereupon there were chosen William de Bristouwe, John de
Hadham, Walter de Brochstone and Robert de Herford, dealers in
the said trade; Henry in the Lane, John atte Marche, William de
Alegate, and Robert de Raughstone, founders and workers of pots;
the which persons made oath that well and lawfully they would
make the assay aforesaid, and lawfully on the Friday next ensuing
present the same.

(Letter Book of the City of London; f. 54)

3.6 Rebuilding the tower of Ely

Between 1323 and 1330, as a result of the old tower collapsing, the crossing of the cathedral at Ely was rebuilt in the form of an octagon, a considerable innovation. That this was largely the result of the decision of an individual, Alan of Walsingham, is suggested by the account given in the *Historia Eliensis*.

One night, after the bretheren had made their procession to the various shrines, in honour of St Ermengilda, and were returning to their dormitory before more than one or two had had a chance to lie down, the central tower collapsed, and destroyed the choir with such a thunder of noise that it seemed like an earthquake, yet nobody was hurt or killed by its fall. Alan, our Sacrist, was sore grieved and afflicted by this lamentable accident, and for some time hadn't the least idea what to do, and how such a disaster could be remedied. But soon, plucking up courage, and putting his trust in the help of God, His most gracious Mother, and the merits of the holy virgin Etheldreda, he 'put his hand to strong things' (Prov.xxxi, 19). First he directed a large force of workmen, at great expense, to clear away from the cathedral all the fallen masonry and woodwork; then he had all the dust and rubbish cleared away. Finally he measured out in eight divisions, with the aid of an architect, the place where he intended to build the new tower, then he set the workmen to dig out and construct the foundations of the eight pillars of stone which would support the whole structure, under which the choir with its stall would afterwards be built, and eventually they found secure ground to support all this. Then, when the places for the foundations had been carefully dug out, and firmly founded with stone and sand, they began to construct the eight large columns, with the stonework which they supported. This he completed in six years, bringing it up to the upper string-course in the year of Our Lord 1328. Then, straightaway the cunningly-wrought timber structure of the new tower was begun, a structure designed with the utmost subtlety of imagination, which would crown all the stonework beneath. This, in its turn, was completed with vast and heavy expense, especially in having to seek far and wide for the huge beams which were needed to support this building, which were eventually found with the utmost difficulty, and at great cost, and brought to Ely by land or sea. These beams were carved and shaped by skilful craftsmen, and incorporated into the structure with marvellous art, and so at long last, with God's help, the tower was brought to that marvellous completion which had been so long desired. The whole cost of this new tower, during the twenty years of Alan de Walsingham's time was £2,400 6s. 11d., whereof £206 1s. came from gifts.

3.7 Royal portraits

There was a considerable industry in the painting of complete sets of royal portraits for dining halls and similar places (by the end of the sixteenth century these were often supplanted or enlarged by similar series of Roman Emperors). The *Chronicles* of Gloucester Abbey record Edward II's visit there *c.* 1323.

In the time of Abbot John Thoky, King Edward II came to Gloucester, and was honourably entertained by the abbot and community. As he sat at table in the abbot's hall, he noted how the Kings his predecessors were painted there, and jestingly asked the abbot whether his own portrait would be added to the collection or not. To which the abbot replied, more in the spirit of prophecy than of jest, that he hoped that he would have the King in a more honourable place than this, as indeed it came to pass. For after the king's death [he was murdered at Berkeley Castle in 1327], his venerable body was refused by certain other monasteries in the region, namely St Augustine's at Bristol, St Mary's at Kingswood, and St Aldhelm's at Malmesbury for fear of Roger de Mortimer and Queen Isabella, and their accomplices. Yet Abbot Thoky fetched his body from Berkeley Castle in his own chariot, sumptuously adorned and painted with the arms of our abbey, and brought it to Gloucester, where the abbot and the whole community clad in their finest vestments received the body honourably, with a procession of all the citizens, and buried it in our church in the north aisle, close by the High Altar.

3.8 Materials for a coronation

State occasions demanded a vast outlay in materials of all kinds, especially sumptuous textiles. Amongst the rolls from the reign of Edward III is an account by John de Feriby and Thomas of Useflete of their expenditure on such materials for the king's coronation on 1 February 1327 in Westminster Abbey. The total cost was formidable: £1,056 19s. 3d.

For the Great Hall of Westminster

Of cloth of Candlewick Street[1] for hangings and bancours, 7 cloths and 12 ells.

The same day of strong cloth for the king's halls, 60 ells;

The same day to be placed under the king's feet, passing with bare feet from his own station to the church, and from the church to his chamber, returning after the coronation, of strong cloth, 15 cloths; Also for the floors of the hall of linen cloth, 300 ells.

The ornament of the king's throne on the day of his coronation in the church of Westminster

For the fitting up and ornamenting of the seat of King Edward III on the day of his coronation in the church of Westminster, Feb. 1st in the first year of his reign; viz. cloth of gold with diaper work on silk, cloth of gold on linen, samite, velvet, tapestry with cushions for the seat by the survey and testimony of John de Feriby, appointed clerk for this purpose by the seneschal and treasurer of the household; for tapestry of different colours to cover the wood-work of the king's seat, 21 tapestries.

The same day for cloth of gold on silk to hang round the seat on every side, and for ornamenting the seat itself, 6 cloths and 1 quarter.

The same day for a veil or curtain to be stretched out over the king's head sitting on the chair in the royal seat, with cords of cloth of gold and purple linen, 2 cloths;

The same day for chamber cushions, for the king's feet when sitting in the chair, 5 cushions.

The same day, to hang between the cloths of gold and silk before-mentioned around the royal seat, at the sides and borders, cloth of gold on linen, 22 cloths.

The same day of striped Tartar cloth for the same, 1 cloth.

The same day of strong lawn for the same, 6 pieces.

---

1. Candlewick Street, which got its name from the fact that its first occupiers were candle-makers, had become, by the fourteenth century, famous for its textile weavers – many of them Flemings. The name is still applied to a type of cloth.

Knights and burghers

For the adorning of the altar-rails of the High Altar, and the floor of the church for coronation day

Item, the same day, for fitting up and ornamenting the rails of the High Altar, and the pavement around it with cloth of gold and diapered silk, 4 cloths.
The same day for purple velvet for the same, 1 piece.
The same day for silk Tartar fabric, 1 cloth.

Ornaments of the king's chamber for his consecration and oblations, and of the Royal seat before the altar

Item, the same day, for fitting up and ornamenting the king's chamber, and for covering the king's faldstool before the altar with cloth of gold from Nakir, 2 cloths.
The same day for cloth of gold on silver with diaper work, 2 cloths.
The same day for the same Samite of Styva, 1 cloth.
The same day for cushions for the king's faldstool; 3 cushions.
Item for cushions for the king's chamber, 4 cushions.
For silk gloves, for the king at his coronation, 1 pair.
For the oblation of our lord the king cloth of gold on silk with diaper work, 1 cloth.

Ornaments of the throne of the Archbishop of Canterbury before the altar

Item for fitting up and ornamenting a chair in which the Archbishop of Canterbury sat at the king's coronation, cloth of gold on silk, 1 cloth. The same day two chamber cushions for the said chair, 2 cushions.
The same day for tapestry to put under the chair, 2 pieces.

For covering the tomb of the late King Edward on the coronation day

The same day for the covering of the tomb of the late Lord Edward, the illustrious grandfather of King Edward III at the coronation, cloth of gold on silk, with diaper work, sewed together on account of the width of the tomb 2 cloths.

Covers for the cushions

Item cloth of Tars for newly covering 3 cushions of the abbot of Westminster, for the king to place his foot on, descending from

the great throne after being annointed on the day of his coronation, 1 ell.

*The ornaments of the king's chamber before his taking the order of
knighthood*

Item for the fitting up and adornment of the king's chamber in his
palace of Westminster, on the last day of January, the night
before he received the order of knighthood, viz. with red
tapestry, and shields of the king's arms in the corners, 5 pieces.
The same day for cushions of new samite for the king's chapel, 3
cushions.
For cushions of the same for the king's chamber after he is
knighted, 6 cushions.
For bancours for the same chamber, ornamented with different
shields, viz. 4 red with green borders, 1 green, and 4 murrey
and blue, 9 banners.
Item for bancours for the chamber before mentioned, ornamented
with tapestry and shields in the corners with the king's arms
bancours.

*Ornaments for the royal throne in the great hall at Westminster on
coronation day*

Item for ornaments for the king's seat, viz. cloth of gold and
Turkey silk 4 cloths, containing 30¾ ells.
The same day for the back of the same to preserve it from the
dampness of the wall, 24 ells of linen.
The same day for 1 piece of velvet, for a curtain with ornaments
attached hanging before the king's table, and strengthened with
red and grey lawn, 4 pieces.
The same day to place under the king sitting, 2 pieces of velvet
containing 14 ells.
The same day cushions of samite for the same, 3 cushions.

3.9 The rules of the tapestry-makers

Essential to the medieval approach to the production of objects of
almost any kind, was a desire to regulate quality as clearly as possible. In 1331 the rules of the Tapicers (who produced carpets and
other types of textiles) were approved by the Court of Common
Pleas of the City of London.

These are the Ordinances of the trade of Tapicers, made by the good folks of the same trade, the which Ordinances were approved and accepted before John de Pulteneye, Mayor, the Aldermen and Commonalty in the Court of Common Pleas held on Monday, the eve of St Hilary [January 13th] in the fourth year of the reign of King Edward the Third:

In the first place, they have ordained, and they pray that no thief or misdoer, acting against the peace of our lord the King, may be found amongst them, and if any such there be, they pray that he be removed, and be punished according to the law. Also they have ordained that no tapice in the said trade shall be made, if it be not of the lawful assize, used in ancient times; that is to say of the common assize every tapice being four ells in length and two ells in breadth; and of the smaller assize the tapice being three ells in length and one and a half in breadth; and that no such tapice be made with arms upon, unless it be made wholly of wool, and that if any tapice be found in any other manner made against the form aforesaid, it shall be forfeited to the Chamber of the Guildhall of London.

Also that no cushions be made with arms thereon, if they be not of wool, and half an ell square, and at least a quarter in width. And if any cushion be found made in any other manner, it shall be forfeit to the said Chamber.

Also that no banker [a cushion or cloth for benches at a dining table] shall be made in the said trade, unless it be the size of the cushions aforesaid; and that if any banker be found made in any other manner, it shall be forfeit to the said Chamber.

Also they have ordained that no man shall keep any manner of handwork of the said trade, if he be not free of the City, and that if any such is found it shall be forfeited to the said Chamber.

And that no man of the said trade, other than a freeman, shall take an apprentice, and that every freeman of the said trade shall maintain his apprentice, according to the usages and franchise of the City. And that if any other person than a freeman shall take an apprentice, the same must be done by permission of the Mayor and Aldermen.

And that from henceforth there shall be used in the said trade nothing but good wool of England and of Spain, and that if any other wool shall be found in the said trade, the same shall be forfeit to the said Chamber.

And that no chalon of ray [striped wool of the sort used for blankets] shall be made if it be not of the lawful assize ordained by the members of the trade; that is to say two ells and half a quarter in length, and five quarters in breadth, and not less.

The article above-written were shown unto the Mayor and Aldermen in the full husting aforesaid by Walter de Stebenhuthe, Richard Merk, Richard Frere, Nicholas atte Forde, John de Bromholme and Nicholas de Southereye, men chosen of the aforesaid trade. And because it seemed that the aforesaid rules had been made to the common interests of the City, it was granted that from henceforth they should be kept, and their points strictly observed.

> How strictly observed they were can be seen by the case brought
> before the Mayor forty-three years later.

On the Monday after the Feast of St Valentine [February 14th] in the forty eighth year of the reign of King Edward III [1374] Henry Clerke, John Dyke, William Tanner and Thomas Lucy Tapicers, and Masters of the trade of Tapicers in London caused to be brought here a coster [a piece of tapestry for the side walls of a hall,or for a table] of tapestry wrought upon the loom after the manner of work of Arras, and made of false work, by Katherine Duchewoman in her house at Fynkeslane, being four yards in length, and seven quarters in breadth, seeing that she had made it of linen thread beneath, but covered with wool above, in deceit of the people, and against the Ordinance of the trade aforesaid, as here in the Chamber enrolled.

And whereas the said Katherine was warned to be here on the morrow to show if she had aught to say why the same coster should not be burnt, for the reason aforesaid, she did not afterwards appear.

Therefore, after due examination thereof by the Masters aforesaid, and other reputable men of the same trade,by assent of the Mayor and certain of the Aldermen, it was ordered that the said coster, as being false work should be burnt, according to the form of the Articles of trade of the Tapicers aforesaid.

And be it known that it was agreed, by assent of the Masters and other reputable men of the trade that the execution of the judgement aforesaid shall not be done on this occasion. [Probably because being a foreigner she was ignorant of the regulations.]

3.10 The pewterer's craft

What is now known as 'quality control' was one of the major preoccupations of medieval craftsmen, and in 1348 the Pewterers drew up a series of ordinances, which specify, *inter alia*, the nature and extent of their activities.

In the first place, seeing that the craft of pewtery is founded upon certain substances and metals, such as copper, tin and lead, of which metals in varying proportions they make vessels, namely pots, salt-cellars, porringers, plates and other things which are ordered by their customers, and these productions demand different alloys and mixtures, according to the nature of the vessel being made. These things cannot be made without the knowledge and skill of a pewterer, who must have been well trained and be knowledgeable in his trade, seeing that many people, not knowing the correct alloys, nor the correct proportions, nor the right rules of the trade, do work and make vessels and other things not in the right manner, to the damage of the people, and to the scandal of the trade. The worthy members of the trade do therefore pray that it may be ordained that three or four of the most lawful and skilful of the trade may be chosen to supervise the alloys; and the quality of the workmanship, and that by their examination and assay, amendment may be made speedily, where a default has occurred. And, if anyone be found guilty of such a default it shall be shown, with the name of the guilty culprit, to the Mayor and Aldermen, and he shall be judged by them with the assistance of the members of the trade.

It must be understood that all types of vessels made of pewter such as salt-cellars, porringers, platters, chargers, pitchers squared, and cruets squared, and chrismatories [vessels for carrying the holy oil for Extreme Unction] and other objects which are made square or ribbed, shall be made of the top quality pewter, with the proportion of copper to tin as much as it will take naturally. All other things which are made by the trade such as pots rounded, cruets rounded, and candlesticks and other rounded things which are produced by the trade must be made of tin, alloyed with lead in reasonable proportions. These proportions for the alloy are 22 pounds of lead to one hundredweight of tin, and these are always to be called 'vessels of pewter'.

Also nobody must meddle with this trade if he has not been sworn in before its members, lawfully to work according to the rules laid down, and he must be an apprentice or otherwise a lawful craftsman, who is known to them by his work. And nobody must accept an apprentice against the laws and usage of the City, and those who are so admitted are to be enrolled according to the said usages.

Nobody – freeman or stranger – shall be allowed to bring into the City any manner of vessel of pewter for sale until it has been assayed, on pain of forfeiture of the wares. If the assay is successful then let the wares be sold for what they are, and not under a false description. Nor must any member of the trade make furtively, or in secret, vessels of lead, or of false alloy, for sending out of the City to fairs or markets for sale, to the detriment of the City's good name and the reputation of the members of the trade. Such things as are to be sent to fairs and markets outside the City shall be sent for assay to the Wardens. Moreover every craftsman must be responsible for the quality of his workmanship and its assay, wherever it may be sold. And if anyone be found carrying such wares for sale to fairs or markets anywhere in the kingdom before it has been assayed, and has been so adjudged by the Mayor and Aldermen, let him receive punishment at their discretion, at the suit of the members of the trade.

Moreover if anyone shall be found doing anything to the detriment of his master, whether apprentice or journeyman, secretly in the form of larceny, if the goods be worth less than 10 pence let him recompense his master; if he offend a second time let him be punished at the discretion of the members of the trade, and if he offend a third time, let him be expelled from the trade.

Those of the said trade who shall be found working in the said trade, otherwise than has before been indicated, and upon assay shall be found guilty thereof, upon the first conviction let them lose the material so wrought, upon the second conviction both lose the material and suffer punishment at the discretion of the Mayor and Aldermen, and on their third conviction, let them be permanently expelled from the trade.

And also the good folk of the trade have agreed that no one be so daring as to work at night upon articles of pewter, seeing that they are aware of the fact that the sight is not so good at night, or so certain as it is by day, and to work by night is to the disadvantage of the community.

(Letter Book of the City of London, 1348, Book F)

3.11 How angels should look

There was no end to the interpretations which could be imposed either by ecclesiastical ordinance, or by the ingenuity of commentators on the shapes which divine and celestial beings could assume in art. Here John de Trevisa (1326–1412) translates from the Latin of Bartholomew de Glanville a section of his *De Proprietatibus Rerum* written in the middle of the thirteenth century. This translation, of what was in effect a kind of encyclopaedia, was one of the books printed by Wynkyn de Worde *c.* 1495.

Howe Angell in bodily shape is peynted. Though angels' kynde have no mater, nother lyneacions [lineaments] and shap of body, yet angels ben paynted in bodily lykenesse, and scrypture makyth mynde that they have diver limmes and shappes. But by denominacyons of limmes that, ben seen unseene werkynges of of hevenly inwyttes [minds] ben understonde. For whan angelles bene paynted with longe lockes and cryspe heer, thereby is understonde theyr cleane affections and ordynate thoughtes. For the heer of the heed tokeneth thoughtes and affections, that sprygen of the roote of thought and mynde. And they bene peynted berdlesse, for to take consideration and hede that they passe never the stage of youth, neyther wexe feble in vertues, neither faile for age. Feete they have, but as it were alwaye bare, for the movyng of theyr affeccyon to godwarde is sequestred from all deedly lykynge. Truly they bene peynted fethered and wynged for that they been aleyne [alien] and clene from all erthly cogitacion, and they ben hoven up [raised up] in effecte and inwytte, and ravyshed to the innest contemplacion of the love of God. They ben clothed in fyrye [fiery] redde clothes, for that they bene wrapped in the lyghte and mantell of the knowledge and love of God.' They be clothed with lyght as with a garment' [Psalm 103]. They ben arrayed in armes and wepyn of batyle and of warre, for that by helpe of them good men ben oft socoured and defended in warre and in batayle of body and soule. And they harpe, for that they that ben worthy to be comforted, by theyre helpe and prayers, falle not into sorowe of despayre and wanhope [hopelessnes?]. They beare trompes in theyr hondes for that they calle and comforte and excyte us to profyte alwaye in goodness. Many such manner thinges ben writen of the araye and doinge of angelles that betokyn theyr marvaylous werkes.

3.12 The King's painters

A whole host of painters was employed by various kings, to undertake many different kinds of work, from the humblest to the most aesthetically elaborate, in a wide variety of media. On 18 March 1350 at the time when the ornamental painting and glazing of St Stephen's chapel, Westminster was being undertaken, Edward III issued the following precept under his own name.

The King, to all and singular, the sheriffs, mayors, officers and other subjects, both within the Liberties and without to whom greeting:

Know ye that we have appointed our beloved Hugh of St Albans, master of the painters assigned for the works to be executed in our Chapel at our Palace of Westminster, to take and to chose as many painters and other workmen as may be required for performing those works, in any place where it may be expedient, either within Liberties or without, in the counties of Kent, Middlesex, Surrey and Sussex, and to cause these workmen to come to our Palace aforesaid, there to remain in our service, at our wages, as long as may be necessary. And therefore we command you to advise and assist the aforesaid Hugh in doing and completing what has been started as often and in such manner as the said Hugh may require.

(*Foedera*, 1825. vol. i, p. 193)

Thirteen years later the King was still having problems pressing painters into service.

The King to all and singular &c.

Know ye that we have appointed our beloved William Walsingham to take so many painters in our City of London (those in the employ of the church excepted) as may be sufficient for our works in St Stephen's chapel, within our Palace of Westminster, and to bring them to our Palace aforesaid, for our employment at our wages, there to remain as long as may be necessary, and we have given him authority to arrest all those who may oppose him, or prove rebellious in this matter, and commit them to our prisons, until we have otherwise ordained their punishment. And therefore we command that you give all assistance to the said William in executing and carrying out all these things before mentioned with your help and counsel, as often as the said William, acting on our behalf, may require you.

The Exchequer Rolls give lengthy details of the payments expended for various works.

1351
June 15th   To John Elham and Gilbert Pokerigh, painters working

on the chapel as well as the tablements, and on the priming of the east end of the king's chapel six days at 10d. per day, each, 10s.

July 4th   To Master Hugh of St Albans and John de Cotton painters, working there on the drawing of several images in the said chapel, four days and a half at 1s. per day each, 9s.

July 11th   To Master Hugh of St Albans, working on the composition of several painted images, two days at 1s. a day, 2s.

October 3rd   To Hugh of St Albans and John de Cotton, painting and drawing several images in the said chapel six days at 1s. per day each, 12s.

1352

March 12th   To John Elham, Gilbert Pokerigh and William Walsingham, painting the tabernacle and images in the chapel, six days at 10d. each per day, 15s.

April 12th   To Wm. Heston and two others, laying on the gold, as well on the said walls, as on the placing of the preynts on the marble columns in the chapel, two days and a half at 5d. per day each, 3s. 1½d.

May 13th   To Hugh of St Albans designer of the works of the painters, working there two days, 2s.

May 28th   To William Walsingham working on the painting of the angels in the chapel, 2½ days at 10d. a day, 2s. 1d.

1357

For the wages of Master Edmund Canon, master stone-cutter, working on the stalls of the King's chapel 364 days at 1s. 6d. per day £27 6s.

> Also recorded are the considerable sums expended on the materials used. The painting of the walls, pillars and tabernacles were executed in oil, The references to tin for the use of 'preynts' seems to indicate that these were templates for repeating figures marbling and designs.

1351

June 26th   To John Lightgrave, for 600 leaves of gold for painting the entablatures of the chapel at 5s. per hundred, £1 10s.
To the same for ten leaves of tin for the borders of the said tablatures, 1s.

For cole and squirrels' tails for the painting of the chapel, 3d.

July 18th   To John Matfrey, for 621 lbs of red lead at 5d. per pounds, £1 5s. 10d.

To Master Hugh of St Albans for four flagons of painters' oil for the painting of the chapel, 16s.

Aug 8th   To the same for a pound and a half of oker, 3d.

To the same for two small earthen jars to put the colour in, 1d.

For half a pound of cynephe, for the painting of the upper chapel, 17s. 3d.

August 15th   To Lonyn of Bruges for 6½ pounds of white varnish at 9d. per pound, 4s. 10½d.

September 5th   To Hugh of St Albans for half a pound of red lead, 8d.

To the same for three pounds of azure, £1 10s.

For thirty peacocks' and swans' feathers, and squirrels' tails for the painters' pencils, 2½d.

For one pair of shears to cut the leaves of tin, 2d.

September 19th   For one pound of hogs' hair for the painters' pencils, 1s.

For 19 flagons of painters' oil at 3s. 4d. per flagon, £3 3s. 4d.

To John Lyghtgrave for 600 leaves of gold at 4s. 6d. per hundred, £1 7s.

For half a pound of cotton for laying on the gold, 7½d.

1352

January 2nd   To John Lambard for two quatern of royal paper for the painters' patterns, 1s. 8d.

For one pair of scales to weigh the different painters' colours, 1s.

April 16th   To John Matfray for 2 lbs of *vert de Grèce*, 2s. 4d.

August 27th   To Nicholas Chauncer for fifteen ells of canvas to cover the images of the king to be painted, 6s. 8d.

3.13 The economics of stained glass

St Stephen's chapel built in the reign of Edward III was richly ornamented with stained glass to designs drawn by Master John of Chester, who was paid 7s. a week. The account Rolls of the Exchequer record in great detail the expenses involved, covering a wide number of different items.

1351

August 15th To William Holmere for 107 ponder of white glass, bought for the windows of the upper chapel, each hundred containing 27 ponder, and each ponder containing 5 lbs at 16s. per cwt £1 0s. 8d.

October 10th To William Holmere for 110 lbs of blue-coloured glass for the windows of the upper chapel at £3 12s. per cwt £3 18s.

Carriage of the same from Candlewick Street 6d.

October 17th To John Prentis for ten hundred of white glass and of various other colours for the windows of the said chapel at 18s. per hundred, £9.

Carriage and boatage of the same from London to Westminster 1s. 3d.

October 30th To John Allemayne for 303 ponder of white glass for the chapel windows at 12s. per hundred, £1 17s. 6d.

Carriage of the same glass from Chiddyngfold to Westminster 6s.

November 21st To William Holmer, for 26 ponder of azure-coloured glass, bought in London for glazing the chapel windows at 3s. each ponder £3 18s.

> The names functions and wages of the craftsmen involved are also recorded.

1351

June 20th To Master John of Chester, glazier, working on the drawing of several images for the glass windows of the king's chapel at 7s. per week, 7s.

To John Athelard, John Lincoln, Simon Lenne, John Lenton, five master-glaziers working there on similar drawings, 5 days at 1s. per day £1 5s.

To William Walton, Nicholas Dadyngton, John Waltham, John Lord, William Lichesfield, John Selnes, Thomas Jonge, John Geddyng, John Halsted, Robert Norwich and William of Lenton, eleven painters on glass, painting glass for the windows of the upper chapel, five days at 7d. per day £1 12s. 1d.

To William Ens and fourteen others, glaziers, on the cutting and joining of the glass for the windows, 6 days at 6d. per day £2 5s.

June 27th To John Geddyng for washing the tables for drawing on the glass, 4d.

To Master John of Chester, working there on the drawing of the images on the said tables, for his week's wages, 7s.

To Nicholas Dadyngton and four other glaziers, painting glass, five days at 7d. per day each, 14s. 7d.

To William Ems and nine other glaziers, joining glass for the windows, six days at 6d. per day each, £1 10s.

July 4th To Simon the Smith for seven *croysours* [cross irons] to break and work the glass at 1½d. each 8½d.

For *cepoarietino* [mutton suet] and filings, to make solder for the glass windows, 6d.

July 11th To Simon the Smith for twelve other *croysours* 1s. 3d.

For *servicia* [ale or wort] for washing the tables for drawing on the glass 7d.

October 3rd To Master John of Chester, John Athelard, John Lincoln, Henry Lichesfield, Simon de Lenne and John Lenton, six master-glaziers, drawing and painting on white tables [i.e. boards] several drawings for the glass windows of the chapel five days at 1s. each per day, £1 16s.

To John Coventry and sixteen others, glaziers, breaking and joining the glass upon the painting tables, five days at 6d. per day £2.2s.

October 10th To Master John of Chester, and five other glaziers, painting on the white tables for the windows of the chapel, at 1s. per day, £1 16s.

To Thomas de Dayngton and Robert Yerdesle, grinding different colours for the painting of the glass, five days at 4½d a day each 3s. 9d.

3.14 No labour problems, 1361

When the king needed builders, masons or the like, there was no problem in the fourteenth century. They were pressed or conscripted like sailors.

The King to the Sheriff of Norfolk and Suffolk, greetings. We command you as strictly as we can that immediately on sight of these present letters you cause to be chosen and attached within the said counties, whether within liberties, or without, of the better and more skilled masons, forty for hewing freestone and forty for laying stone, and cause them to be brought or sent, with the tools belonging to their trade to our castle at Windsor, so that you have them there by the first of May at the latest, to be delivered to our beloved Clerk, William of Wyckeham, Clerk of our works there, to remain at our works for as long as may be necessary at our wages. And you shall take from all the said masons such security as you would be willing to answer for to us that they will remain continuously in our aforesaid works and will not depart therefrom without our special license. And all those masons whom the aforesaid William shall certify to you as having left our said works without leave and returned to the aforesaid counties you shall cause to be bodily taken and arrested, wherever they may be found in your bailiwick, whether within liberties or without, and kept securely in our prison, so that without our special mandate, they will in no way be loosed from the same. And you shall inform us clearly, and without concealment by the first of May of the names of the masons aforesaid and of the security you take from each of them to remain at our works aforesaid. And this you shall in no wise omit on pain of forfeiting everything you can forfeit to us. Witness the King at Westminster April 12th 1361.

3.15 London work for Durham

It was by no means invariably the case that local craftsmen were employed. When between 1370 and 1380 Sir John de Nevill made some important gifts to Durham Cathedral, they were made in London, and transported by sea to Newcastle, then by land to Durham.

Sir John de Neville commissioned an important new work of marble and albaster to go under the shrine of St Cuthbert, for which he paid more than £200. He had it packed in crates in London, and then sent by sea to Newcastle, whence the Prior of Durham had it carried by land to the cathedral. And when this work was completed, and in place, he gave a new reredos for the high altar, at the suggestion of Prior John and the monastic community, and this cost him five hundred pounds. This too he had packed in crates in London, and at his own cost sent it by sea to Newcastle, where the Prior had it collected. Prior John Fossor however died before the work was set up, and it was completed by his successor Robert Berrington, being dedicated on the feast of the Four Kings in 1380

(*Historiae Dunelmis Scriptores*)

3.16 Painting at Durham

The demand for painters was continuous. The Durham Account Rolls (Surtees Society) record the work done by various artists, and the amounts they were paid.

1377 For a painting showing the image of St Thomas of Canterbury for the chapel at Bienlwe, 20s.

1370 For painting an image of St Mary Magdalene, 25s.

1380 To a painter from Newcastle for a painting of St Cuthbert to adorn the reredos, 12d.

1397 For a painting of St Andrew, 6s. 8d.

1403 To William the painter for an image commissioned for the High Altar, 3s. 8d.

1412 For an armorial painting of St Andrew, 16d.

1420 For painting the picture of St Andrew 6s.; for making a tabernacle for the same 12d.; for painting the said tabernacle 16d.; for two candlesticks in front of the images of St Andrew and the Blessed Mary, 20d.; for painting them, 12d.

1439 Spent for painting one small crucifixion standing on the altar with the images of St Andrew, St Anne, and St John the Baptist and for work in other places within the Infirmary, 40s.

1441 For painting one panel-picture standing on the altar in the chapel 13s. 4d.

1449 Paid to William Browne for a picture of the image of the Blessed Mary Magdalene, 15s. 1d.

1469 For restoring the image of the Trinity at the end of the Infirmary Hall, 12d.

3.17 A haul of jewellery

On 15 August 1382 two men appeared before the Mayor Aldermen and Coroner of the City of London accused of being in possession of jewellery stolen from John Frensshe a goldsmith. The list of their booty gives some indication of the range and variety of objects of a secular nature made in precious metals in the fourteenth century. (Riley H. T. *Memorials of London Life* 1868, pp. 470–71.)

Walter atte Watre, goldsmith and Nicholas Somersete of Phelipe Norton [Norton St Philip, near Bath] in the county of Somerset were taken at the suite of John Frensshe of London, goldsmith, with the mainour [goods found on the person] of divers goods and chattels belonging to him, John Frensshe, namely two silver girdles with red silk braid, value 46s.; one silver girdle, with a blue silk braid, 30s.; one other small silver girdle with green braid 16s.; one silver chalice with patten 38s.; one chain of silver gilt 40s.; other small silver chain 5s.; one girdle of red silk, with a buckle, and studded with silver gilt 16s.; 2 sets of phials of silver their necks gilt, 20s.; one osculatory [a metal circular object for passing round the kiss of peace at mass] 20s.; two mazer cups, bound with silver gilt, 33s.4d.; 6 silver spoons, 14s.; 2 gold rings with two diamonds £15; one gold ring with a balas [a pale rose-coloured ruby]; 3 strings of pearls 70s.;6 gold necklaces 100s.; and other goods and chattels such as rings of silver gilt, broken silver, girdles set with silver, buckles and pendants for girdles, and *paternosters* of silver and pearls to the value of £40, which goods and chattels the same Walter atte Watre and Nicholas Somersete on the Wednesday next after the Feast of the Assumption of the Blessed Virgin Mary [August 15th] feloniously stole by night at the corner of Friday strete in Westcheape, in the Parish of St Matthew, in the Ward of Farndone Within, in London, and there feloniously broke into the shop of him John Frensshe.

And also the same Walter atte Watre and Nicholas Somersete were taken at the suit of Thomas Stoke of London, goldsmith, with the mainour of goods and chattels of him, Thomas Stoke; namely one mazer cup, bound with silver gilt, value 10s.; one other small mazer cup, bound with silver gilt 5s.; 3 buckles with three pendants for silver girdles, 15s.; one other buckle and one silver girdle, 6s. 8d. and one knife called a *copegorge* [cut throat] with one *loket* and *chape* [the metal top and tip of a scabbard] of silver 6s. 8d. by them stolen at night on the Wednesday in the sixth year of the reign of King Richard II from the shop of the aforesaid John Frensshe goldsmith in the same place.

The jury by Henry Markeby and eleven others declared upon their oath the said Walter atte Watre and Nicholas Somersete to be guilty of the felonies aforesaid. But because they were clerks, and judgement could not lawfully be proceeded to without the Ordinary [the bishop] they were committed to the Prison of Neugate, there to be kept in safe custody. They had no chattels.

3.18 An ideal castle

In his *Troy Book* of 1412–20 John Lydgate described the rebuilding of Troy, and in his account of the palace which Priam built for himself clearly expresses the kind of architectural ideals – the concept of the ideal home – and its construction as it appeared to men of the early fifteenth century.

He made it bilde highe up-on a roche,
It for tassure in his fundacioun,
And callyd it the noble Ylyoun.
The site of whiche, justly circuler,
By compas cast rounde as any spere,
And who that wold the content of the grounde
Trewly accounten of this place rounde,
In the theatre first he most entre,
Takying the line that kerveth thorugh the centre,
By gemetrie, as longeth to that art,
And trebild it, with the seventhe part,
He fynde might by experience
The mesour hool of the circumference,
What lond also, pleynly eke with al,
Contened was withinne the stronge wal –
The crest of whiche, wher it lowest was,
Hadde in highte full sixe hundred pas,
Bilt of marbil, ful royal and ful strong,
And many other riche stoon among;
Whose touris wern reysed up so highe,
That they raght almost to the skye;
The werk of whiche no man myght amende,
And he that list by grecis up ascende,
He myghte seene in his inspeccioun
To the boundis of many regioun
And provincys that stoode rounde aboute.
And the wallys withinne and withoute
Endelong with knottis grave clene,
Depynt with azour, gold, zinopre & greene,
That verraily, whan the sonne schon,
Up on the gold meynt among the stoon,
Thei gaf a light, withouten any were,
As Phybus doth in his mydday spere –
The werke of wyndowe and eche fenestral,
Wrought of berel and of clere cristal.
And amydds of this Ylyoun,
So fresche, so riche of fundacioun,
Whiche clerkys yit in her bokis preyse,
King Pryam made an halle for to reyse,
Excellyng alle in bewte & in strengthe
The latytude accordyng with the lengthe.
And of marbil outwarde was the wal;

75

And the tymbre, most nobil in special,
Was half of cedre, as I reherse can,
And the remenant of the riche eban,
Whiche most is able as I dar specyfye
With stoon to joyne by craft of carpentrie;
For theye of tymbre have the sovereynte.
And for to tell of this Eban (ebony) tre,
Liche in bookes soothely as I fynde,
It cometh out of Ethiope and Ynde,
Black as is get, and it will wexe anoon,
When it is korve, harde as any stoon,
And evermore lasten and endure,
And natt corrupt with water nor moysture.
And of thys halle ferther to diffyne,
With stonis sqayre by level and by lyne
It pavid was with grete diligence
Of masownry and passyng excellence.
And al above, reysed was a se,
Ful curiously of stonys and perre,
That callid was, as chefe and principal,
Of the regne the sete most royal.
To fore whiche was seyt by gret delyt
A borde of Eban and of yvor whyt,
So egaly joyned and so clene,
That in the werk there was no ryfte seene;
And sessions wer made on every syde,
Only the statis by ordre to devyde.
Eke in the halle as it was covenable,
On each partie was a dormant table
Of evor eke, and this eban tre;
And even ageyn the kynge's royal see,
In the party that was there-to contrarie,
I-reised was by many crafty stayre,
Highe in the halle in the tother syyt,
Righte as lyne in the opposyt,
Of pured metal and of stonys clere
In brede and lengthe a ful rich auter.
On which ther stood, of figure and visage
Of masse gold, a wonderful ymage,
To ben honoured in that highe sete,
Only in honour of Jupiter the grete.
And the statue, for al his huge weyghte,
Fifteen cubites complet was of heighte,
A crowne of gold highe up-on his hed,
With hevenly saphirs & many rube red
Fret envyroun with other stonys of Ynde;

And amon were medeled as I fynde,
Whyte perlis massyf, large and rounde;
And for most chefe al dirkness to confounde,
Was a charbuncle, kynge of stnys alle,
To recounfort and gladyn all the halle,
And it tenlumyn in the blake nyght,
With the freshnesse of his rody light.
The valu was ther-of in-estimable,
And the ryches pleynly incomperable;
For this ymage by divisioun,
Was of shap and proporcioun
From hed to foot so maisterly entayled,
That in a point the werkeman hath nat failed
It to parforme by crafty excellence.

3.19 A Chaucerian chamber

With his keen eye for detail and his visual sensibilities, Chaucer is
an invaluable source of information for various aspects of fourteenth and fifteenth-century architectural detail. It may well be that
his account of his own room in *The Dreame* is optimistic –
representing what he would have liked to have had, rather than
what he did possess.

And sooth to saine my chamber was
Full well depainted, and with glas,
Were all the windows well yglased
Full clere and not a hole ycrased
That to behold it was a great joy,
For holly all the story of Troy
Was in the glaising ywrought thus
Of Hector and King Priamus
Of Achilles and of King Ladmedon
And eche of Medea and Jason
Of Paris, Heleine and of Lavine
And all the walls of color fine
Were paint, both text and gloss
And all the Romaunt of the Rose,
My windows weren that echone
And through the glasse the sunne came.

3.20 A contract for building a church

The amount of detailed instructions contained in this contract for
the building of the nave of Fotheringay church in 1434 suggests

the high degree of sophistication which clients displayed, and also emphasises the fact that masons working in one county did so in close collaboration with each other, and possessed some kind of central organisation.

This indenture maad betwix Will. Wolston sqwier, Thomas Pecham, clerk commissaries for the hy and mighty prince, and my right redoutith lord, the duc of Yorke on the too part, and Will. Horwood freemason, dwelling in Fodringhey on the tother part; wytnessith that the same Will. Horwood hath granthid and undertaken, and by thise same hath indenthid, graunts and undertakes to mak up a new body of a kirk, joyning to the quire of the college of Fodringhey of the same hight and brede that the said quire is of, and in length iiij xxx fete from the said quere donward withyn the walles a metyerd of England accounteth alwey for iij fete. And in this cuvenant the said Will. Horwood shal also wel make all the groundwerk of the said body,and take hit and void hit at his own cost, as latlay hit suffisantly as hit ought to be by oversight of maisters of the same craft, which stuff [is] suffisantly ordeigned for him at my seide lord's cost, as belongeth to such a werke. And to the said body he shall make two isles which shall be according to heght and brede to the isles of the saide quere, and in hight to the body aforesaid, the ground of the same body and isles to be maad within the end under the ground-table-stones with rough stone; and fro the ground-stone batiments, and all the remanent of the said body and isles to the full hight of the said quire with clene hewen ashler altogdir in the outer side unto the full hight of the said quire; and all the inner side to be of rough stone, except the bench-table-stones, the soles of the windows, the pillars and chapetrels that the arches and pendants shall rest upon, which shall be altogedir of free-stone wroght tewly and dewly as hit ought to be.

And in eche isle shall be wyndows of free-stone, accordying in all points unto the wyndows of the said quire, sawf hey shal no bowtels haf at all. And in the west-end of aither of the said isles, he shal mayke a wyndow of four lights, according altogedir to the wyndows of the said isles. And til aither isle shall be as sperware enbattailement of freestoon thrwoghout, and both the end enbattailed butting upon the stepill. And aither of the said isles shall have six myghty botrasse of free-stone, clene-hewn; and every botrasse fynnisht with a fynial, according in all points to the fynials of the sayd quire, safe onlie that the botrasse of the body shal be more large, more strong and mighty than the botrasse of the said qwere.

78

And the cler-story both withyn and without shal be mayde of clene asheler growndid upon ten mighty pillars, with four respounds; that ys to say two above joyning to the qwere, and two benethe joyning to the end of the sayd bodye. And to the two respownds of the sayd qwere shall be two perpeyn walls joyning of free-stone, clene wrought; that is to say oon on aither side of the middel qwere dore; and in eyther wall three lyghts, and lavatoris in aither side of the wall, which shall serve for four auters, that is to say oon on aither side of the myddel dore of the said qwere and oon on aither side of the said isles.

And in eche of the said isles shall be five arches abof the stepill, and abof every arch a window, and every wyndow to be of four hyghts, according in all poynts to the wyndows of the clere-story of the said qwere. And either of the said isles shall have six mighty arches, butting on aither side to the clere-story, and two mighty arches butting on aither side to the said stepull, according to the arches of the qwere, both in table-stones and crestis with a sqware embattlement thereupon.

And in the north syde of the chirche the said Will. Horwode shall make a porche, the outer side of clene assheler, the inner side of rough stone, conteining in length xij fete, and in brede as the botrasse of the said body wol soeffre, and in hight according to the isle of the same side, with raisonable lights in aither side, and with a sqware embattlement thereupon.

And in the south syde of the cloystre-ward another porche, joyning to the dore of the said cloystre, berynge wydenesse as the botrasse will soeffre, and in hight betwixt the chirch and the sayd cloystre dore with a dore in the west side of the said porche to the townward, and in aither side so many lights as will suffice, and a sqware embattailment above, and in hight according to the place where hit is set.

And to the west of the sayd body shall be a stepyll standing above the chirche upon three strong and mighty arches vawthid with stoon, the which steepil shall haf in length iiijxxx feet after the mete-yard of three fete to the yard above the ground are to be table-stones and it shall be xx fote sqware wythin the walls, the walles berying sixe fete thicknesse abof the said ground table-stones. And to the hight of the said body of the cherche, hit shall be sqware with two myghty botrasses joyning thereto, oon in either side of a large dore, which shall be in the west end of the same stepil.

And when the said stepill cometh to the hight of the said bay then it shall be changid and turned in vii paynes and at every souchon a boutrasse, fynysht with a fynial according to the fynials of the said qwere and body, the said chapell to be embattailed with a square embattailment large; and abof the dore of the said stepill a wyndow rising in hight al so high as the gret arch of the stepill, and in brede as the body will issue. And in the said stepill shall be two floores, and above each floore viii clerestoral windows set yn the myddes of the walle, eche window of three lights, and all the owter side of the stepill of clene-wrought free stone; and the inner syde of rough stone. And in the said stepill shall be an ulce towrnyng, servingt till the said body, isles and qwere, both beneth and abof, with all manner other werke necessary that logyth to such a body, isles, stepill and porches, also well nought comprehendit in this endenture as comprehendit and expressyed.

And of all the werke that in this same endenture is devysed and rehersyd, my said lorde of Yorke shall fynde the carriage and stuffe, that ys stone, lyme, sond, ropes, boltes, ladderis, tymbre, scaffolds, gynnes and all manner of stuffe that belongeth to the seyde werke, for the which werke, well and truly and duly to be made and finysht in wyse as it was afore devised and declayrd, the said Will. Horwode shall haf of my lord ccciii Sterlingues, of whych somme he shall be payd in wyse as hit is declayrd hereafter, that ys to say when he hath takyn his ground of the said kirke, isles, botrasse porches and stepill, hewyn and set his ground table-stone and his ligements and the wall thereto wythin and without as hit ought to be well and duly made, then he shall haf vi poundes, xiis. iiijd. And when the said Will Horwode hath set xxi fote abof the ground-table-stone, also well thoughout the outer side as the inner side of all the saide werke, then he shall haf payment of c pounds Sterling and so for every fote of the said werke, aftir hit be fully wroght and set, as hit ought to be, and as yt is afore devysed, till hit come to the full hight of the highest of the fynials and battaylment of the seyd body, he shall have but xxx s. Sterlingues till hit be fully endyed and performed in wyse as it is afore devysed.

And when alle the werk abof wrytten rehersyd and devised is fully fynisht as hit ought to be and hit is above accordyd and devysed betwix the said commissaris and the sayd William; then the seid Will. Horwode shall haf full payment of the said ccc pounds Sterling, if any be due or left unpayd thereof until hym; and during all the sayd werke the seid Will. Horwode shall neither set more nor fewer free masons, rogh setters ne leyes thereupon, but such as shall be ordeigned to haf the governance and ofersight of the said werke, undre my lord of Yorke well ordeign him and assign him to haf.

And yf so be that the seyd Will. Horwode make noght full payment of all or any of his workmen, then the clerke of the werke shall pay hem in his presence and stoppe als mykell in the said Will. Horwode's hand as the payment that shall be dewe unto the workmen cometh to.

And duryng all the said werke, the setters shall be chosyn and takyn by all such as shall haf the governance and oversight of the sayd werke by my seyd lord; they to be payd by the hand of the seyd Will. Horwode, in forme and manner abofwrytten and devysed. And yf so be that the sayd Will. Horwode wol complayn and say at any tyme that the two seyd setters or any of them, be noght profitable ne suffisant workmen for my lordys avale, then by oversight of master-masons of the countre they shall be demyed; and yf they be found fawlty or unable, then they shall be chawnghyt and others takyn and chosen in, by such as shall haf the governance of the sayd werke by my seyd lordys ordenance and commandement.

And yf it so be that the sayd Will. Horwode make nought fulle end of the sayd werke withyn tyme reasonable, which shall be lymyt him in certain by my seyde lorde, or by his counseil, in forme and manere as is afore-written and devysed in thise same endentures, then he shall yeilde his body to prison at my lorde's wyll, and all his moveable goods and heritages at my lordys disposition and ordenance.

In wytness &c the sayd commissaries as well as the sayd Will. Horwode to these present endentures haf sett theie sealles interchangeably &c the XXIVth day of Septembre, the yere of the reign of our sovereign lord King Henry the Sixt after the conquest of England xiiij.

(Reproduced in *Masonic Monthly*, July 1882.)

3.21 Marriage sampling

Portraits played an important role in the arrangement of marriages at a distance, due to a natural human reluctance to buy a pig – or a sow – in a poke. In the journal of Thomas Beckington (Rolls Series 1872) there is an account of a mission sent by Henry VI in 1441 to contract an alliance of marriage with one of the three daughters of John, Count of Armagnac. At Bordeaux the mission was joined by one Hans, described as a workman, whose instructions from the king in the summer of 1442 are quoted below. It is perhaps worth noting that amongst the excuses put forward by Hans for his delay in completing the mission in the winter of that year was that because of the intense cold his colours were freezing. Nothing was heard of the portraits, and Henry actually married Margaret of Anjou, daughter of the Duke of Lorraine.

That ye do portraie the iii daughters in their kertelles, simple, and their visages like as ye see their stature and their beaulte and color of skynne, and their coutenances with almaner of features and that i of you be delivered in all haste with the said portratur to bring it unto the kyng and he to appointe and signe whych him liketh, and thereupon to send you word how ye shall be governed.

3.22 Designing Eton College

Henry VI was not only an active and enlightened patron, but he took the keenest interest in the minutiae of architectural designs. The instructions issued in 1447 for the building of Eton, were clearly issued with the advice of master-builders, but they are sufficiently specific to show the same degree of interest as Henry III had shown some two centuries earlier.

I will that the Quire of my said College at Eton shall contain in length 103 feet, whereof behind the High Altar shall be 8 feet, and from the side altar to the choir door 95 feet.

Item the said Quire shall contain in breadth from side to side 32 feet.

Item the foundation of the wall shall be raised higher than they are now on the outer side before coming to the level of the clear walls, to three feet and on the inner side, until it comes to the line of the first stone of the clear wall to a height of 10 feet.

Item the walls of the said Quire shall contain in height from the ground-works up to the top of the battlement 80 feet.

Item in the east end of the said Quire shall be set a great gable window of 7 daies and two buttresses, and on either side of the same Quire 7 windows, every window of 4 daies and 8 buttresses, containing in height from the ground-works unto the over parts of the pinnacles, 100 feet of stone.

Item that the said plans be so carried out that the first stone lie in the middle of the High Altar, which shall be twelve foot long and five foot wide. And that first stone must not be removed, touched nor stirred in any way.

Item the vestry to be set on the north side of the said Quire, which shall contain in length 50 feet divided into two houses, and in breadth 24 feet, and the walls in height 20 feet, with gable windows and side windows convenient thereunto. And the ground-works to be set in height of the ground of the cloister.

And I will that the edification of the said building of my College at Eton proceed in large form, clean and substantial, well replenished with goodly windows and vaults, leaving aside any superfluity of too greatly intricate works of engraving and over-busy moulding.

Item in the said Quire on either side 32 stalls and the rood loft there, I will that they be made in like manner and form as be the stalls and roodloft in the chapel of St Stephen at Westminster, and of the length of 32 feet and in breadth 12 feet clear.

And as touching the dimensions of the said church of my College of Eton, I have devised and appointed that the body of the said church between the aisles shall contain in breadth within the limits of 32 feet, and in length from the Quire to the west door of the said church 104 feet. And so too the side body of the church shall be longer than the Quire shall be longer than is the choir from the reredos at the High Altar unto the quire door by 9 feet, whichever dimension is thought to be right or good, convenient and due proportion.

Item I have devised and appointed that the aisle on the either side of the body of the church shall contain in breadth, from respond to respond, 15 feet, and in length 104 feet, according to the said body of the church.

Item in the south side of the body of the church a fair large door with a porch over the same for christenings and weddings.

Item in the width of the churchyard from the church door unto the walls of the churchyard within the wall at the west end, which must be taken off the street in the highway 16 feet.

Item the grounds of the cloister to be raised higher than the old ground 8 feet to where it comes to the pavement, so that it be set but 2 feet lower than the paving of the church. Which cloister shall contain in length east and west 200 feet and in breadth 160 feet north and south.

Item the said cloister shall close up to the church on the north side at the west end, and on the north side at the east end of the church it shall close up to the college, with a door into the same college.

Item the same cloister shall contain within the walls in breadth 15 feet, and in height 20 feet with clerestories round about the inside, and vaulted and battlemented on both sides. Item, the same cloister shall contain 39 feet, which is left for to set in certain trees and flowers, beholdful and convenient for the service of the said church.

Item the cemetery of the church shall be lower than the paving of the church by four feet, with as many steps up into the church door as shall be convenient thereto.

Item in the middle pane of the west cloister a great square Tower, with a fair door in the cloister, which tower will contain clear within the wall 20 feet and in the height with the battlement and pinnacles 140 feet.

Item from the highway on the south side up to the walls of the College a good high wall with towers convenient thereto. And in likewise from thence by the waterside, and about the gardens and all the precincts of the place round about by the highway until it come to the end of the cloisters on the west side again.

Item that the water at Baldweyne bridge be turned outwards into the river Thames by a ditch 40 feet wide. And the ground between the ditch and the College to be raised to a great height so that in times of flood it may be clear and dry ground.

And as touching the dimensions of the housing of my said college of Eton, I have devised and appointed that the south wall of the precinct of the said college, which will extend from the tenement that Hugh Dier now holdeth and occupieth unto the east end of the gardens along the waterside shall contain in length 1,450 feet with a large door in the wall to the waterside.

Item the east wall of the said precinct which shall extend from the waterway unto the highway at the new bridge at the east end of the gardens shall contain in length 700 feet.

Item the north wall of the said precinct which shall extend from the east end of the gardens beside the highway into the south west corner of the same precinct shall contain in length 1,040 feet in which there shall be a fair gate out of the outer court into the highway.

Item the west wall of the said precinct which shall extend from the said west corner of the same precinct unto the said tenement, which the said Hugh Dier now occupieth shall contain in length 600 feet, and so the outer walls of the said precinct shall occupy in length 3,503 feet.

Item, between the said north wall of the said precinct and the walls of the College in the outer court, on the west side of the gate, and the way into the College shall be built various housing necessary for the bakehouse brewhouse gardeners stables and hayhouse with chambers for the stewards, auditors and other learned counsel and ministers of the said College as shall happen to be diseased with infirmities.

Item in the west part of the said gate and the way into the college 8 chambers for the poor men. And in the west part 6 chambers, and behind the same a kitchen, buttery, pantry with gardens and a ground for fuel for the said poor men.

Item the north part of the College shall contain 155 feet within the walls in the middle of which will be a fair tower, and a gatehouse with 2 chambers on either side, and 2 chambers above, vaulted, containing in length 40 feet and in breadth 24 feet. And in the east side of the above gate 4 chambers, 2 beneath and 2 above, each of them in length 35 feet, and in breadth. And in the west side of the same gate a schoolhouse beneath of 70 feet in length and in breadth 24 feet and above the same two chambers either of them in length 35 feet and in breadth 24 feet.

Item the east pane in length within the walls 230 feet in the middle whereof directly against the entry to the cloister a library containing in length 52 feet and in breadth 24 feet with 3 chambers above on the one side, and 4 on the other, and beneath 9 chambers each of them in length 24 feet and in breadth 18 feet with five outer towers and five inner towers.

Item the west pane of the said College 230 feet in length in which shall be directly against the library, a door in to the cloister, and above 8 chambers and beneath another 8 with three outer towers beyond the north side of the cloister and 5 inner towers with a way into the quire for the ministers of the church between the vestry and the same quire.

Item the south pane in length 155 feet in which shall stand the hall, with a vault underneath for the buttery and cellar containing 82 feet in length and 32 feet in breadth with two bay windows one on the inward one on the outer side with a tower over the hall door. And at the east end of the hall a pantry with a chamber beneath containing in length 70 feet, and at the west end of the hall the Provost's lodging above and beneath, containing in length 70 feet with a corner tower inward and another without. And on the south side of the hall a goodly kitchen and in the middle of the quadrangle within a conduit, well designed to the ease and profit of the said College.

Item all the walls of the college of the outer court and of the

85

precinct about the gardens and as far as the precinct shall go to be made of hard stone of Kent.

(Modernised from C. Willis and H. Clark, *Architectural History of Cambridge*, vol. I Cambridge, 1887, p. 368)

3.23 A heaven of timber

The elaborate nature of many church monuments seems often to have been influenced by the trappings of the medieval stage, an example being that created for the church of St Mary Ratcliffe, Bristol, and recorded in the church records.[1]

Memorandum

That Master Cumings hath delivered the 4th day of July in the year of Our Lord 1470 to Mr. Nicholas Bettes, vicar of Ratcliffe, Moses Couteryn, Philip Bartholemew, and John Brown, procurators of Ratcliffe aforesaid, a new sepulchre well-gilt, and cover thereto, an image of God Almighty rising out of the same sepulchre, with all the ordinance thereto belonging, that is to say:

A lath made of timber and iron work thereto:

Item; thereto belongeth *Heaven* made of timber and stained cloth.

Item: *Hell* made of timber and iron work with devils to the number of thirteen.

Item: Four knights armed, keeping the sepulchre with their weapons in their hands, that is to say two spears, two axes, two paves [large shields].

Item: Four pairs of angel's wings, for four angels, made of timber, and well-painted.

Item; The Father, the crown and the visage, the bell with a cross upon it, well-gilt. with fine gold.

Item; The Holy Ghost coming out of Heaven into the sepulchre.

Item; Belongeth to the angels, four chevelers [wigs].

3.24 Peeces of Arras

The import of luxury objects from Europe and the Near East was continuous. The royal household was especially fortunate since it

---

1. The construction was clearly intended for Holy Week services, the events of which were in fact the frequent subject of mystery plays.

was able to exempt its imports from taxes, as this letter from Henry VII to the bishop of Exeter, who was Keeper of the Privy Seal in March 1488, shows.

Whereas we of late bought of John Grenier, of the town of Tournay, tapysser, two awterclothes and ix peeces of cloth of Arras of the hystorye of Troye, for which we are graunted unto him that he therefor shuld paye no custome or othre dueties; we therefore wol and charge you that, under oure prive seal beying in youre keping, ye doo make oure several letters in due forme to be dirccted aswel unto the custumers of oure towne and port of Sanewiche, where the said clothes were discharged, willing and charging theym by the same, utterly to acquitte and discharge the same John Grenier of alle suche customes and other dueties as might be due unto us for the said twoe awter clothes and ix peeces of cloth of Arras as unto the treasurer and barons of our Exchequier, for to geve due allowance thereof unto the sayd customers and aswel theym and the said John Grenier, and alle other utterly discharge and acquitte for ever.

(In May 1488 the king disbursed £180 16s. 4d. to 'a certain merchaunt of Tournay.')

3.25 The king's chapel and the king's tomb

The chapel of Henry VII in Westminster Abbey is one of the great achievements of late medieval architecture in England, and the last great piece of pre-Reformation ecclesiastical architecture. The concept and the design were very clearly laid down by the king some considerable time before his death, with appropriate plans and pictures.

And foreasmoche as we have received our solempe coronacion, and holie Innuncion within our abbey of Westm', and that within the same monasterie is the comen sepulture of the Kings of this Realm, and specially because that within the same, and among the same Kings, resteth the holie bodie and reliques of the glorious King and Confessor Sainct Edward, and diverse others of our noble progenitours and blood, and specially the body of our graunt Dame of right noble memorie Quene Kateryne, wif to King Henry the Vth and doughter to King Charles of France, and that we by the grace of God propose right shortely to translate into the same, the bodie and reliques of our Uncle of blissed memorie King Henry the VIth. For theis and diverse other causes and consideracions us

specially moevying in that behalf, we wol that whensoever it shall
please our Salviour J'hu Crist to calle us out of this transitorie life,
be it within our Royme, or in any other Reame, or place withoute
the same, that oure bodie bee buried within the same monasterie;
That is to saie in the Chapell were our said graunt Dame laye
buried; the whyvhe chapell wee have begoune to buylde of newe
in the honour of our blessed Lady. AND we wol that our
TOWMBE bee in the myddes of the same Chapell before the high
Aultier, in such distaunce from the same as it is ordred in the plat
mayde for the same Chapell, and signed with our hande; In which
place we wol, that for the said Sepulture of us and our derest late
wif, the Quene, whose soule God pardonne, be made a Towmbe
of Stone, called touche, sufficient in largieur for us both; And upon
the same oon ymage of our figure, and another of hers, eyther of
them of copure and gilt, of such faction, and in suche manner as
shall be thougt moost convenient by the discretion of our executors, yf it not before doon by ourself in oure daies. And in the
borders of the same towmbe, bee made a convenient scripture,
conteigning the yeres of our reigne, and the daie and yere of our
decesse. And in the side and booth ends of our said towmbe, in
the said touche under the saide bordours wee Wol tabernacles bee
graven, and the same toi be filled with Ymages especially of our
said avouries of coper and gilte. Also we Wol that incontinent after
our decesse, and after that our bodye be buried wythin the saide
towmbe, the bodie of our said late wif the Queen be translated
from the place where it is nowe buried, and brought and laide with
owre bodie in our seyd towmbe, if it not bee done by our self in
our daies. ALSO we wol that by a convenient space and distance
from the grees of the high Aultier of the said Chapell there be
made in length and brede about the said towmbe, a gate in manner
of a closure of copure and gilt, after the faction which we have
begonne, which we wol by our said Executours fully accomplisshed and perfourmed. And within the said gate, at owre fete,
after a convenient distaunce from our Towmbe, be made an aultier,
in the honour of our Salviour Jesus Crist, streight adjoyning to the
seyd gate. At which Aultier we Wol certeine preists daily saie
masses for the weale of our soules and remission of our synnes,
under such manner and fourme as is couvenanted and agreed
betwext us and the Abbot, Priour and Convent of our said
monasterye at Westminster, as more specially appereth by certaine
writings indented, made upon the same, and passed, agreed and
concluded betwixt us and the said Abbot, Priour and Convent,

under our grete Seale and signed with our owen hand for our partie, and the Convent Seale of the said Abbot, Priour and Convent for their partie, and remayning of record in the Rolles of our Chauncellary.

AND if our seyde Chapell and towmbe and our said wif's Ymagies, grate and closure be not fully accomplisshed and perfectly finished, according to the premisses by us in owre lifetime, then we Wol that not oonly the same chapell, towmbe, ymagies, grate and closure, and every of theim and al other things to them belonging, with al spede, and asson as our decease as goodly as may be doone, be by our executors hooly and perfectly finished in every behalve, after the manner and fourme before rehersed and sutingly to that is begun and doone of them, but also that the seid Chapell be desked and the windowes of our seid Chapell be glased with stores, ymagies, armes, bagies and cognoisaunts, as is by us redily divised, and in picture delivered to the Priour of sainct Bartilimews beside Smythfield, maister of the workes of our said Chapell, and that the walles, doores, windowes, Archies and Vaults and ymagies of the same our chapell, within and without be painted, garnisshed and adorned with our armes, bagies, cognois-saunts and other convenient painting, in as goodly and riche maner as such a werke requireth, and as to a King's werk apperteigning.

(Neale J. M., *Gleanings from Westminster Abbey*, vol. I, 1864, pp. 7, 8)

4. The new spirit

Merchants and courtiers in the Tudor period

4.1 Sources of patronage

The immense artistic wealth of the church was based not only on
the patronage of kings and nobles, but on that of ordinary farmers,
yeomen and traders, who, on the approach of death sought to lay
up treasures in heaven by legacies, often disproportionate in
amount to their wealth, to churches and religious institutions.
Sometimes they were specific about the uses to which they wanted
their bequests to be put; more usually however they were generalised. The extent and nature of these bequests can be gauged from
the following extracts from wills in the Bedfordshire Public
Records Office covering the period between 1500 and 1526.

In the name of God, Amen. The iiij day of the monthe of
September the yere of our lord millesimo VC[1500], I Agnes
Newbold in my hole mynd makyth this my testament in manner
foloyng. Fyrst I bequeath my soule to Allmyghty God, to Owr
Ladye Sancte Mary, and to all the company of Hevyn. And my
bodye to be buryed in the chirchyard of Sancte Peter Dunstable in
Bedford. And I beqwythe to the High Auter of the same church
iijd. Also I geve and bequeth to the chirch of Lincoln iid. Also I
give and beqweth to a canapy xijd. Also I geve and beqweth to the
belles off Sainct Peter beforesaid xij. Also I geve and beqweth to
the chirch of St Peter beforenamed a quarter of malt. Also I geve
and biqueth to Our Ladye in St Peter Church, before rehersed, my
best gyrdyll. Also I geve and bequeth to Goldyngton chirch xiid.
Also I give and bequeth to Thurlee chirch xiid.

To the parson for tithes forgotten 20d.; to the lights of the
Assumption of Our Lady, the rood and St Thomas 6s. 8d. and 2
bush malt respectively; to the church of Lincoln 4d.; to the painting
of the rood loft 3s. 4d.; to the high altar a cloth; to St Laurence
chapel repairs, 1 qutr. malt.
Jn. Sloo; 10 March 1502/3 (Latin original)

For his sepulchre in the church 6s. 8d.; to the high altar for tithes forgotten, 6s. 8d.; every other altar 20d.; to the north porch 40s.; to the making of the seats 20s.; to the cathedral of Lincoln 3s. 4d.; to St John's church 6s. 8d.; to every other church in Bedford 3s. 4d.; to Renhoild church 6s. 8d.; to the prior, sub-prior and cellarer of Newnham, 6s. 8d. each; to every other canon, being a priest there 20d., and for every novice 12d.; to St Thomas' chapel on the bridge 20s.

Wm. Joyce, Bedford; 20 October 1503

To the high altar for things forgotten 3s. 4d.; to the bells 20d.; to the torches 20d.; to the guild of the Trinity 12d.; to the guild of Mary Magdalen 12d.; to the church of Lincoln 4d.; to a 'seclary' priest to pray in the church of Riseley for him and his friends' souls one year 8 marks; to the church £4 to buy 'a cope of qwyte branchyt damask'; to the church of St Laughton 12d.; to the priest of St Laughton 4d; to the church of Higham Ferrers 20d.; to the sub-warden of Higham Ferrers 8d. to pray for his soul; to the making of the sepulchre 6s.; to the 'payntyng' of the same 6s.; to his lying in the church 6s. 8d.; to the friars of Bedford 5s. for half a trental.

Wm. Gadman, Risely, 26 August 1509

To the painting of the image of Our Lady in Houghton 33s. 4d.; to the church where he was born 10s.; to the church of Toddington 40s.; to the lights in the church of Houghton a cake of wax of 10 lbs; to Friar John Coke, prior of the friars in Dunstable to pray for his soul for 1 year, 8 marks 6s. 8d.; for a trental if it may be done daily 20s.; to the friars of Dunstable for a trental on day of burial his pile of wood that lies before his door.

Wm. Walle, vicar of Houghton Regis; 24 March 1506/7

To the high altar for tithes forgotten, 3s.4d.; to the lights of Our Lady of the Assumption and the nativity a ewe each; to the 'sustentacion' of St Thomas of Canterbury, 'the whych fygure stondeth in the chancell,' 2 bushels of barley; towards the painting of the dome in the rood loft 3s. 4d.; to sweet Jesus' altar an ewe; to the church for such things as are necessary, 13s. 4d.; to the Trinity Chapel 3s. 5d.; to St Laurence Chapel 3s. 4d.; to the church of Lincoln 12d.; to the torches a cow; to the bells 3s. 4d.

Wm. Wodil of Marstone Moretaine; 20 November 1505

To the high altar for tithes forgotten 3s. 4d.; to the church of
Lincoln 2d.; to the making of a new aisle 'now negening of the
north side of the church' 40s.; to the making of the new tabernacle
of Our Lady of Grace, 20s.; to the painting of the tabernacle of All
Hallows £4; to the friars of Bedford for a trental for his soul 10s.
Jn. Maynard, Broom, Southill; 21 April 1522.

To the church at Lincoln 2d.; to the high altar 12d.; to the torches
20d.; to Our Lady of Pity a ewe and a lamb; to the painting of the
tabernacle of Our Lady 3s. 4d.; to the sepulchre light a sheep; to
Kempston Church 1 quarter of malt.
Harry Goditot, Wooten; 31 October 1522.

4.2 'Like an earthly paradise'

The richness and magnificence which tapestry added both to the
ordinary life of the rich and powerful, and to state occasions, are
clearly described in a poem, *The Life of St Werburgh* written by
Henry Bradshaw, who died in 1513. In it he describes the feast
given by Ulfer, King of Mercia in the hall of the Abbey of Ely, on
the occasion of his daughter, Werburgh becoming a nun in 710,
but it clearly refers to a fifteenth-century context.

Clothes of golde and arras were hanged in the hall,
Depainted with pyctures, and hystoryes manyfolde,
Well wroughte and craftely with precious stone all,
Glyttering as Phebus, and the beaten golde,
Lyke an earthlye paradyse, pleasaunt to beholde;
As for the sayde moynes [nun], was not them amonge
But prayinge in her cell, as done all novice yonge.

The story of Adam there was goodly wrought,
And of his wyfe Eve, bytwene them the serpent,
How they were deceyved, and to theyre peynes brought,
There was Cayn and Abell, offeryng theyr present,
The Sacryfyce of Abell accepte ful evydent,
Tubal and Tubalcain were purtrayed in that playce,
The inventours of musyke and crafte, by great grace.

Noe and his schyppe was made there curyously,
Sendynge forth a raven, whiche never came agayne;
And how the dove returned with a braunche hastily,
A token of comforte and peace to man certeyne;
Abraham was there, standyng upon the mount playne,

To offer in sacryce, Isaac his dere sone,
And how the shepe for hym was offered in oblacyon.

The twelve sons of Jacob were there in purtrayture
And how into Egypt yonge Joseph was solde,
There was imprisoned by a false conjectour,
After all in Egypt, was ruler (as is tolde).
There was in pycture, Moyses, wyse and bolde,
Our Lorde apperynge in bushe flammynge as fyre,
And nothing bernt thereof, lefe, tree nor spyre.

The ten plagues of Egypte were well embost,
The children of Israel passyng the Reed see,
King Pharoo drowned with all his proude hoost,
And how the two tables at the mounte Synaye
Were gyven to Moyses, and how soon to idolatry
The people were prone, and punyshed were therefore;
How Datan and Abryon were full youre [burnt].

Duke Josue was joyned after them in pycture,
Leding the Isrehlytes to the land of promysson,
And how the seyd land was divided by mesure
To the people of God by equall sundry porcyon;
The judges and bysshops were there every chone,
Theyr nobles actes and Tryumphs marcyall
Freshly were browdred in these clothes royall.

But over the high desse [dais] in the pryncypall place,
Where the sayde three kynges sat crowned all,
The best hallynge hanged as reason was,
Whereon were wrought the ix orders angelicall,
Dyvyded in thre ierachys, not cessynge to call
Sanctus, sanctus, sanctus, blessed be the Trynite,
Dominus Deus Sabaoth, thre persons in one Deyte.

Next in order ensuynge, sette in goodly purtrayture,
Was our blessed Ladye, flowre of femynte,
With the twelve apostles, each one in his fygure,
And the foure Evanylstes, wrought most curyously;
Also the dyscyples of Christ in theyr degre,
Preching and tecynge unto every nacyon
The fyathes of holy chyrche, for their salvacyon.

Upon the other syde of the hall sette were
Noble auncyent storye, how the stronge Sampson
Subdued his enemyes by his myghty power;
Of Hector of Troye, slayne by false treason,
Of Arthur kynge of this regyon

With many other more, whych it is to longe
Playnly to expresse this tyme you amonge.

4.3 Sartorial splendour

The role of dress and accoutrements for political and social ends in
the sixteenth century reached an apogee which produced raiment of
unparalleled splendour. On 30th April 1515 Pasqualigo, the Venetian Ambassdor Extraordinary in London described to a Venetian
correspondent how he was received by Henry VIII at Richmond.

We were conveyed to the palace of Richmond, where they led us
into a kind of hall, and though it was before mass, they made us
breakfast, for fear we should faint; after which we were conducted
to the presence, through sundry chambers, all hung with most
beautiful tapestry, figured in gold and silver and in silk, passing
down the ranks of the body-guard, which consisted of three
hundred halberdiers in silver breast-plates and pikes in their hands;
and, by God, they were all as big as giants, so that the display was
very grand.

We at length reached the King, who was under a canopy of cloth
of gold, embroidered at Florence, the most costly thing I ever saw.
He was leaning against his gilt throne, on which was a large
brocade cushion covered in gold embroidery, where the sword of
state lay; he wore a cap of crimson velvet, in the French fashion,
and the brim was laced up with strings on the ends of which were
gold, enamelled tags. His doublet was in the Swiss fashion, striped
alternately with white and crimson satin, and his hose were scarlet
and all slashed from the knee upwards. Very close round his neck
he had a gold collar, from which there hung a round cut diamond,
the size of the largest walnut I ever saw, and to this was suspended
a most beautiful and very large round pearl. His mantle was of
purple velvet, lined with white satin, the sleeves being open, and
with a train verily more than four Venetian yards in length. This
mantle was girt in front like a gown, with a thick gold cord, from
which there hung large tassels entirely of gold, like those suspended
from a cardinal's hat; over this mantle was a very handsome gold
collar with a pendant St George, entirely of diamonds. On his left
shoulder was the garter, which is a cincture buckled circular-wise,
and bearing in its centre a cross gules on a field argent, and on his
right shoulder was a hood with a border, entirely of crimson
velvet.

Beneath the mantle he had a pouch of cloth of gold, which covered a dagger, and his fingers were one mass of jewelled rings.

To the right of His Majesty were eight noblemen, they dressed like himself also being knights [of the Garter]. To the left were a number of prelates in their rochets. Then there were six men with six gold sceptres, besides ten heralds with their tabards of cloth of gold, wrought with the arms of England, and moreover a crowd of nobility, all arrayed in cloth of gold and silk.

Subsequently we attended high mass which was chanted by the bishop of Durham with a superb and noble descant choir, and afterwards we accompanied the King to table the courses contained in sixteen massive dishes of gold.

4.4 Graphic art

Although by the sixteenth century in England illuminated liturgical manuscripts were rarely produced, legal documents, deeds and the like could be works of calligraphic art, often adorned with portraits. The subject is dealt with extensively in Erna Auerbach's *Tudor Artists* (London 1954) where the following accounts are recorded in connexion with two of Cardinal Wolsey's foundations.

Expenc' laid owt by Thomas Crumwell about my Lorde his Colledge of Oxford (Christ Church)

Ffirst paid to Hert for vellum, parchemyn and drawinge of great letters xxxixs. iid.

To Gerarde xvis.viid.

To Stepehn Vaughen for writing of sondry thinges xls.

To Mr. Jude for laces of silver and golde xviiis.

For more Vellome and drawyng of great Lettres vis.

Expence layd out by Thomas Crumwell aboute the charges of my lorde Hys Colledge in Gypswyche anno Henrici Octavi, as hereafter it doth appeare First for xxviii skynnes of velome for drawyng and floryshyng letters in the same as well for the Kynge's patents as for my lords deades and charters at iiiis. the peace one with another vl.xs.

Item payd to Garard for wrytyng out of xii deades that ys to saye the originalles and duplicattes iiil.xixs.

Item pade for paper and parchyment that ys to saye twoo dosen parchyment at vis. and one reame of paper at iiis. ixs.

4.5 A cardinal entertains

In October 1527 Cardinal Wolsey entertained the French ambassadors, who had come to negotiate a treaty between Francis I and Henry. VIII against the Emperor Charles V. The account of the event given by the Cardinal's biographer George Cavendish gives some indication of the wealth of patronage to architects, artists, craftsmen and designers that the activities of such personages afforded.

Then my Lord Cardinal sent me, being his gentleman usher, with two other of my fellows to Hampton Court, to foresee all things touching the rooms to be nobly garnished accordingly. Our pains were not light but kept us daily moving from chamber to chamber. Then the carpenters, the joiners, the masons, the painters, and all other artificers necessary to glorify the house and feast were set to work. There was carriage and re-carriage of plate, stuff and other rich implements, so that nothing was lacking or to be imagined or devised for that purpose. There were also fourteen score beds provided and all manner of furniture to them belonging, too long particularly here to rehearse. But to all wise men it sufficeth to imagine, that knoweth what belongeth to the furniture of such triumphant feast or banquet.

The day was come that was to the Frenchmen assigned, and they ready assembled at Hampton Court something before the hour of their appointment. Wherefore the officers caused them to ride to Hanworth, a place of the King's, there to hunt and spend the time till night. At which time they returned again to Hampton Court, and everyone of them conveyed to his chamber severally, having in them great fires and wine ready to refresh them, remaining there till their supper was ready, and the chambers where they would sup were ordered in due form. The first waiting-chamber was hanged with fine arras, and so were all the rest, one better than another, furnished with tall yeomen. There was set tables round about the chambers, banquet-wise, all covered with fine cloths of diaper. A cupboard [a kind of buffet] of plate, parcel gilt; having also in the same chamber to give them more light, four plates of silver, set with lights upon them, and a great fire in the chimney.

The next chamber, being the chamber of presence, hanged with very rich arras, wherein was a gorgeous and precious cloth of state hanged up, with many goodly gentlemen ready to serve. The boards were set as the other boards were set in the other chamber before, save that a high table was set beneath the cloth of estate, towards the midst of the chamber, covered with fine linen cloths of damask work, sweetly perfumed.

There was a cupboard, made for the time, of the length of the chamber, six desks high, full of gilt plate, very sumptuous, and of the newest fashions; and upon the nethermost desk garnished all with plate of clean gold, having two great candle-sticks of silver and gilt, most curiously wrought, the workmanship whereof, with the silver, cost three hundred marks, and lights of wax, as big as torches burning upon the same. This cupboard was barred in round about that no man might come nigh to it; for there was none of the same plate occupied or stirred during this feast, for there was sufficient besides. The plates that hung on the walls to give light in the chamber were of silver and gilt, with lights burning in them, a great fire in the chamber, and all things necessary for so noble a feast . . .

Before the second course my Lord Cardinal came in among them, booted and spurred, all suddenly and bade them welcome, at whose coming they would have risen, and given place with much joy. Whom my Lord commanded to sit still and keep their rooms. Anon up came the second course, with so many dishes, subtleties and curious devices, which were above a hundred in number, of so goodly and costly that I suppose the Frenchmen never saw the like. The wonder was no less than that it was worthy indeed. There were castles with images in the same; Paul's church and steeple in proportion for the quantity as well counterfeited as the painter should have painted it upon a cloth or wall. There were birds, beasts, fowls of different kinds, and personages, most lively made and counterfeit in dishes; some fighting as it were with swords, some with guns and cross-bows; some vaulting and leaping, some dancing with ladies, some in complete harness, jousting with spears, and with many more devices than I am able with my wit to describe. Among all, one I noted; there was a chess-board subtiley made of spiced pastry with men to the same, and because Frenchmen be very expert in that play, my Lord gave the same to a gentleman of France, commanding that a case be made for the same in all haste to preserve it in the conveyance thereof into his country.

Then went the cups merrily about that many of the Frenchmen were fain to be led to their beds. And whilst they were in communication and other pastimes all their liveries were served to their chambers. Every chamber had a bason and ewer of silver, some gilt and some parcel gilt, and some two great pots of silver in like manner, and one pot at the least with wine and beer, a bowl or goblet, and a silver pot to drink beer in, a silver candlestick or two with both white lights, and yellow lights of three sizes of wax.

4.6 A contract for windows

In 1526 the authorities of King's College, Cambridge commissioned four London glaziers to adorn the chapel with stained-glass windows in the chapel. The contract is printed in T. J. P. Carter's *King's College Chapel* (Cambridge, 1867).

The said glasyiers shalle at their own propre costes and charges well, suerly, clenely, workmanly, substauncyally, curyously and sufficiently glase and sett up, or cause to be sett up eightene wyndowes of the upper story of the great churche within the kynges college of Cambridge, whereof the wyndowe in the este ende of the seid churche to be oon, and the wyndowe in the west ende of the same churche to be another, and so seryally [in sequence] the resydue with good, clene, sure and perfyte glasse and oryent [brilliant] colors and imagery of the story of the olde lawe and of the newe lawe, after the forme, maner, goodness, curiositie, and clenelyness in every poynt of the kynge's new chapell at West-mynster; and also accordingly and after such manner as oon Barnard Flower, glasyer, late deceased, by indenture stode bounde to doo; that is to sey, six of the seyd windowes to be clerely sette up and fynyshed after the forme aforeseid within twelve monthes next ensuying after the date of these presentes, and that the seid Galyon, Richard, Thomas Reve and James Nycholson shall surely bynde all the seide wyndowes with double bonds of leade for defence of great wyndes and outragious wetheringes. The aforeseid shall have for the glasse, workmanship, and setting up of every foote of the seid glasse by them to be provided, wrought, and sett up after the forme aforeseid eighteen pence sterlings.

4.7 A painted head

The responsibility for painting statues, and most were painted, rested with the sculptor, and it is interesting that in the following lawsuit, recorded in volume three of the Records of the Borough of Nottingham, the plaintiff was himself a stainer (1529).

John Nicholson, stainer, complains of John Cottingham, image-maker, of a plea that he render him a head of St John the Baptist and half a quarter of gold, value 10s. which he unjustly witholds from him. And whereupon the same plaintiff complains in his own proper person that whereas he, on the Monday next after the feast of St Andrew the Apostle in the 21st year of the reign of our Lord the King, here at Nottingham delivered to the aforesaid John Cottingham the aforesaid head of St John to paint before Christmas then following, and then to redeliver it to the aforesaid John Nicholson.

4.8 'Payntyng of dyvers tabulls'

In the extensive account books in the Public Records Office which record in great detail the money Henry VIII spent on Hampton Court, after taking it over from Wolsey, there are the following payments made to Anthony Tote – in effect Toto del Nunziato, a Florentine artist then working in England *c.* 1530.

Payntynge of dyvers tabulls [i.e. wooden panels, a generic word for most paintings] as ensuyeth:
To Antonye Tote, paynter for the payntyng of 5 tables in the King's Lybrarye;
Ffyrst; one table of Joachym and Sent Anne.
Item; another table how Adam dylffed in the grownde.
Item; the third table how Adam was dryven owght of Paradyce.
Item; the fourth table of the buryenge of our Lord.
Item; the fyfth table beynge the last table of the buryeng of our blessyd Lady.
The sayd Antonye takynge for the sayd 5 tables by a bargain £6.13.4. Item; to Antonye Tote paynter for the payntyng of 4
Item; to Antonye Tote paynter for the payntyng of 4 grate tablys – that is to saye one table of our Lady of peyte; another table of the 4 Evanglysts; the thyrd of the Mawndyth; the fourt [illegible]. The sayd Antonye tayking for the sayd tables by a bargain £20.

4.9 A garden to walk in

It had become generally accepted that a garden was essential for a comfortable, civilised life, and on 20 September 1532 the Master and Fellows of Queen's College, Cambridge passed the following Order.

It is thus agreid also, and by the hole assent and consent of the said Master and felowse determined: That whereas the Presydent of the college hath before yis tyme no garden appointid severailly for hymself, nother for frute, nor to walk in, but wyth the felowse both in walkis and in divident of frute. Now at the desire of the said Presydent the felowship or cumpani of this College hath agreid and grawnted yt the said presydent shall have enjoy, and take from hensforth the Garden or Ortzard over agaynst the College brode gates with all the frutes growing wythyn the same to his own proper use. Under yis condition the sayd President from hensforth shall have no parte or divident of such frutes as groweth wythyn the College grate ortzard.

Teste Simine Heynes, *manu propria*

4.10 Embellishing Hampton Court

In 1535 and 1536 Henry VIII embarked upon an ambitious programme of improving Wolsey's palace of Hampton Court. Amongst the various expenses were the following (Chapter House Accounts).

Carving of the Stalls

1. Carvers upponn the stalls in the chappell Edmond More and Peter Cleff at 12d. the day.
2. Ryding costs. Also payd to Eddy More, Carver, for his costs and Expenses Rydyng to Ammeersham, to Cehynys, to Penley, to Thatcham and to Kynges-Clere with the Kynge's commysson, to rest and take up workmen by the space of 4 dayes at 12d. the day over and besydes hes dayes wayges for hymsself and his horsse — 4s.
3. Harry Corant of Kyngston, karver for cuttyng, carvyng, joynyng, framing, setting up and fenesshying oon of the sydes of the stall of the chappell, savyng the crest backing above.

Chappell Doore

1. Also payd to Wylliam Raynoldes, fremason for entayling of too crownys in freston stadyng over the Kyng's armes and the quenys at the Chappell dore at 5s. the pece, by convencyon.

2. The new payntyng, gyldyng and garnesshyng of the too pieces of armes at the Chappell-dore with the Kynges and Quenys armes, pryce the peece 20s.
3. For a lowng bolt of Iron tynned conteyning 3 footes in length, servyng for the Chappell-dore pondering 11 lb.

Windows

1. In the Chappell wyndow before the hyghet altar is 16 footes of Immagere, pryce the foote 2s.
2. Item there is in the hede of the sayd wyndow 3 badges whiche doth emounte to 4 footes pryce the foote – 2s.
3. Item in the wyndowes of the sayd chappell ys sett 3 of the Queny's badges in a skutchen, pryce the peece 12d.
4. Mendyng and paynttyng of fyve peces of images in the wyndowes in the chappell pryce the peece 8d.
5. In the Chappell ys 2 of the Queny's half armes new sett at lyke pryce.

Carved Roof of the Chappell

For payntyng, gyltyng and varnesshyng of the vought in the Kinge's new Chappell: payd to John Hethe and Harry Blankston of London guylders and painters for gyltyng and garnesshing of the vought in the chappell, wyth grate arches bourd, great pendaunts, wyth angels holding schichens wyth the Kynge's armes and the Quenes, and wyth great pendantts of boyes playing with instruments, and large battens set with antyke of lead, gylt with the Kynge's wordde also gylt with fynne gold sett out with other ffyne collers, and for casting of the antyke and letters of lead, and for the pyn nayll, with all other necessaryes belowngyng to the foresaid chappell rowff, wyth too grate baye windowes of the Kynge's and the Quenes Holydaye Closettes, for the side next unto the chappell, garnesshed and gwylte wyth the Kynges armys and the Quenys, wyth beests guylte with fyne golde sett outt wyth other fyne collers.

4.11 The expenses of a princess

The account books of Mary Tudor during the period between 1536 and 1544 (published by Frederick Madden in 1831) give a meticu-

lous account of her expenses as a young Princess. A selection of
them gives a very clear idea of the kind of involvement with
various aspects of art and design which a person of her standing
had in the sixteenth century.

1536

January. Item; payd for mending of the Clocke which My Lady's
Grace had of my Lady Rochford 5s.

Item; payd to Blase for broidering a payre of sleves for My Lady's
Grace, 20s.

February. Item payd to a goldsmyth of Chepe for 7 peeces of goldsmyth's work and two pair of aiglettes 26s. 8d.

March. Item; payd for goldsmyth's works for My Lady given to
John of Andwarpe [Antwerp] £4 16s. 7d.

Item; for 3 yds of Satten given to Mr Paston techyng my ladye of
the virginalls 21s. 6d.

April. Item; payd to Frauncis goldsmith for the fascion of a brooch
20s.

1537

July. Item; given to the qwene's gardner at Hampton Court 5s. 4d.

Item; Payd for making a Dore to My Lady's Grace's chamber at
gulford 3s. 4d.

1537

August. Item; payd for a Salt of gold £13.

September. Item; payd for a Brasse pot 7s. 2d.

October. Item; payd for a Payr of Claspis of Sylver and gilt sent to
the Lady Butler 4s.

November. Item; given at the Cristenyng of Dr. Michael's childe,
a Salt Gilt and silver my Lady's grace being Godmother to the
same, 66s. 8d.

December. Item; Bought of Farnando at my Lady's grace last
comyng to the Courte a hundred perles at 13s. 4d. the peece
£66 13s. 4d.

Payd to Orton Goldsmythe for certain goldsmyth's work of him
bought £16.

Item; payd to the myllenar for 2 Tabletts and one broche of gold
£6.

Item; payd for golde to embraudre a qwyssion [cushion] for Mr
Wriothesley 20s.

Item; payd for Silver to embradre a boxe for my Lady Elizabeth's grace 12s.

February. Item; given to George Mountjoye drawing my Lady's grace to his valentyne 40s.

1538

March Item; Pyd to Abraham of London for 6 yds. of Cloth of Silver £12.

Item; payd for a broche of gold 26s. 8d.

September. Item; payed for Venes [Venice] golde for my Lady's grace 20s.

1540

February. Item; Firste payd for a payre of Braccletts of golde 110s.

Item; payd for 3 broches £9.

Item; for the fascion of a little chene 5s.

Item; for the fascion of 2 payr of Clasps 2s.

Item; payd for 2 gilt potts weying 16¼ ounces at 3s. 4d. the ounce 50s. 1d.

Item; peyd to pecocke of London for 9 yerds of Cloth of Gold at 38s the yard £37 10s. 6d.

April. Item; payd to the King's Brawderer for Embrawdring a Cote for the Prince his grace 53s. 4d.

1542

January. Item; given to 3 Venetians giving my Lady's Grace a fayr stele glass 15s.

Item to maisress Daker's servunt bringing a Table with a picture 7s. 6d.

January. Item; payd to Cornelys the goldesmyth in full payment for plate of hym bought as new yeres gifts £20.

Item; given to the keeper of the kyng's garden 5s.

Item; pd to the Boke bynder for a Boke lymed with golde the same given to the prince's grace for a newyeres gift 29s.

1542

May. Item; Payd to [blank] goldesmythe for the fascion of a girdle set with Rubyes and perles 73s. 4d.

January. Item; payd to greene of London for covering of a chaire, the same given to the kinges maiestie for a newyere gift 86s. 7d.

Item; given to John Hayes for draweing a Patterne for a qwyssion for the quene 6s. 6d.

1543
February. Item; payd to gullyam Brellont for th' embrodering of a chaire for the King's maiestie £18.

1544
April. Item; gevin to John Hayes for draweing of a quyshun 10s.
June. Item; payd to Reynolds the goldsmythe for setting of a Jewell with 4 diamonds and for gold that he put thereto £4 4s. 4d.
November. Item; pd to one John that drue her grace in a table £5.

4.12 Domestic images

Private individuals of quite modest status often possessed religious objects of some value. In 1539, for instance Anne Buckenham of Bury St Edmunds made the following bequest; the pathos of the last sentence hardly needing any underlining.

I give and bequeath to the chapel in the manor of Buckenham in Lyvermore Magna, my table of alabaster with the images of the Trinity, Saint Peter and St Nicholas, there to remain as long as it may endure.

4.13 The pursuits of Henry VIII

In his own way a Renaissance man, Henry VIII was interested in the arts, literature and music, acquiring a reputation as a composer. In 1539 the French ambassador wrote to Francis I.

The King, who in recent years has been somewhat solitary and pensive, now gives himself up to amusements, going to play every night upon the Thames with harps, chanters and every kind of music and pastime. He evidently delights now in painting and embroidery, having sent to France, Flanders, Italy and elsewhere for masters of the art and other experts in these fields. All his people think that this is a sign of his desire to marry if he can find a suitable match.

4.14 A tomb for King Henry VIII

Any notion of specialisation in art was very slow in coming. The King's Sergeant-Painter was expected to paint anything from a picture to a wall, as well as to gild frames, furniture and ornaments. He had to undertake decorations for revels and masques, to be responsible for the exterior decoration of royal palaces as well as the interior. In 1604 Leonard Fryer, who held the post was paid 52s. 'for laying clere colouring, guilding and varnyshyng fyve greate frames for Mappes in the Gallery'; 40s. 'for latering a picture in the Chapple and made it Joseph and a superscrition to yt'. He was also paid for 'the washing and cleneing of the picture of our ladie in the chapple'. In 1574 William Hearne was entrusted with the creation of a tomb for Henry VIII and the payments made to him (quoted in Erna Auerbach's *Tudor Artists*, London 1954) and the carver indicate the variety of work involved.

Also allowed to the saide Accomptaunte for money by him disbursed and payde for the charges don upon the modell of a Tombe for kinge Henrye the eighte wythyn the tyme of this Accompte, viz in emptyon of parchment and paystpaper 25s.; drye pearetree 3s; tape 14d.; for pearetree wainscott, clapborde and the wagies of one man 6 dayes 28s. 6d.; for hire of a horse twise to Windsoure 13s.; two sqyres 2s.; cariage of the modell by water to Hampton Courte, and to and fro the painters and to my Lorde Treasorers at sundrie tymes 11s. And to William Hearne for payntyng and gyldying of the small modell £6 13s. 4d.; to Richard Rowlande, carver for carvinge of 12 figures, 60s.; for the pictures of the kinge and enrichinge the bodye of the Tombe 26s. 8d.; for gravinge the mouldes and workinge of 8 pillers 60s.; for workinge of 22 tie pannells 44s.; for enrichinge 12 petistalles on bothe sides 24s.; making the moldes and the bases that goe about the petistalles 10s.; workinge of fyve smalle fygures withe the carvinge; for fyve paire of the queenes armes of the queen's armes at 5s. the paire 25s.; for enrytchinge of the balles and the cornyshe 4s.; for turninge of 4 pillers with carvynge 8s.; for waxe 15s.; for paistbord 4s.; for 9 smale pendittes 12s.; for drawinge three plattes 30s.; to Cure for drwainge the ground playtes and uprightes for the Tombe 4l. and for turninge of 8 pillers, capitals and ballisters 13s. 4d.; and for making letters and a Calender to knowe what is wraughte and what ys wanting about the modell 3s. 4d. In all 34l. 5s. 4d. And for wagies of joyners workinge by the daye at 14d. the daye about the same Tombe 7l 9s. 4d. In all the chardges of the sayd modell done by the space of 38 dayes endinge the last daye of September 1574

Anno regni dominae Elizabethe Regine 16 to. as by a Booke thereof subscribed by the officers aforesaid more plainely may appear 41l. 14s. 8d.

4.15 The Royal Collection

In 1542 Sir Anthony Denny was appointed Keeper of the Palace of Westminster, and he drew up an inventory of the contents of the Palace, initialled by the King, which is now amongst the Miscellaneous Books of the Augmentation Office in the Public Records Office (reproduced in *Courtauld Institute Texts for the Study of Art History*, 1937). It reveals that the Tudor monarchs possessed a very large collection of works of art more varied in content, more diverse in its variety than one would have expected. Not only are there the religious works, the ancestral and family portraits, but images, probably of a rather untutored kind, of classical subjects; not only are there 'tables' (i.e. panels) but bas-reliefs, statues in stone and 'erthe', marble heads, pictures painted on board, cloth, glass and paper, as well as numerous tapestries and 'embraudered' pieces. Catalogued in the inventory, but omitted from all but the early extracts, there are the curtains, usually of 'white and yellow sarcenet' which seem to have been drawn in front of paintings when rooms were not in use. The language in which the subjects are described indicates a certain simplicity of outlook amongst people not yet entirely acquainted with the sophistication of Renaissance iconography.

Tables with picture[1]

Item; oone table having in hit the five woundes embraudered upon black satten.

Item; oone table with the picture of St Hierome pointing upon a dede man's head.

Item; oone table with the picture of a naked woman holding a table with a scripture in hit in the one hand and a bracelet upon thother arme at thupper part thereof.

Item; oone table of the Decolacion of Seynt John Baptiste.

Item; oone table with the picture of a woman playing the lute and an olde man holding a glass in the one hand and a ded man's hed in thother hande.

---

1 'Table' usually meant a panel.

Item; oone table with the picture of a woman playing upon a lute, with a book before her and a lyly pott with lylies springing out thereof.

Item; oone table with the picture of St Michaell and St George, being in harness holding a streemer.

Item; oone table with the picture of the French Queene Elienora in Spanysh aray, and a cap on her hed and an oringe in her hand.

Item; Oone table with the picture of the French kyng having a doublet of crimson colour and a gowne garnished with knotts made like perle.

Item; oone table with the picture of the 3 childerne of the King of Denmarks with a curtain of white and yellow sarcenet paned.

Item; oone table with the pictures of the hangeman holding St Jon's hed in his hand and a woman holding a dish to receive it with a curteyne of white and yellow sarcene.

Item; oone great table with the picture of the Duches of Mylane being her whole stature.

Item; oone table with the picture of St George on horseback embraudred with Venice gold and silver.

Item; one table with the picture of a naked woman sitting upon a rocke of stone with a scripture above her head.

Item; oone table of the naked truth with the works of the busshop of Rome set forth in it.

Item; oone table of the ould Emprouer and the emprourer that nowe is, and Ferdinando with a curten of yellowe and white sarconet paned togethers.

Item; oone table with the picture of our Lady holding our Lord taken downe from the crosse in her armes, with a curtain of white and yellow sarconet paned togethers.

Item; oone table with the picture of an old man dalieng with women and a pheasant cocke hanging by the bill.

Item; oone table with the picture of a woman with a monkey on her hand.

Item; oone table with the pictures of our Ladye and Christ sucking and Joseph looking on a booke.

Item; oone table of alabaster with the picture of John the Evangelist.

Item; oone table of the 3 kings of Culloyne [the Magi were supposed to be buried in the cathedral at Cologne]

Item; oone table with two folding leavis with the picture of the King his Majestie being yonge wearing his here with a flower of silver upon the locke.

Item; oone table with the whole stature of my Lorde Prince his grace stayned upon cloth.

Item; oone table with the picture of King Henry VII his mother, being Countess of Richemont.

Item; oone table with the picture of Henry the Vth.

Item; oone table with the picture of Henry VIth.

Item; oone table with the picture of King Edward the iijth.

Item; oone table of the Passion of cloth of gold embraudred and garnyshed with small peerles lacking in sundry places and ix counterphet rubies and two counterphet turquoses.

Item; oone table with the picture of Lucrecia Romana in a gowne like crymson vellvat, with greene foreslevis cutt.

Item; oone table of russet and black of the parable of the xviiith chapter of Mathewe reyzed with liquid golde and silver.

Item; oone table of the buriall of our Lorde, all of sundry woodes joyned togethers.

Item; oone table of King Mides and misery reyzed with liquid gold and silver.

Item; oone table of the Salutacion of our Ladye embossed upon black velvat, garnished with sundry small perles and counterphet stones, lacking sundry stones, the frame being of blac ebonet garnyshed with silver and lacking in sundry places, both leavis and scrowla, and uponn the toppe thereof the father and the sonne with beams of silver and gilt.

Item; oone table with the picture of our Ladye holding our Lorde in her armes, with divers angells and children of alabaster, our Ladye divers angells and children, standing in a tabernacle of wood gilt with burnyshed golde, the ground thereof being of purple velvat with a curten of yello and white sarconet paned together.

Item; oone table with the picture of oone having long here being crowned, and having a roobe like clothe of golde and the furre being white.

Item; foure tables of parchment sett in frames of wodde with figures in them and in every oone of them a manor place, videlicet in oone of them is written Hampton Courte, and in another of them is written Amboyse, in another is written Cognat End, and in thother is written Gandit.

Item; thre tables with the picture of our Lord enbraudred upon cloth of golde, two of them with borders of crimson velvat and thother with a border of blac vell.

Item; oone table with Pilat bringing forth our Lorde scourged before the people embraudred upon cloth of golde with a border of black vellvat.

Item; oone table of the Decolacon of St John Baptist painted upon glass the border thereof gilt with burnished gold.

Item; oone table with the picture of our Lady holding our Lorde in her lappe and a pomegarnett in her hand, and an angell playing upon a lute, and Joseph standing by.

Item; oone table with the picture of Julius Caesar.

Item; oone table with the Salutation of our Lady enbraudered upon black satten with ij pillours and an arch of crymson satten enbraudered with Venice golde and in the top of the same on each side an angel.

Item; oone table of mother of peerle in roundels of the birth and passion of Christ garnished with glasse instead of stones with pinecles of wood gilt.

Item; oone table of the siege of Pavy [Pavia].

Item; oone table of the story of Orpheus with sundry strange bests and Monsters stayned on cloth.

Item; two square tables made of sundry colourid wodds either of them having ix lidds to open and within every lidde sundry divises carved with white wodde set fourth with colours of blewe and silver.

Item; oon cloth stayened with the historye of Hester submitting herself to the king Atraxes and he laying his septer upon her hed.

Item; oone picture of a woman made of erthe, her garment being crimson, her hed tyred after Flaunders fashion, sett in a boxe of wodde.

Item: oone picture of Balthasar oone of the thre kings of Colloyne, his head being blac touche sett in brass gilt with a crownet on his head of copper and gilt.

Item; oone picture of a woman with a child in her armes sucking and another at her fote all of blac towche partly gilt sett upon a foote of wood and alabaster.

Item; oone picture of a hed of white marble sett in a roundel of wood.

Item; the description of Venice stayned upon paper and pasted on cloth.

Item; a long mappe of paper pasted upon canvas, conteigning the description of Constantynople Venice and Naples.

4.16 'A newe churche'

On her accession Queen Mary started to show keen interest not only in re-establishing Catholicism, but in building churches on a scale commensurate with the past. She was especially concerned with the building of a new Chapel at Trinity College, Cambridge, and on 30 April 1556 'in the seconde and thirde yeares of the Raignes of Philipp and Marye by the grace of god Kinge and Quene of England, France, Naples, Hierusalem and Irelande, Defenders of the Faithe, Princes of Spaine and Sicilie, Archdukes of Austriche, Dukes of Mylan, Burgundye and Brabante, Countes of Hapsburge, Flaunders and Tirolle' a contract was drawn up between the Master and Fellows and Steven Walles of Cambridge burgess and joiner for the woodwork in the new chapel, for which he was to be paid three hundred pounds. It specified as follows.

FIRSTE uppon the entry of the stalles a border of antique with a double creste, one greater above and another lesse beneath. And the said crestes to return aboute the throwen pillers of waynscott, the back playne of waynscott with a haunce above cutt with antique, the upper seetes to be rysing and falling as they are at the Kinge's College, and after the same fourme, and betwixt every seete a turned piller of oke, and ye vautes over ye said seetes to be playne, the bought of the seetes to be after the same wourke they bee at the King College. The gret desks to be of feyre oke and thre inches thicke, and of brede to be half a yarde besyde the crestes, and to have a border of antique runnyng upon the foredge of the said deskes, and under the deskes to be turned pillers to bere them upp throwout, and the end of the partitions to be with turned pillers as they be at the Kinge's College.

The nether set to have a playne seete of feyre oke, the holle length of the partition, and the back behinde underneth the turned pillers of the stalles to be frenche pannell. The desks of the same stalles to be half a yard brode and two inches thicke, with turned pyllers underneth to beare them upp. The endes of the partitions to be with turned pillers as they are at Kinge's College.

And further the said Steven Walles doth covenaunt and graunt that he shall make the doore into the quere of the said churche with turned pillers upp to the toppe, and to sele the vaut over the entrye and the sydes thereof with two dores of frenche pannell to the outer edge of the rode lofte; And the entry to be ix or x fete from the edge of the stalls to ye edge of the rode lofte. Towards the furnysing thereof the said Master, Fellowes and Schollers to fynde the gymmers for the said doors.

AND also the said Steven Walles covennaunteth that he shall worke make and frame a frette to hang uppon the roofe with croked battones and straye battones, thorowe the holle roofe of oke inbowed with forescore and one pendauntes hanging downe two foote from the said roofe, the brede of the said roofe to be xxxiiii foote and in lengthe one hundred and fyftie and vii foote. And the said roofe to be made and framed at the proper costes and charges of the said College for the foresaid Steven to sette his worke uppon. AND FURTHER the said Steven Walles covenaunteth that he shall fynde all manner of stuffe as well apte and mete belonging to the said stalles as to ye said frettes battones and pendauntes as tymbre, nayles workmanship and all other thinges necessary for ye sayd Joyners worke, and the same worke and every part and parcell thereof to be holly wrought and fynished at the proper costes and charges of the said Steven Walles according to the pattron shewed to the Master and others of the said College for the said battones and pendaunts. And the said Master Fellowes and Schollers conventeth and graunteth by these presentes to make redye the place to sett the stalles uponn, and a scaffolde or stage of tymbre for the erecting and fraymyng of the said frettes, battonnes and pendantes at the costes and charges of the said Master, Fellowes and Scholers and their successors.

4.17 Decorating a ship

Colour and ornamentation played a great role in many aspects of life, and just as jousts and other chivalric activities were pretexts for elaborate displays of decorative art, so, as can be seen by this advice given by Jehan Bythorne, Gunner in Ordinary to the King in 1543 (published in *The Naval Miscellany* vol. I, 1902) ships were equally magnificently decked out.

On touching the ornamentation of your ship, on the outside from the main wale [planking on the outside of a ship] in the water-line to the top of the castle, she should be painted in your colours and devices, as also the forecastle and the aftercastle as splendidly as maybe. And all the shields round the upper parts of the castles – both the forecastle and the aftercastle – ought to be emblazoned with your arms and devices. And above the forecastle, on a staff inclining outwards, you ought to have a pennon of your colours and devices; as also at the two corners of the castle. Amidships there ought to be two square banners emblazoned with your arms. On the aftercastle, high above the rudder, you ought to have a large square banner, larger than any of the others. And on each side of this castle, as you face towards the mast, there ought to be five or six square banners, not so large as that above the rudder, which I have just spoken of, all emblazoned with your arms, quarters and devices. All round the main top – *videlicet*, of the main mast – you ought to have top-armour of the full length of the top, and emblazoned with your arms; and from it there must fly a broad swallow-tailed standard, of such length as to reach to the water, and similarly emblazoned with your arms and devices. And on the top of that maste [main top must] there ought to be a square banner emblazoned with your arms. And no one is permitted to carry such a banner except you, for it is by it that you are recognised by day. Likewise on the foremast there ought to be a top with armour all round, like to that of the main top. And above there ought to be a pennon, like to the great standard, but not so long.

Some there are who hang a great number of small banners or pennons from the mainstay or from the forestay, as also from the main mizzen stay; likewise from both sides of the vessel in the waist, according to their pleasure.

And for celebrating a triumph, your ship ought to be covered in and curtained with rich cloth, and the same on the two sides, as low down as the guns; and within board, below the deck it should also be draped and canopied, so that the beams cannot be seen; and underfoot there should be a rich carpet, as in a room on shore; and the aftercastle should be richly draped, as also the forecastle, but not so richly. You may also paint your sails with such devices and colours as you choose; or with the representation of a saint if you prefer it. And in my opinion, Sir, your ship will thus be prepared in the best possible way, whether for the campaign or an actual battle.

4.18 Post-Reformation treasures

Despite the changes introduced by the Reformation the church was still to retain, although in a depleted way, some of the immense wealth of treasures it had accumulated. An inventory taken at York Minster in the reign of Edward VI records some of the masterpieces of the goldsmith and embroiderer's arts, even though it is only about quarter of the length of a similar one taken in 1500, and by the time Elizabeth I died most of the objects recorded here had vanished, either for reasons of liturgical odium, or more private forms of greed.

An inventory of all the jewels, plate, coupes, vestments and other ornaments as well within the Revesterye of the Cathedrall Church of St Peter in York, and also appertaigning to the High Altar therein in the reigne of King Edward VI

PLATE. A chalice of gold, with a pataine, 47 oz. A chalice of gold with a pataine of gold, dayly used 23 oz. A chalice of silver and guilt 58 oz. A chalice of silver guilt with a lyon and three scallop shells on the foot, 29 oz, and patten, 22 oz. A round footed chalice of silver and guilt, with a crucifix on the foot, 19 oz. A round footed chalice of silver and guilt 13 oz. A round chalice parcell guilt, 9 oz. A chalice of silver and guilt with a crucifix on the foot, 19 oz. A pair of censors of gold, 17 oz. A shell of silver for the same censors, 11 oz. A box for singing bread, silver guilt, 11 oz. A box for singing bread, silver 10 oz.[1] A pair of great censors of silver and guilt 64 oz.; Another pair of great censors 100 oz. A pair of olde censors, silver and guilt, 38 oz. Another pair of old censors, silver and guilt, 46 oz. Another pair of censors, silver and guilt, 44 oz. Two basons of gold for the High Altar 42 oz. Two little basons of silver guilt, with keys upon them, 30 oz. A sconce of silver, parcell guilt, 27 oz.. Another sconce of silver, 18 oz. A ship, with a spoon of silver and guilt 21 oz., two little crewitts of silver, parcell guilt, 7 oz. A shell of silver guilt for salt 2 oz. A bell of silver 5 oz. A hat piece of silver, 3 oz. A pax of silver and guilt, 9 oz. Three ampulles of silver, 40 oz. A tablet of silver and guilt, unmelted, to sett on the altar 110 oz. A pectoral of gold, with a rich stone in the middest, 13 oz. A pectoral of gold with a great stone in the middest, and 6 perfect rubies, all weighing 14 oz. A pectoral of silver and guilt with a stone of silver and guilt with the Acension 80 oz. Two candelsticks of beryll. A superalter garnished about with silver guilt and stones. A handle of silver and guilt 5 oz. A superalter, with a black stone, garnished with silver and guilt. A chrystamatory of silver and guilt 8 oz. A standyng cupp with a cover, silver and guilt with a berryle in the middest, 43 oz. A pair of crewetts, silver and guilt, with four great precious stones in the middest, 51 oz. A pair of crewetts, silver and guilt, with swannes,

---

1. 'Singing bread': the wafers for the Holy Communion, so-called because they were cooked in *singing irons*, metal containers made for that purpose. In 1429 Annas Wells of York left 'tria instrumenta ferri vocata *syngynirons*, ii instumenta ferri pro pane ad Eucharistiam ordinando'.

35 oz. A pair of crewetts silver and guilt, 27 oz. A pair of candlesticks with the Lord Scrope's arms, 100 oz. A pair of little crewetts
silver and guilt, 25 oz. A paire of silver candlesticks, parcel guilt,
80 oz. A holy water pott, with a sprinkle of silver, 101 oz. A holy
water pott of silver with a sprinkle, 36 oz. A holy water pott with
a sprinkle of silver, 40 oz.

In the inner vestrey

RED COPES. A red cope of clothe of tishewe with orphry of pearl.
Another red cope of clothe of tishewe with orphry of needlework,
with the five woundes. A cope of clothe of tisshew having our
Ladye on the backe with orphrey. A cope of raised clothe of
goulde, of the Lord Darcye's gift [1467–1537]. A cope of fine red
clothe of tishewe with 21 apples with orphry. A cope of clothe
of gold of the gift of Martin Collins. Two rich copes of cloth of
goulde, one having St Oswalde on the hoode, the other the
Assumption of our Lady. A cope of clouthe of goulde *ex dono
Prioris de Bardforde* [the gift of the Prior of Bradford]. Two copes
of cloth of goulde, one haveing the Assumption, the other the Puri-
fication of our Lady. Two copes of sanguine purple clothe of
goulde. Two copes with daisies. Two copes of red velvett with
eagles. Two red copes with images of needlework, one cope of red
cloth of goulde *ex dono* Thomas Arundell. One red cope with
arches sett with pearls. One cope of red sattin with pearle. One
cope of clothe of tishew ex dono Richardi Layton, Deacon [Dean].
A cope of cloth of goulde, *ex dono* Gulielmi Hobyill. A cope of
clothe of tisshew ex dono Thomas Magus (Magnus) archdeacon.
Two copes of red velvett with angells, one with Trinity, the other
with our Lady, with orphreys on the back. Four copes of crimson
velvett plaine, with orphreys of cloth of goulde for standers.

WHITE COPES. Two copes of clothe of tishewe, one having the
Resurrection, the other St Peter on the backe. A cope of damask
clothe of goulde with St John Baptiste on the backe. Three copes
of damaske, one given by Martin Collins, and one other by Dr
Simson, and the third by Mr Newman. A cope of white velvet of
Mr Molton's gift. Two damaske white copes with angells. A white
velvett cope with a broad orphry on the back and starrs on the
cape. A cope of white clothe of goulde of Mr Carver's guifte, one
of white velvett with starres all of one sute.

BLUE COPES.[2] A principall goodly cope, all with needlework, the orfrey of pearl with birdes. Another of the same making, the orfrey with pearle and goulde connected. A cope of needlework, with orfrey of the old fashion, the cell [cowl?] couched with pearle. Two copes of clothe imperiall, of Deane Higdon's guifte, as Mr John Wither's. Four blew copes, one with the Resurrection, one with the Assumption, the third with the Trinitye, and the fourth with the Salutation on the back, with orfry. Six copes of blew cloth of tissewe of Mr Andrew Hollis, archdeacon of York, his guift. A cope of cloth of goulde *ex dono* Hugonis Ashton. A blew cope of goulde needlework with angells upon it. A blew cope of velvet with flowers upon it. A blew cope of velvet with torches. A cope of clothe of goulde *ex dono* Edm. Lee, Archiepiscopi.

GREEN COPES Four riche copes of fine clothe of tissewe, one with the image of Our Saviour, the second with the conception of our Lady and her sonne in her armes, and the fourth with the Assumption of our Lady on the orfreye. Two copes of clothe of tissewe greene, with eahgles on. A cope of cloth of tissewe with swannes on the orfreye, needlework. A cope of greene cloth of goulde *ex dono* Thomas Dalby. Six copes of clothe of goulde of divers mens' gifts.

COPES IN THE CHAMBER ABOVE. Four green copes of damask with orfreye of cloth of goulde. One greene cope with a partriche. One greene cope of velvett with bulls' heads.

BLEW COPES THERE. A cope of blew tinsell sattin. A cope of blew sattin with king Richard's badge. A cope of blewe velvett, orfreye, cloth of tissewe. A blew cope of velvett with garter and esses. A blew sattin cope with angells.

REDD COPES. A riche cope for the Bishope. Another for his chaplaine. A cope with dolphins and pearles in the orfreye. A cope of imagery work with starres of goulde.

BLACK. One cope of black clothe for obites. Six black damaske copes with red orfreys. A black velvet cope *ex dono* Mr Whiat. A chaire of purple velvet. Two cushions of cloth of goulde. A clothe of estate with coverall of cloth of goulde. A train of red sarsnett.

---

2. Blue was the liturgical colour for feasts of the Virgin Mary.

A canopie of red and greene sattin to be borne over St William's head. A Turkey carpet. A rich sudarye [towel] embroydered with gold.

(*The Fabric Rolls of York Minster*, Surtees Society, vol. 35, 1858/9)

4.19 How a man should build his house or mansion, 1547

Architectural and artistic advice kept cropping up in the most unlikely places. *A Dyatorie, or Regiment of Health by Andrew Boorde of Physicke, Doctor*, published in 1547, contained the following advice.

Make the hall of such fashion that the parlour be annexed to the head of the hall; and the buttrye and pantrye at the ende thereof; the cellar under the pantrye at the lower ende thereof; the cellar under the pantrye sett somewhat at a base; the kechyn sett somewhat at a base from the buttrye and pantry; coming with an entrie within, by the wall of the buttrie; the pastrie house and the larder annexed to the kechyn. Then dyvide the loginges by the circuit of the quadrivial courte, and let the gatehouse be opposite, or against the hall doore; not directly but the hall doore standing abase of the gatehouse, in the middle of the fronte enteringe into the place. Let the prevye chamber be annexed to the great chamber of estate, with other chambers necessary for the buildinge, so that many of the chambers may have a prospect into the chappell.

4.20 Deface and destroy

The desire of the Tudor reformers to efface every kind of imagery went beyond the public domain, and the Act of January 1550 against so-called superstitious books and images spelt this out at some length.

And be it further enacted by the authority aforesaid, that if any person or persons of whatever estate, degree, or condition whatsoever, he, she or they be, body politic or corporate, that now have, or hereafter shall have in his, her, or their custody any books or writings of the sort aforesaid, or any images of stone, timber, alabaster or earth, graven, carved or painted, which heretofore have been taken out of any church or chapel, or yet stand in any church or chapel, and do not before the last day of June next ensuing deface and destroy or cause to be defaced and destroyed the same images and everyone of them shall be therefore convict, forfeit and lose to our Sovereign Lord the King, for the first offence twenty shillings, and for the second offence shall forfeit and lose, being thereof lawfully convict, four pounds, and for the third offence shall suffer imprisonment at the King's will.

4.21 Royal possessions

On Queen Mary's accession in 1553 the Keepers of the Palace of Westminster were asked to account for various royal possessions from the place which were missing. A selection of these gives some idea of the range and diversity of the objects accumulated by Tudor kings and queens.

Stuff delivered to the Lady Jane, usurper, at the Tower

One sable skin, with a head of gold, muffled, garnished and set with four emeralds, four turquoises, six rubies, two diamonds and five pearls; four feet of gold, each set with a turquoise, the tongue being a ruby.

A cap of black velvet, having a fair brooch with a little square table ruby, and divers pictures enamelled with red, black and green with xviii buttons, with small rock rubies, and xviii buttons also of gold with three small pearls the piece. Two little images of box, graven, representing the King's majesty, and the late King Henry, his father.

One fair striking clock, standing upon a mine of silver, the clock being burnished with silver and gilt, having in the top a crystal, and also garnished with divers counterfeit stones and pearls, the garnishment of the same being broken and lacking in sundry places.

One alarum of silver enamelled, standing upon four balls.

One alarum of copper, garnished with silver, enamelled with divers colours, having in the top a box of silver, standing upon a green molehill, and under the molehill, a flower of silver, the same alarum standing upon three pomegranates of silver.

One sable skin with a head of gold, containing in it a clock, with a collar of gold, enamelled black, set with four diamonds, and four rubies, and two pearls hanging at the ears, and two rubies in the ears, the same skin having feet of gold, the claws thereof being sapphires, two of them being broken, and with a diamond upon the clock.

Stuff delivered by Arthur Sturton, deceased, without warrant to sundry persons, who have subscribed his book for the same

The physmanye [physiognomy] of King Henry the eight painted in a table [i.e. panel] like an antique broken because it was the destruction of the Bishop of Rome.

One paper of the Passion, painted. [Delivered to Mrs Clarencius]

Seventy nine tables, with pictures, some of pearl, some embroidered, and some painted; six stained cloths; eight pictures of earth; twelve maps, or descriptions of cities, towns and countries.

Stuff remaining in the custody of George Brydeman, viewed by the Lord Chamberlain and laid apart to be shown to the Queen her majesty

A picture of the Lady of Suffolk in a yellow box; another picture of Andrew Dorye in another box, and a picture of Queen Katherine that last died in a box. All which parcels aforesaid are within a coffer of murrey [dark red] velvet, plated with copper.

A picture of the Princess Dowager.

The picture of King Edward in a little box.

Sundry kinds of jewels, plate and other stuff of the king's majesty's borrowed by Sir Andrew Dudley, for the furniture of his pretended [i.e. intended] marriage to the Lady Clifford

One fair tablet of gold, to open in the back, made like a castle, garnished with xxvii diamonds, eight rubies and four sapphires, cutlozenze-wise, with a picture of a woman and an agate holding a small diamond in her hand like a glass.

A flower of gold, with a diamond in the middle, and eight small diamonds on the borders, and three pearls pendant.

A table of Diana and nymphs bathing themselves, and how Actaeon was turned into a hart.

An ewer of antique work of silver and gilt garnished with pearls, jacinths, amethysts and other stones of small value (22½ ounces).

Three combs, a glass, an earpick and a bodkin, all of white bone garnished with damascene work.

4.22 Tergiversations

Changes in political power and religious convictions played havoc with the great legacy of religious imagery and liturgical objects which had been built up during the Middle Ages. The Henrician Reformation destroyed much – notably rood-lofts, but in the reign of Philip and Mary these were, at least in part, restored. Then, with the advent of Elizabeth, the process was reversed as the Audit Books of St John's College, Cambridge for 1559 reveal.

Inprimis to Baxster the stationer for twelve English saulters xxixs.

Item to hym for 2 Communion Books xs.

Item to Johne Walker and his man for a daye's workinge pulling down the hye alter and carting it away xxd.

Item to a poore fellowe wch helpede to carie awaie ye stone of ye alter iiid.

Item to ye glasier for setting xxi peynes of new glasse in ye windowes of ye chappell and for altering ye crucifix iis. ixd.

Item for pulling down ye aulter in doctor Ashton chappell vid.

Item to ye mason for leyinge downe certain stones about the high alter vid.

Item to Underwood and other for pulling down ye alter on ye south side of ye lower chappell and carrying ye grauell to ye causye of ye backe syde xiid.

4.23 Ancient monuments

The impetus behind the destruction of statues and images was purely sectarian, and, it was felt, had gone too far. On 19 September 1560 Elizabeth issued a proclamation from Windsor restraining the destruction of secular monuments and the like.

The Queen's Majesty, understanding that by means of sundry people, partly ignorant, partly malicious, or covetous, there hath of late years been spoiled and broken certain ancient monuments, some of metal, some of stone, which were erected up as well in churches, as in other public places within this realm, only to show a memory to the posterity of the persons there buried, or that had been benefactors to the buildings or donations of the same churches or public places, and not to nourish any kind of superstition:

By which means not only the churches and places remain at this present day spoiled, broken, and ruinated, to the offence of all noble and gentle hearts and the extinguishing of the honourable and good memory of sundry virtuous and noble persons deceased; but also the true understanding of divers families in this realm (who have descended of the blood of the same persons deceased) is thereby so darkened as the true course of their inheritance may be hereinafter interrupted, contrary to justice, besides many other offences that do ensue to the slander of of such as either gave or had charge in times past only to deface monuments of idolatry, and false, feigned images in churches and abbeys; and therefore, although it be very hard to recover things broken and spoiled, yet both to provide that no such barbarous disorder be hereafter used, and to repair as much of the said monuments as conveniently may be:

Her Majesty chargeth and commandeth all manner of persons to forbear the breaking or defacing of any parcel of any monument, or tomb, or grave, or other inscription and memory of any person deceased being in any manner of place, or to break any image of Kings, princes or noble estates of this Realm, or of any other that have been in times past erected and set up for the only memory of them to their posterity in common churches and not for any religious honour, or to break down or deface any image in glass windows in any church without consent of the ordinary.

Upon pain that whosoever shall herein be found to offend to be committed to the next gaol, and there to remain without bail or mainprize unto the next coming of the justices for the delivery of the said gaol, and then to be further punished by fine or imprisonment (besides the restitution or re-edification of the thing broken) as to the said justices shall seem meet, using therein the advice of the ordinary and (if need be) the advice also of Her Majesty's Council in her Star Chamber.

As for such as be already spoiled in any church or chapel now standing Her Majesty chargeth and commandeth all archbishops, bishops and other ordinaries or ecclesiastical persons which have authority to visit the same churches or chapels, to inquire by presentments of the curates, churchwardens, and certain of the parishioners what manner of spoils have been made sithen Her Majesty's reign, of such monuments, and by whom, and if the persons be still living how able they be to repair and re-edify the same; and thereupon to covent the same persons, and to enjoin them, under pain of excommunication, to repair the same by a convenient day, or otherwise, as the cause shall further require, to notify the same to Her Majesty's Council in the Star Chamber at Westminster, and if any such shall be found and convicted thereof, not able to repair the same, then they be enjoined to do open penance in the church two or three times as to the quality of the crime and party belongeth, under like pain of excommunication.

(Hughes, P. L. & Larkin, F. J. *Tudor Royal Proclamations*, Yale 1969, vol. 2, p. 146.)

4.24 A woman painter *c.* 1560

There are several references in Elizabethan documents to Levina Teerlinc 'pictrix', who had come to England from Flanders in the reign of Henry VIII, and was a gentlewoman of the Privy Chamber to the Queen, and as such in 1563 received a New Year's gift from the Queen of 'two guilt spoones'. In 1552 she had been sent by Henry VIII to draw a portrait of Elizabeth, for £10, and was paid that sum quarterly during the reign of Edward VI. With the accession of the Queen, this was increased to £40 a quarter. In 1563 she was recorded in the Lord Chamberlain's accounts as being paid for 'a Carde with the Quenis Maiestie and many other personages' and in 1577 a document under the Privy Seal recorded:

To the Treasouror and Chamberlayns of our Exchequire greetinge. Wheras wee by our Letters Petente datid the Tenth day of October in the first yere of our Reigne did geve and grantte unto Levyne Terlinge latelie deceased and late wyffe unto George Terlyne one of our gentlemen Pencioners one Annutie of fortie poundes by yere duringe her Lieffe Payable at fowre equall partes, forasmuche as wee are credyblie enformed that the saide Levyne died the xxiith of June lastepaste one day onlie one day before tene powndes parcell of the same annutie should have been due unto her, wee as well in respecte of previous service done unto us by the said Levyne Terlinge, as of the presente service of our said Servaunte George Terlinge are pleased that the said George shall have payment of the saide Tene poundes. Geaven under our Privie Seale at Halingsburie Morley the eleventh day of Auguste in the eighteenthe yere of our Reigne.

4.25 Worthy of his hire

In theory, at least, wages were subject to government regulations contained in Royal Proclamations. From one of these promulgated on 3 August 1563, we may get some notion of the economic standing of artists and craftsmen in relation to a selection of other workers.

Goldsmiths, with meat and drink; by the year £8; by the week 3s. 4d. By the day 7d. Without meat and drink by the week, 6s.; by the day 12d.

Painter-stainers with meat and drink, by the year £4; by the week 4s.; by the day 9d. Without meat and drink, by the year £8; by the week 6s.; by the day 14d.

Broderers [embroiderers], with meat and drink; by the year £5; by the day 8d.; without meat and drink, by the week 6s. 8d.; by the day 13d.

Tilers with meat and drink; by the week 4s.; by the day 9d.; without meat and drink by the week 6s.; by the day 12d. His apprentices, with meat and drink; 3s. 4d.; the day 7d.; without meat and drink; the week 5s.; the day 11d.

Plasterers with meat and drink, by the day 9d.; without meat and drink, by the day 13d.

Glaziers with meat and drink, by the day 9d. Without meat and drink 13d.

Barbers, with meat and drink, by the year £3; by the week 20d.

Joiners with meat and drink; by the year £5; by the week 4s. 6d.; by the day 9d; without meat and by the week 7s.; by the day 14d.; his servant with meat and drink by the year £4; by the week 2s.; by the day 4d. Without meat and drink, by the week 4s.; by the day 10d.

Carpenters; with meat and drink by the week 4s.; by the day 9d.; without meat and drink by the week 6s.; by the day 13d.

Carpenter's apprentice that hath served three years, with meat and drink; by the week 3s. 4d.; by the day 7d; without meat and drink by the week, 5s. by the day 11d.

Longbow string-makers, with meat and drink, by the year £4; by the day 8d.; without meat and drink by the day 12d.

Common labourers, with meat and drink, by the day 5d.; without meat and drink by the day 9d.

4.26 Elizabethan stained glass

The ambivalences of the Elizabethan religious settlement were illustrated by the fact that though an excess of religious imagery was frowned upon, stained-glass windows were still installed in churches, even though they tended to be much simpler than their medieval predecessors. Between 1562 and 1564 William Blithe and Miles Jugg, of Thaxted in Essex installed windows in the new chapel of Trinity College, Cambridge, the cost of which were noted by the Bursar in his accounts. The glass removed had presumably been religious in nature.

In primis paide to William Blithe of Thacksted for xvi top pieces for the west wyndowe which he drewe to xxi fote of glass at vd. the fote ixs. viid.

Item paide to hym for 80 fote of white glass, sett upp in the xi lightes of the second storie in ye west wyndowe at vd. the fote xlvs. iiiid.

Item payde to hym for fyve score and eight fote of white glass at vd. the fote, set up in nyne lightes of the lowest storie in the west windowe lxixs. vid.

Item for a greate Rose, flowerdelice and a purcholis at vis. the piece set upp in the weste wyndowe and iii letteres in gold iiis. xxs.

Item for two tables for sentences at vis viid the peece xiis. ivd.

Item paide for eight score and eight fote of white glass, and half a fote at vd. the foote for the first windowe of the sowth side iiili. xviis. iid.

Item for the ii Armes in the sayde windowe xiis.; for the ii Ranges iiiis; and for xii paynes of the foures [flowers?] having letters or prynces arms in them summa xiis. xxviiis.

Item for the white glass of six other wyndowes on the sowth side everye windowe conteining eight score and eight fote et dimid and for xii Armes and xii Ranges and three score and twelfe quarrels paynted with gold worke xxxli. xis. iiiid.

Item to Miles Jugg the glasier for the painted glass of syx wyndowes of the northe side of the chappell, vizt. for xii Arms and lxxii greate paynted quarrels and xii Ranges viii.li. viiis.

Item for syx windowes of glass for the north syde of the chappell xxiiili. iiis. iiiid.

Item my charges and horshier to Thacksted when I wente to bargen with the glasier for the wyndowes yet to glase iis. vid.

Item to two glasiers iiii daies takyng downe the glasse of the old chappell viiis.

Item given to William Blithe of thacksted in ernest of a bargein for glassing the wyndowes of the new chappell wyth burgundie glass at vid the fote, to be done between this and ester if passydge by sea be had before the feaste of the nativitie next coming, but if it happen the passedge before ye feast but between chistenmas and fastingham, then owr windowes to be glassed before pentycost next. iis.

In November 1565 an entry reads:

Item for repayring of the places which were broken furth in all places where did appear Superstition.

4.27 Preserving the royal image

Portraits of the sovereign had, indeed they still have to a certain extent, an almost liturgical significance as symbols of royal power, with which they were identified. It was not merely the Queen's vanity which provoked the following proclamation in 1563. (*Archaeologia*, vol. ii, p. 169 *et seq.*)

For as much as through the natural desire that all sorts of subjects, both noble and mean, have to procure the portrait and picture of the Queen's Majestie, great number of Paynters and Gravers and some Printers have allready and doe daily, attempt to make divers manners portraictures of hir Majestie, in paynting, graving and printing, wherein is evidently shewn that hytherto none hath sufficiently expressed the naturall representation of Hir Majestie's person, favor or grace, but for the most part have also erred therein, as thereof daily complaints are made amongst Hir Majestie's loving subjects, in so much, that for ridress thereof Hir Majestie hath lately bene so instantly and unfortunately sued by the Lords of her Consell, and others of hir nobility, in respect of the great disorder herein used not only to be content that some special coning paynter might be permitted by access to Hir Majestie to take the naturall representation of Hir Majestie, whereof she hath been allwise of her own right disposition very unwilling, but also to prohibit all manner of other persons to draw, paynt, grave or pourtray Hir Majestie's person or visage for a time until by some perfect patron [pattern or prototype] and example, the same may be by others followed.

Therefor Hir Majestie being herein as it were overcome with the contynual requests of so many of hir Nobility and Lords, whom she cannot well deny, is pleased that for their contentations [requests] some coning persons mete thereof shall shortly make a pourtraict of her person or visage, to be participated to others for the satisfaction of her loving subjects; and furdermore commandeth all manner of persons in the meantyme to forbear from paynting, graving, printing and making of any pourtraict of Hir Majestie until some speciall person that shall by hir allowed shall have first fynished a pourtraicture thereof, after which fynished Hir Majestie will be content that all other paynters, printers or engravers that shall be known men of understanding, and so thereto licensed by the hed officers of the plaices where they shall dwell (as reason it is that every person without consideration attempt the same), shall and maye at their pleasure, follow the said patron or first pourtraicture. And for that Hir Majestie perceiveth that a great number of her loving subjects are much greved, and take great offence with the errors and deformities allready committed by sondry persons in this behalf, she straightly chargeth all hir officers and ministers to see the observation hereof, and as soon as maybe to reform the errors allready committed, and in meantyme to forbydd and prohibit the showing and publication of such as are apparently deformed until they are reformed which are reformable.

4.28 Royal advice

Queen Elizabeth's interest in art obviously went beyond her concern for a faithful representation – even a flattering one – of her own appearance. In his *The Art of Limning*, a contribution which Nicholas Hilliard made to Richard Haydocke's translation of the *Trattato dell'Arte della Pittura, Scultura ed Architettura* by Giovanni Paolo Lomazzo, and which was written *c.* 1590, he recounted a conversation with the Queen.

This makes me to remember the wourds also and reasoning of Her Majestie when first I came into her Highnes' presence to drawe, whoe, after showeing me how shee noticed great differences of shadowing in the works and diversity of drawers of sundry nations, and that the Italians [who] had the name to be cunningest, and to drawe best shadowed not, requiring of me the reason for it, seeing that best to showe onesselfe nedeth no shadowe, but rather the oppen light; to which I graunted [and] afirmed that shadowes in pictures weare indeed caused by the shadow of the place or coming in of the light as only one waye into the place at some small or high windowe, which many workmen covet to worke in for ease to their sight, and to give unto them a grosser lyne, and a more aparent lyne to be deserned, and maketh the worke imborse well, and shew very well afare off, which to liming worke needeth not, becawse it is to be veewed of nesesity in hand neare unto the eye. Heer her Majestie conseved the reason, and therfor chosse her place to sit in for that purposse in the open ally of a goodly garden, where no tree was neere, nor any shadowe at all, save that the heaven is lighter than the earthe, so must that littel shadowe that is from the earthe. This her Majestie's curious demane hath greatly bettered my jugment, besids diverse other like questions in art by her most excellent Majestie, which to speake or writ of weare fitter for some better clarke.

> Hilliard then went on to discuss 'shadowes' in more particular ways.

This matter only of the light let me perfect, that noe wise man longer remain in error of praysing much shadowes in pictures after the life, especially small pictures which are to be viued in hand; great pictures place high or farr of, requier hard shadowes or become the better than nearer in story worke better than pictures of the life, for beauty and goode favor is like cleare truth, which is not shamed with the light, nor neede to bee obscured, so a picture a littel shadowed may be bourne withal for the rounding of it, but so greatly smutted or darkened as some use disgrace it, and is like trith ill-towld. If a very weel favoured woman stand in [a] place her is great shadowe, yet showeth she lovely, not because of the shadowe, but because of her sweet favor, consisting in the line or proportion, even that little which the light showeth greatly pleaseth, moving the desire to see more, *ergo* more would see more; but if she be not very fayre, together with her good proportion, as if too paile, too red or frekled etc, than shadowe to show her in doeth her a favore. Wherefore I conclude greate shadowe is a good signe in a picture, after thc life of an ill cause, and sheweth plainly that either the drawer had no good sight to diserne his shadowes, except they weare grosse, or had a bad light to drawe in, to high or to lowe, or to littel, or else the party drawne needeth and choose thosse shadows for the causes above sayd, or it was perhaps some speciall device or affection of the stander to be drawne in so standing.

Knowe this also, that to shadowe sweetly (as we well calle it) and round well, is a far greater cunning than shadowing hard or dark, for to round awork well cannot be without some shadowe, but so to shadowe as if it weare not at all shadowed is best shadowed, for a round ball is a round ball in the oppen light, where the light cometh every way, as well as in a seller, where it cometh in at a little grating. But everything in his true kind is to be allowed of, as is required of necesity in the story or device, that is where the matter consisteth more in a strange light then in the likeness of the party to drawne as if one must be drawne or painted blowing the coalle in the darke to light a candel wee must them shadowe accordingly, making no light but that which comes from the coalle untill the candel be lighted, so when the action in the story or devyse in the pycture requireth it, then I should highly comend it, and discommend theire absurdyty which omit it. As if one should mayke the troup of Judas going to steel Christ in the garden by night with torches and landthornes or any fier works, or assaulting a citie by night, and should make a cleare sky and faire day one of them, and all the landskip wear it never so well paynted it weare not to the purpose or matter, but reddiculous and false; for there the matter consisteth chifly one the trayterous act done by night and any such provision as they had for light. Paulo Lamatzo mainteneth my opinion more than any other I heard in his bouck saing 'What is a shadow, but the defect of light?'.

4.29 Romish images

Religious preoccupations could influence art and its appreciation. Despite her artistic sensitivity, Elizabeth was occasionally subject to them, and in his *Annals*, published in the seventeenth century, John Strype related a conversation (probably based on fact) between the Queen and the Dean of the Chapel Royal.

The Dean, having gotten from a foreigner several fine cuts and pictures representing the stories and passions of the saints and martyrs, and placed them against the epistles and gospels of their festivals in the Common Prayer-book, and this book he had caused to be richly bound, and laid on the cushion for the Queen's use, in the place where she commonly sat, intending it for a new year's gift to her majesty, and thinking to have pleased her fancy therewith. But it had not that effect, but the contrary; for she considered how this varied from her late open injunctions and proclamations against the superstitious use of images in churches, and for the taking away of all such images of popery.

When she came to her place she opened the book and perused it, and saw the pictures, but frowned and blushed, and then shut it (of which several took notice) and calling the verger she bade him bring her the old book wherein she was formerly used to read. After sermon, whereas she was wont to get immediately on horseback or into her chariot, she went straight to the vestry, and applying herself to the Dean, thus she spoke:

Q. Mr Dean, how came it to pass that a new service book was

placed on my cushion? To which the Dean replied 'May it please your majesty, I caused it to be placed there'.
'Then' said the queen' wherefore did you so?'.
D. *To present your majesty with a new year's gift.*
Q. You could never present me with a worse.
D. *Why so, Madam?*
Q. You know I have an aversion to idolatry, to images and pictures of this kind.
D. *Wherein is the idolatry, may it please your majesty?*
Q. In the cuts resembling angels and saints, nay, grosser absurdities, pictures resembling the Blessed Trinity.
D. *I meant it no harm, nor did I think it would offend your majesty when I intended it for a new year's gift.*
Q. You must needs be ignorant then. Have you forgot our proclamation against images, pictures and Romish reliques in the churches? Was it not read in your deanery?
D. *It was read. But be your majesty assured, I meant no harm when I caused the cuts to be bound up with the service book.*
Q. You must be very ignorant to do this after our prohibition of them.
D. *It being my ignorance, your majesty may the better pardon me.*
Q. I am sorry for it, yet glad to hear it was your ignorance rather than your opinion.
D. *Be your majesty assured it was my ignorance.*
Q. If so, Mr Dean, God grant you his Spirit and more wisdom for the future.
D. *Amen, I pray God.*
Q. I pray Mr Dean, how came you by these pictures? Who engraved them?
D. *I know not who engraved them, I bought them.*
Q. From whom bought you them?
D. *From a German.*
Q. It is well it was from a stranger. Had it been from any of our subjects, we should have questioned the matter. Pray let no more of these mistakes or of this kind be committed within the churches of our realm for the future.
D. *There shall not.*

This matter occasioned all the clergy in and about London, and the churchwardens of each parish, to search their churches and chapels, and caused them to wash out of the walls all paintings that seemed to be Romish and idolatrous, and in lieu thereof they caused suitable texts taken out of Holy Scripture to be written.

4.30 A priest's vestments

Not all ecclesiastical treasures belonged to institutions or had been destroyed at the Reformation, and individual priests often commissioned vessels and vestments for their own use. In 1563 John Howe a priest of Plymouth made the following bequest.

This bille made the last days of September in the yere of Our Lorde Godd 1563 is to testifye that I John Howe of Plymouthe, priest have geven, and by these geve unto Mr John Derry maier of Plymouth, and to Mr John Ford, one of the aldermen of the said towne these parcells of good here specified, to wete one clothe of blewe velvett, imbradered with flowers of Venys gold and silke also one whytt sute of vestments for preist, deacon and subdeacon, with one cope of the same sute of silke. Also one other sute of red vestments for priest, deacon and sub deacon with x copes of the same redd sute. Also another red sute of vestyments for preste, deacon and sub deacon with one cope of the same sute to this entent and ende that these foresaid parcells of goods may be solde by the said Mr John Derry and Mr John Ford, and that the money received for the same goods be distributed unto the poore accordyng to their wisdom and discrecion. In witness of my wyll hereunto I have wrytyn this bylle with myn hande and subscribed my name, and put my seale the daye and yeare above wrytyn. John Howe.

(Historical MSS. Commission Report, vol. IX, part I)

4.31 Reluctance to reform

Despite the Elizabethan enactments against religious imagery and such relics of Popery, old habits died hard as the Visitation Books of the Archbishop of York showed. (*Memorials of Ripon*, Surtees Society, vol. 81 1886),

October 29th 1567. Office against Thomas Blackburne, Richard Tirrie, Ninian Atkinson, Christopher Bawdersbie, John Carver, alias Browmflet, vicars of the church of Ripon . . .

They do not communicate together when the Communion is ministered as they ought to do, and the said vicars on a night toke the keis of the church from one John Daie, the sacristane ther, and that night all the imageis and other trumperie were conveied furth out of the said churche and bestowed where it is not known.

Whereunto the said Vicars the dressinge of the saide church apperteinithe, they yet suffer the stones and rubies of the altares to remain in divers closetts in the said church, not yet carried away . . .

Ther is a howse within a vawte of the said churche yet remain-
inge reserved vi great tables of alabaster full of imageis, and xlix
bookes, some Antiphoners, and such bookes as are condemned by
publicque authoritie.

> The unfortunate Blackburne was hauled before the High Court of
> Commission at York and sentenced to make the following state-
> ment from the pulpit.

'Whereas I, goode people a most blinde guide of an old and superstitious custom . . . I am now most hartilie sorry therefore and
desyreth God for ye love of Jesus Christ to forgyve me a penytent
sinner bewaling my offences into his bountefull mercie. Also I
desyre you to beware that you be no more seduced by me, and to
forgive me my former offences towardes you, and I do renounce
my said evill and superstetiois dealings being penytent therefore.
And also for that I, unto whom the charge of the fabrick of this
church is committed, have hithero suffered that olde, abominable
and superstitious vawte called the Wilfrid's needle, and the alter
therein, and certaine other alters also to remaine hitherto within this
church undefaced, undestroyed, and not taken away, contrary to
the lawes of this realm, my dewty and to the great danger of my
soule.'

4.32 Glass popular

The demand for window glass in England rose sharply towards the
end of the sixteenth century. The reduced price of glass helped to
stimulate the demand, and enabled more people to buy it. Till that
time little was made in England, but this too increased sharply after
1567. The following figures are revealing.

IMPORTS

Date	Amount	Origin	Value
1567/8	110 cases.	Normandy.	£110.0.0.
	250 cases.	Burgundy.	£50.0.0.
	56 cases.	Rhineland.	£55.0.0.
1571/2	138 cases.	Normandy.	£138.0.0
	75 cases.	Rhineland.	£75.0.0.
1600	3 cases.	Normandy.	£3.0.0.
1615	26 cases.	Normandy.	£26.0.0.
1621	225 cases.	Scotland.	£224.0.0.
	20 cases.	Normandy.	£20.0.0.

CRYSTAL

Date	Amount	Value	Origin
1567	43 doz.	£1400	France.
1571	50 doz.	£10.0.0.	Amsterdam.
1600	8 doz.	£1.12.0.	Holland.
1621	280 doz.	£94.0.0.	
1626	890 doz.	£267.0.0.	Scotland.
1630	430 doz.	£129.0.0.	France.

ORDINARY

Amount	Value	Origin
2,942 doz.	£93.13.4.	France.
717 doz.	£35.17.10.	Amsterdam.
1,000 doz.	£50	Holland.
1,800 glasses	£7.10.	France.
54,400 glasses	£18.15.	Scotland.
300 glass bowls	£5	Caen.
142,500 glasses	£593.	Scotland.
35,000 glasses	£147.	France.
250 doz.	£12.10.	Flanders
48,400 glasses	£201.	France.
1 doz. glass dishes	£3.15.	Amsterdam.

EXPORTS.

1634   About 40 cases. New England £40.0.0.

Table glass was also becoming popular and widely used as the following figures for drinking glasses show.

(Extracted from the Port Book of Customs, printed in Eleanor S. Godfrey, *The Development of English Glassmaking, 1560–1640*, Oxford 1975)

Harrison confirmed this tendency in his *Description of England*:

As for drink, it is usually filled in pots, goblets, jugs, bowls of silver in noblemens' houses, also in fine Venice glasses of all forms, and for want of these elsewhere, in pots of earth of sundry colours and moulds, where of many are garnished with silver, or at the least-wise in pewter. It is a world to see in these our days, wherein gold and silver most aboundeth, how that our gentility, as loathing those metals (because of the plenty), do now generally choose rather the Venetian glasses, both for our wine and beer, than any of those metals or stone wherein beforetime we have been accustomed to drink.

4.33 The Elizabethan home

William Harrison's *Description of England* of 1577 was published in Holinshed's *Chronicle* the following year, and gives a clear and detailed picture of the homes of the time.

The greatest part of our building in the cities and good towns of England consisteth only of timber; for as yet few of the houses of the commonality, except here and there in the west country towns, are made of stone, although they may (in my opinion) in divers other places be builded so good cheap of the one as of the other.

Our houses are commonly strong and well timbered, so that in many places there are not four, six or nine inches between stud and stud, so in the open and champaign countries, they are forced, for want of stuff to use no studs at all, but only frankposts, raisins, beans, prickposts, groundsels, summers, transoms and such principals, with here and there a girding, whereunto they fasten their splints or raddles, and then cast it all over with thick clay to keep out the wind, which otherwise would annoy them.

As every countryhouse is thus apparalled on the outside, so it is inwardly divided into sundry rooms above and beneath, and where plenty of wood is, they cover them with tiles, otherwise with straw, sedge or reed, except some quarry of slate be at hand, from whence they have for their money as much as will suffice them. The clay wherewith our houses are inpannelled is either white, red or blue. Within their doors also, such as are of ability do, oft make their floors and parget of fine albaster burned, which they call plaster of Paris. In plastering we used to lay a line or two of white mortar, tempered with hair upon laths, which are nailed one by the other, and finally cover all with the aforesaid plaster. The walls of our houses on the inside in like sort be either hanged with tapestry, arras work, or painted cloths, wherein either divers histories, or herbs, beasts, knots and such like are stained, or else they are ceiled with oak of our own or wainscot brought hither out of the East countries. As for stoves, we have not used them greatly, yet they now do begin to be made in divers houses of the gentry and wealthy citizens, who build them not to work and feed in, as Germany and elsewhere, but now and then to sweat in, as occasion and need shall require it.

Horn in windows is now laid down in every place, so our lattices are also grown in less use, because glass is come to be so plentiful, and within a little so good cheap, if not better than the other. Heretofore also the houses of our princes and nobles were often glazed with beryl, and in divers other places with fine crystal. But now these are not in use, so that only the clearest glass is esteemed.

Moreover the mansions of our country towns and villages are builded in such sort generally as that they have neither dairy, stable, nor brewhouses annexed to them under the same roof (as in many places beyond the sea and some of the north parts of our country) but all separate from the first and one from the other. And yet for all this they are not so far distant in sunder but that the goodman lying in bed may lightly hear what is done in each of them with ease, and call quickly to his man if any danger should attack him.

The ancient manors and houses of our gentlemen are yet, and for the most part, of strong timber, in framing whereof our carpenters have been and are worthily preferred before those of like science among all other nations. Howbeit such as be lately builded are commonly either of brick or stone or both, their rooms large and comely.

The furniture of our houses also exceedeth, and is grown in manner even to passing delicacy; and herein I do not speak of the nobility and gentry only, but likewise of the lowest sort in most places of our south country that have anything at all to take to. Certes in noblemen's houses it is not rare to see abundance of arras, rich hangings of tapestry, silver vessels, and so much other plate as may furnish sundry cupboards to the sum often times of a thousand or two thousand pounds at the least, whereby the value of this and the rest of their stuff doth grow to be almost inestimable. Likewise in the houses of knights, gentlemen, merchantmen and some other wealthy citizens it is not geson [unusual] to behold generally their great provision of tapestry, Turkey work, pewter, brass, fine linen and thereto costly cupboards of plate worth five or six hundred or a thousand pounds to be deemed by estimation. But herein as in all things these sorts do far exceed their elders and predecessors, and in neatness and curiosity the merchant all other, so in times past the costly furniture stayed there, whereas now it is descended yet lower, even unto the inferior artificers and many farmers, who by virtue of their old and not of their new leases, have for the most part learned also to furnish their cupboards with plate, their joined beds with tapestries and silk hangings, and their tables with carpets and fine napery, whereby the wealth of our country (God be praised therefore, and give us grace to employ it well) doth infinitely appear.

There are old men yet living in the village where I remain which have noted three things to be marvellously altered in England within their sound remembrance, and other three things too much increased.

One is the multitude of chimneys lately erected, whereas in their young days there were not above two or three, if so many in most uplandish towns of the realm (the religious houses and manors of the lords, always excepted, and peradventure some great personages) but each one made his fire against a reredos in the hall, where he dined and dressed his meat.

The second is the great (though not yet general) amendment of lodging; for, said they, our fathers, yea and we ourselves also, have lain full oft upon straw pallets, or rough mats, covered only with a sheet, under coverlets made of dogswain, and a good round log under their heads, instead of a bolster or pillow. If it were so that our fathers, or the goodman of the house, had within seven years of his marriage purchased a mattress or flock bed and thereto a sack of chaff to rest his head upon, he thought himself to be as well lodged as the lord of the town that peradventure lay seldom in a bed of down or whole feathers, so well were they contented with such bare kind of furniture. Pillows (said they) were meet only for women. As for servants if they had any sheet above them it was well, for seldom had they any under their bodies to keep them from the pricking straws that ran oft through the canvas of the pallet and rased their hardened hides.

The third thing they tell of is the exchange of vessel as of treen platters into pewter and wooden spoons into silver or tin. For so common were all sort of treen stuff in old time that a man could hardly find four pieces of pewter (of which one was peradventure a salt) in a good farmer's house, and yet for all this frugality (if it may so be justly called) they were scarce able to live and pay their rent at their days without selling of a cow or a horse or more, although they paid but £4 at the uttermost a year. Such also was their poverty that if some one odd farmer or husbandman had been at the alehouse, a thing greatly used in those days, amongst six or seven of his neighbours, and there in a bravery to show what store he had did cast down his purse, and therein a noble or 6s. in silver unto them, (for few such men cared for gold, because it was not so ready payment, and they were often enforced to give a penny for the exchange of an angel) it was very likely that all the rest could not lay down so much against it; whereas in my time, although peradventure £4 of old rent be improved to £40, £50, or £100, yet will the farmer, as another palm or date tree, think his gains very small toward the end of his term if he have not six or seven years' rent lying by him, therwith to purchase a new lease, beside a fair garnish of pewter on his cupboard, with so much more in odd vessels going about the house, three or four feather beds, so many coverlets and carpets of tapestry, silver salt, a bowl for wine and a dozen spoons to furnish up the suit [set].

4.34 Modest possessions

Harrison's description of the possessions of the small farmer and men of his kind is borne out by inventories for probate of estates less than £10, which prove how frequently such homes contained not only furniture, but 'peynted cloths', pewter and other artefacts. The following are typical.

A horse, 13/4; certeyne hay, 8s. 0d.; 2 lyttle pannes, 5s. ; 2 potts, 5s.; sheets, 16s 0d.; yren, 9s. 0d.; 18 peeces of pewter, 5s. 0d.; 4 candylsticks, 1s. 4d.; 2 canvasses, 3s. 0d.; a coverlet, 2s. 2d.; 5 shurts, 4s. 0d.; 9 treene dyshes and a ladel, 2d.; a peyre of hamps,

10 d.; peynted clothes, 12 d.; a rope and a bucket, 6d.; 3 kern-chieffes, 12d. (Thomas Greene, Old Swynford Parish, Stourbridge, 1544.)

2 formes, a bedsted and 2 bordes, 1s. 8d.; 2 coffers and a pyne chest, 1s. 6d.; A nowld broken coffer, 2d.; owl Ierne, 1d.; 2 pewter platters, A dysshe, a sawswer, a pyntpot, 2 lettel candulsteckes, a ston salte, 1s. 6d.; A nowld ladder, 1d.; A saw, 4d.; A payle, A lome, A pere of bellowes, A pere of scales an A nowld hatchet, 6d.; A bras pot, 3 owld kettuls, A pyt and a choppyng knyfe, 2s. 0d.; A pere of sheres, 2d.; A red kyrtull, 2 owld petycotes and A wastcot and A hat and A cap, 1s. 3d.; a mattress, 2 pyllowes, 2 wynowshetes; 3 shetes and a halffe, and A nunder cloth, A rowlyng pyn and a Stamper, A stole and a kusshyn, 4s. 0d.; a tabull bord, a pere of tressulsmand 4 li. of wool, A nowld peynted cloth, 1s. 0d.. (Elizabeth Sly of Banbury, 1575.)

One cowe and a heafer £1 10s. 0d.; 3 kettels, one skellet, 2 brase potts, 9s. 0d.; 2 cendelstick, 17 pieces of pewter, one flock bed, 2 bolsters, 2 pelaes, 3 twellies, one covering, 10s. 0d.; 10 sheetes, 8s. 0d.; one Jerkine, one dublet, one perei of hose, 3s. 4d.; 2 table Clothes and 3 shortes, 2s. 8d.; one peare of shewes, one Cappe, 1s. 0d.; 2 lommes, 2 stoppes, 2 barrels, one paile, 3 Cheese fatts, 2s. 4d.; one table bord, 3 stolles, one forme and 2 trestles, 1s. 0d.; 9 small painted Clothes, 2 boxes, 2s. 11d.; teane potts and milk pans, 2d.; one friing pan 3d. (William Downing, Dudley, 1588.)

4.35 Hanged with tapestry

In *Cymbeline* (Act II Sc. 4) Shakespeare described Imogen's room in a manner which suggests that it was based on his own experience of such a place as being typical of an affluent room of the time.

First her bedchamber . . . it was hanged
With tapestry of silk and silver; the story
Proud Cleopatra, when she met her Roman,
And Cydnus swelled above the banks, or
For the press of boats or pride; a piece of work
So bravely done, so rich that it did strive
In workmanship and value; which I wondered
Could be so rarely and exactly wrought,
Since the true life on't was.
. . . The chimney

Is south the chamber, and the chimney-piece
Chaste Dian bathing; never saw I figures so likely to report
themselves;
. . . The roof o' the chamber
With golden cherubins is fretted; her andirons –
Of silver, each on one foot standing nicely
Depending on their brands.

4.36 Building restrictions, 1580

An awareness of the building problems inherent in the growth of
towns and cities had been apparent since the fourteenth century,
and in 1580 Elizabeth issued a proclamation which showed that
even then property developers were not untramelled by regulations.

The Queen Majesty, perceiving the state of the city of London
(anciently termed her chamber) and the suburbs and confines
thereof to increase daily by excess of people to inhabit in the same
in such ample sort as thereby many inconveniences are seen
already, but many greater of necessity like to follow; being such
as her majesty cannot neglect to remedy, having the principal care
under Almighty God to foresee aforehand to have her people in
such a city and confines not only well governed by ordinary justice
to serve God and obey her majesty.

Which by reason of such multitudes lately increased can hardly
be done without device of more new jurisdictions and officers for
that purpose, but to be also provided with sustentation of victual,
food and other like necessaries for man's life upon reasonable
prices, without which no city can long continue; yet where there
are such great multitudes of people brought to inhabit in small
rooms (whereof a great part are seen very poor, yea, such as must
live by begging or worse means, and they heaped up together, and
in a sort smothered with many families of children and servants in
one house or small tenement) it must needs follow if any plague
or popular sickness should, by God's permission, enter amongst
those multitudes that the same would not only spread itself and
invade the whole city and confines, but would also be dispersed
through all other parts of the realm to the manifest danger of the
whole body thereof, out of the which neither her majesty's own
person, can be but by God's special ordinance exempted, nor any
other whatsoever they be:

For remedy thereof, as time may now serve until by some further good order to be had in Parliament or otherwise, the same may be remedied, her majesty by good and deliberate advice of her council, and being also moved thereto by the considerate opinions of the Lord Mayor, aldermen and other grave and wise men in and about the city, doth charge and straightly command all manner of persons, of what quality soever they be, to desist and forbear from any new buildings of any house or tenement within three miles from any of the gates of the said city of London to serve for habitation or lodging for any person where no former house hath been known to have been in the memory of such as are now living, and also to forbear from letting or setting or suffering any more families than one only to be placed or to inhabit from henceforth in any house that heretofore hath been inhabited.

And to the intent this her majesty's royal commandment and necessary provision may take place and be duly observed for so universal a benefit for the whole body of the realm, for whose respect all particular persons are bound by God's law and man's, to forbear from their particular and extraordinary lucre; her majesty straightly chargeth the Lord Mayor of the city of London, and all other officers having authority in the same, and also all justices of the peace, lords and bailiffs of liberties not being within the jurisdiction of the said Lord Mayor of London, and all others to foresee that no person do begin to prepare any foundation for any new house, tenement or building to serve, to receive, or hold any inhabitants to dwell or lodge or to use any victualing therein, where no former habitation hath been in the memory of such as do now live, but that they be prohibited and restrained so to do; and both the persons that shall so attempt to the contrary and all manner of workmen that shall (after warning given) continue in such work tending to such new buildings to be committed to close prison, and there to remain without bail until they shall find good sureties with bonds for reasonable sums of money (to be forfeitable and recoverable at her majesty's suit for the use of hospitals in and around the said city) that they shall not at any time attempt the like. And further the said officers shall seize all manner of stuff so (after due warning given) brought to the place where such new buildings shall be intended, and the same cause to be converted and employed in any public use for the city or parish where the same shall be attempted.

And for the avoiding of the multitudes of families heaped up in one dwelling house, or for the converting of any one house into a multitude of tenements for victualing or dwelling places, the said Lord Mayor and all other officers in their several liberties within the limit of three miles shall commit any person giving cause of offence from the day of the publication of the present proclamation to close prison as is aforementioned . . . Such undersitters or inmates may provide themselves other places abroad in the realm where many houses rest uninhabited to the decay of divers ancient good boroughs and towns.

4.37 Art in the service of the law

It is an indication of the improving quality of both portraiture and reproduction processes that when orders were issued for the arrest of the conspirators in the Babington Plot of 1586, it was ordered that posters should be put up throughout the kingdom with their 'living portraiture'.

And for the better apprehending of those abovesaid persons, it is ordered that the portraits of their faces, agreeable even to such living portraiture as both they themselves, and other conspirators of their company which are taken for their mischiefs caused to be made in the city of London, shall be in open places in the city of London published, and shall also be, dispersed to sundry other places of the realm

(Proclamation issued on August 2nd 1586.)

4.38 One of the most beautiful houses in England

In 1592 Frederick, Duke of Wurtemberg came on a visit to England, and an account of his journey was published ten years later by Jacob Rathgeb, his private secretary (reprinted in William Brenchley Rye's *England as seen by Foreigners*, London 1865). The account of their visit to Theobalds, the great house which Burghley had built for himself, and which was to become the favourite residence of James I, gives some indication of the glories of this vanished monument of the Elizabethan age.

On the morning of 30th of August his Highness proceeded to London (from Ware) and on the way he went to see the magnificent palace Theobalds, belonging to the Lord High Treasurer of England, which is reckoned one of the most beautiful houses in England, as in truth it is.

First of all his Highness inspected the handsome and delightful hall, which is so ornamental and artistic that its equal is not easily to be met with; for, besides other embellishments in it, there is a very high rock, of all colours, made of real stones, out of which gushes a splendid fountain that falls into a large circular bowl or basin, supported by two savages. This hall has no pillars; it is about 60 feet in length, and upwards of 30 wide.

The ceiling or upper floor is very artistically constructed; it contains the twelve signs of the zodiac, so that at night you can see the stars proper to each; on the same stage the sun performs its course, which is without doubt contrived by some concealed ingenious mechanism. On each side of the hall are six trees, having the bark so artfully joined, with birds's nests and leaves as well as fruit upon them, all managed in such a way that you could not distinguish between the natural and these artificial trees, and, as far as I could see, there was no difference at all, for when the steward of the house opened the windows, which looked upon the beautiful pleasure garden, birds flew into the hall, perched themselves upon the trees and began to sing. In a word, this hall is so elegantly adorned with paintings and otherwise that it is right royal and well worth the seeing.

There are also many other spacious halls and fine galleries in this splendid palace, with very artistic paintings, and accurate landscapes of all the most important and remarkable towns in Christendom, as well as tables of inlaid-work and marble of various colours, all of the richest and most magnificent description.

In another hall is depicted the kingdom of England, with all its cities, towns and villages, mountains and rivers; as also the armorial bearings and domains of every esquire, lord, knight and noble who possess lands and retainers to whatever extent. In short, all the apartments and rooms are adorned with beautiful tapestries and the like to such a degree that no king need be ashamed to dwell there.

Some rooms in particular have very beautiful and costly ceilings, which are skilfully wrought in joiner's work and elegantly coloured, the ground being prettily ornamented with blue colours, but the roses and other ornaments are gilded.

The garden is close adjoining and of immense extent, and as the palace is really most magnificent, so likewise in proportion is no expense spared on the garden; in a summer-house there is a table made of a solid piece of black touchstone, fourteen spans long, seven wide, and one span thick.

4.39 Royal powers

The power of the crown to appropriate supplies and services for
its needs in the area of building, painting etc. survived beyond the
Middle Ages. An undated commission from Elizabeth to George
Gower, who was Sergeant-Painter from 1581–96 gives some indication of them.

Elizabeth, by the grace of god Quene of England, Fraunce and
Ireland, Defender of the faith. To all and singular our justices of
peace, maiors, sherifs, Bayliffes, constables, Hedboroughs and all
other our officers, mynisters and subiectes to whome this patente
shall come greetings. Wee lett you witt that wee have authorisesd
and appointed, and by this patent doe give full power and auctority
unto our well beloved servaunt George Gower, our Sargeant
paynter, and to his sufficient Deputies and Deputies bearers hereof
in his name from tyme to tyme hereafter, for the better execution
of his office to take up and provide for us and in our name, for
the only provision of our service to be done in and about the same
office, all manners of colors, oyle, varnysh, workmen and laborers
as well free as forreigne, and all manner of stuffe and necessaries
whatsoever mete and convenient to be emploied for that service.
And also to take up all manner of Carrieges as Barges, boats,
cartes, waynes, carres, horses and all other cariages wyth their furn-
yture and necessaries nedeful for the conveyghance of the premises,
as well by water as by land, for reasonable prises and payments to
be mayde in that behalf. And in case any person or persons shall
obstinatlie or disobediently withstande or repugne this our
commission, Then to comyt everie such person to warde or
pryson, there to remayne untell such tyme as the imprisonment
shall be thought convenient and condygne for his or their offence
or offences, and thereuponn to put them at large and libertie,
Wherefore wee will and commaunde you and every of you by theis
presents to be aidinge, helpinge and assistinge our said servant and
his said Deputie or Deputies bearers hereof in the due execution
of the premisses. As ye and every one of you tender our pleasure,
and will answer to the contrarye at your uttermost perills. In
witness whereof wee have caused thies our letters of Commission
to be sealed with our great Sele, Witness our selfe at Westminster
etc.

(Lansdowne MS 105, no. 37)

In a Patent of 1584 the Queen further specified the duties of the
Sergeant-Painter:

He shall have a monpolie of all manner of purtraictes and pictures of our person and proporcyon of our bodye in oyle cullers upon bourdes or canvas, or to grave the same in copper, or to cutte the same in woode or otherwyse.

4.40 Use before uniformity

The preoccupation with building, and the ideals which informed it in Elizabethan and Jacobean times were perfectly reflected in Francis Bacon's essay 'Of Building' (1597), with its precocious notions of functionalism.

Houses are built to live in, and not to look on; therefore let use be preferred before uniformity, except where both may be had. Leave the goodly fabrics of houses for beauty only, to the enchanted palaces of the poets, who build them with small cost. He that builds a fair house upon an ill site committeth himself to prison. Neither do I reckon it an ill seat only where the air is unwholesome, but likewise where the air is unequal, as you shall see many fine seats upon a knap of ground environed with higher hills around it; whereby the heat of the sun is pent in, and the wind gathereth as in troughs; so as you shall have, and that suddenly, as great diversity of heat and cold as if you dwelt in several place . . .

To pass from the seat to the house itself. First therefore I say, you cannot have a perfect palace, except you have two several sides; a side for a banquet, as is spoken of in *The Book of Hester*, and a side for the household; the one for feasts and triumphs, and the other for dwelling. I understand both these sides to be not only returns, but parts of the front; and to be uniform without, though severally proportioned within; and to be on both sides of a great stately tower in the midst of the front, that, as it were, joineth them together on either hand. I would have on the side of the banquet in front, one only goodly room above stairs of some forty foot high, and under it a room for a dressing or preparing place at times of triumphs. On the other side, which is the household side, I wish it divided at first into a hall, and a chapel, with partition between, both of good state and bigness, and those to go not only to go all the length, but to have at the further end a winter and a summer parlour, both fair. And under these rooms, a fair and large cellar, sunk under ground, and likewise some privy kitchens, with butteries and pantries and the like. As for the tower, I would have it two stories of eighteen foot high a piece, above the two wings;

and a goodly lead upon the top, railed with statuas interspersed, and the same tower to be divided into rooms, as shall be thought fit. The stairs, likewise to the upper rooms, let them be upon a fair open newel, and finely railed in with images of wood cast into a brass colour, and a very fair landing place at the top. But this to be, if you do not point any of the lower rooms for a dining place for servants. For otherwise you shall have the servants' dinner after your own, for the steam of it will come up, as in a tunnel. And so much for the front. Only I understand the height of the first stairs to be sixteen foot, which is the height of the lower room.

Beyond this front is there to be a fair court, but three sides of it of a lower building than the front. And in all the four corners of that court, fair stair-cases, cast into turrets on the outside, and not within the row of buildings themselves. But these towers are not to be the height of the front, but rather proportionable to the lower building. Let the court not be paved, for that striketh up a great heat in the summer, and much cold in the winter. But only some side alleys, with a cross and the quarters to graze, being kept shorn, but not too near shorn. The row of return on the banquet side, let be all stately galleries, in which galleries let there be three or five fine cupolas in the length of it, placed at equal distance, and fine coloured windows of several works. On the household side chambers of presence and ordinary entertainments, with some bed-chambers; and let all three sides be a double house, without through lights on the sides, that you may have rooms from the sun, both for forenoon and afternoon. Cast it also that you may have rooms both for summer and winter; shady for summer and warm for winter. You shall have sometimes fair houses, so full of glass, that one cannot tell where to become to be out of the sun or cold. For inbowed windows, I hold them to be of good use (in cities indeed, upright do better, in respect of the uniformity towards the street); for they be pretty retiring places for conference, and beside they keep both the wind and the sun off; for that which would strike almost through the room, doth scare pass the window. But let them be but few, four in the court, on the sides only.

Beyond this court, let there be an inward court, of the same square and height, which is to be environed with the garden on all sides; and on the inside, cloistered on all sides, upon decent and beautiful arches, as high as the first story. On the under story, towards the garden, let it be turned to a grotto, or place of shade or estivation, and only have opening and windows towards the garden; and be level upon the floor, no whit sunk under ground, to avoid all dampness. And let there be a fountain, or some fair work of statuas in the midst of this court, and to be paved as the other court was. These buildings to be for privy lodgings on both sides, and the ends for privy galleries. Whereof you must foresee that one of them be for an infirmary, if the prince or any special person be sick, with chambers, bed-chamber, ante-camera, and recamera joining to it. This upon the second story. Upon the ground story a fair gallery, open, upon pillars, and upon the third story likewise, an open gallery upon pillars, to take the prospect and freshness of the garden. At both corners of the further side, let there be two delicate or rich cabinets, daintily paved, richly hanged, glazed with crystalline glass, and a rich cupola in the midst, and all other elegancy that may be thought upon. In the upper gallery too, I wish that there may be, if the place will yield it, some fountains running in divers places from the wall, with some fine avoidances. And thus much for the model of the palaces, save that you must have before you come to the front three courts. A green court, plain, with a wall about it; a second court of the same, but more garnished with little turrets, or rather embellishments, upon the wall, and a third court, to make a square with the front, but not to be built, nor yet enclosed with a naked wall, but enclosed with tarrasses, leaded aloft, and fairly garnished on three sides, and cloistered on the inside, with pillars, and not with arches below. As for offices, let them stand at distance, with some low galleries to pass from them to the palace itself.

4.41 Tenements

As the population increased and cities grew perceptibly in size, speculative building made its appearance, and in September 1595 the *Remembrancia* of the City of London recorded the disquiet this was occasioning.

There continue to be erected great numbers of poor tenements, which they call 'pennyrents' in Southwark and Kentish Street, wherein are placed a great number of poor people. These having no trade or honest endeavour to maintain themselves, nor to pay their rent (which must usually be done at the week's end), make it their occupation to beg in the streets of the city. At this time one Mr Sawyer hath given leave to a bricklayer to build a great number of tenements upon his grounds within Kentish Street, whereby he has encroached three feet on the common street.

4.42 'A kind of true gentility'

The emphasis on the connexion between art and 'gentility' which was emphasised in so many Renaissance writings, and found its most famous expression in the works of Peacham, first appears in English in Hilliard's *Treatise*, though Gild regulations of the previous century had exempted 'gentlemen' from their regulations.

Now therefore I wish it weare so that none should meddle with limning, but gentlemen alone, for that it is a kind of gentill painting, of less subjection than any other, for one may leave when he will, his coullers nor his work taketh any harme by it. Moreover it is a secreet; a man may use it, and scarecely be perceaved of his own folke; it is sweete and cleanly to use, and it is a thing apart from all other painting or drawing, and tendeth not to common mens use, either for furnisshing of howses, or any patternes for tapestries or building, or any other worke whatsoever, and yet it excelleth all other painting whatsoever in sondry points, in giving the true lustre to pearle and precious stones, and worketh the metals gold or silver with themselves, which so enricheth and enobleth the work, that it seemeth to be the thinge itselfe, even the worke of God, and not of man, being fittest for the decking of princes' bookes, or to put in jewells of gold, and for the imitation of the purest flowers, and most beautifull creatures in the finest and purest collors which are chargeable, and is for the service of noble persons very meet in small volumes in private manner for them to have the portraits and pictures of themselves.

It is a kind of true gentility, when God calleth, and though doubtless gentlemen be the meetest for this gentil calling or practize, yet not all, but naturall aptness is to be chosen and preferred, for not every gentleman is so genteel spirited as som others are. Let us therefore honore and preferre the election of God in all vocations and degrees, and surely he is a very wise man that can find out the naturall selection of his children in due time, and so applie him that waye which nature most inclineth him, if it be goode, or may be made goode, as it may be used, though in childhood abused, and as for a naturall aptness of or to painting after the life, those surely which have such a gift from God ought to rejoyce with humble thankfulness, and to be very wary and temperat in diet and other government, lest it be soon taken waie from them by some sudden mischance or by their evell customes, their sight or hand decaie.

Then this exhortation give I, more that he be diligent, yea, ever diligent, and putt his whole uttermost and best endaevours to excell all others, for a stronge man that putteth not forth his strength, is often foyled by weeker, and the most sunningest must doe the same diligence, or rather more, to effect and performe his worke better than he did at the first learninge. For it cannot be sayd that a man be never so cunning by teaching or naturall learninge, yet it will growe out of him as haire out of the head, or fall from him, whether he will or no, but with great labour, and this comfort shall he have that above all others, even an heaven of joye in his hart to behold his own well-doings remaining to his credit for ever. Yea, if men of worth did know what delight it breedeth, howe it removeth melancholy, avoideth evell occasiouns, putteth passions of sorrowe or greefe awaye, cureth rage, and shorteneth the times they would never leave till they had attained in some goode meassur a more than comfort. Maie he have both praise and fame for ever after, and princes commonly give them competent menes, by which not the workmen, soe much as themselves are eternized, and famously remembered as the nursses of vertue and arts.

4.43 Magnificently built

If not the most massive, Hampton Court was certainly the most ostentatiously magnificent building to have been constructed in England, a fact made all the more remarkable in that it was built of brick. In its Elizabethan state it greatly impressed the German traveller Hentzner whose *Journey into England* was published in 1598.

Hampton Court is a royal palace, magnificently built with brick by Cardinal Wolsey in ostentation of his wealth, where he enclosed five ample courts, consisting of noble edifices, in very beautiful work. Over the gate in the second court is the Queen's device, a golden rose with the motto *Dieu et Mon Droit*. On the inner side of this gate are the effigies of the twelve Roman Emperors in plaster. The chief area is paved with square stone; in its centre is a fountain that throws up water, covered with a gilt crown, on the top of which is a statue of Justice, supported by columns of black and white marble.

The Chapel of this Palace is most splendid, in which the Queen's closet is quite transparent, having its windows of crystal. We were led into two Chambers called the Presence, or Chamber of Audience, which shone with tapestry of gold, silver and silk of different colours; under the canopy of state are these words embroidered in pearl; VIVAT REX HENRICUS OCTAVUS. Here besides is a small chapel richly hung with tapestry, where the Queen performs her devotions. In her bed-chamber the bed was covered with very costly coverlets of silk. At no great distance from this room we were shown a bed, the tester of which was worked by Anne Boleyn, and presented by her to her husband Henry VIII.

All the other rooms, being very numerous, are adorned with tapestry of gold, silver and velvet, in some of which are woven history pieces; in others Turkish and American dresses, all extremely natural.

In the Hall are these curiosities; a very clear looking-glass, ornamented with columns and little images of alabaster; a portrait of Edward VI, brother to Queen Elizabeth; the true portrait of Lucretia; a picture of the battle of Pavia; the History of Christ's passion carved in mother-of-pearl; the portraits of Mary, Queen of Scots, who was beheaded; the portrait of Ferdinand, Prince of Spain, and of Philip, his son [sic]; that of Henry VIII, under it placed the Bible curiously written upon parchment; an artificial sphere; several musical instruments; in the tapestry are negroes riding upon elephants; the bed in which Edward VI is said to have been born, and where his mother Jane Seymour died in childbed; in one chamber were hung excessively rich tapestries, which are put out when the Queen receives Ambassadors. There were numbers of cushions ornamented with gold and silver; many counterpanes and coverlets of beds lined with ermine; in short all the walls of the palace shine with gold and silver. Here is also a certain Cabinet called *Paradise* where, besides that everything glitters so with silver, gold and jewels, as to dazzle one's eyes, there is a musical instrument made all of glass, except the strings.

4.44 Fashions regulated

Nowhere was the influence of the state on matters of taste more apparent than where dress and fasion were concerned. Since the thirteenth century rules and regulations about what people might wear had been issued, but in the sixteenth century they reached almost hysterical proportions, and, oddly, almost completely ceased with the accession of the Stuarts. A proclamation issued from Greenwich on 6 July 1597 was the last, and almost the most detailed of a long series of rules about apparel which had been issued in the course of the Queen's reign.

For mens' apparel her majesty doth straightly charge and command that none shall wear in his apparel cloth of gold or silver tissued silk of colour purple under the degree of Earl, except Knights of the Garter inn their purple mantles only.

Cloth of gold or silver, tinseled satin, silk, or cloth mixed or embroidered with gold, pearl or silver, wool cloth made out of the realm, under the degree of a baron, except Knights of the Garter and Privy Councillors to the Queen's majesty.

Passement lace, or other lace of gold or silver or mixed with gold and silver, or with silver and silk; spurs, swords, rapiers, daggers, skeans, woodkives, hangers, buckles, or studs of girdles gilt, or damasked with gold or silver, silvered, under the degree of a baron's son, except gentlemen in ordinary office attending on the Queen in her house or chamber, such as have been employed in embassage to foreign princes, such as may dispend 500 marks a year for term of life in possession above all charges, and knights for wearing only of spurs, swords, rapiers, daggers, and those other things there with ensuing, and likewise captains being in her majesty's pay.

Velvet in gowns, coats, cloaks, or other uppermost garments, embroidery with silk, netherstocks of silk, under the degree of a knight, except gentlemen in ordinary office attending the queen in her house or chamber, such as have been on embassage to foreign princes, the son and heir apparent of a knight, captains in her majesty's pay, and such as may dispend £200 a year for term of life in possession above all charges.

Satin, damask, grosgrain, taffeta in hose, doublet, under the degree of a gentleman bearing arms, except gentlemen in ordinary office attending upon her majesty in her house or chamber, such as have been employed in embassages to foreign princes, and such as may dispend £20 by the year for term of life in possession above all charges.

None shall have in their saddles, bridles, stirrups, trappings, harness, footcloth or other furniture of the horse any velvet, gilding, damasking with gold or silver, silvering, studs, buckles, or other garniture gilt, damasked with gold or silver, silvered, under the degree of a baron's son, except knights and gentlemen in ordinary office attending on her majesty in her house or chamber, such as have been employed in embassages to foreign princes, captains being in her majesty's pay, and such as may dispend 500 marks a year for term of life in possession, above all charges.

None shall wear in their apparel any caps, hats, hatbands, capbands, garters, boots, silk netherstocks, trimmed with gold, silver or pearl, enameled chains, buttons, aiglets, except men of the degrees aforementioned, the gentlemen attending upon the Queen's person in her highness' privy chamber, or in the office of cupbearer, carver, skewer, esquire for the body, gentlemen ushers, or esquires of the stable.

Note that the Lord Chancellor, Treaurer, President of the Council, Privy Seal may wear any velvet, satin, or other silks except purple, furs, except black genets.

These may wear as have heretofore used, viz. any of the Queen's Council, Justices of either Bench, Barons of the Exchequer, Master of the Rolls, Sergeants at Law, Masters of the Chancery, apprentices at law, mayors and other head officers of any town corporate, Barons of the Five Ports, except velvet, damask, satin of the colour crimson, violet or purple, blue

Note that her majesty's meaning is not by this order to prohibit in any person the wearing of silk buttons, the facing of cloaks, hats and caps for comeliness only with taffetas, grosgrains, velvet or other silk as is commonly used.

For womens' apparel her majesty doth straightly charge and command that:

None shall wear in her apparel cloth of gold or silver tissued, silk of colour purple under the degree of a countess, except viscountesses to wear cloth of gold or silver tissued in their kirtles only.

Cloth of gold, cloth of silver, tinseled satin, satins branched with silver, or gold, satins striped with silver or gold, taffetas branched with silver or gold, taffetas with gold or silver grounds, tinseled taffetas, tufted or plain, tinselled cypresses, cypresses flourished with silver or gold, gold or silver camlets, networks wrought with silver or gold, tabinet branched or wrought with silver or gold, or any other silk or cloth mixed or embroidered with gold, silver or pearls, under the degree of a baroness, except the wives of barons' eldest sons and barons' daughters to wear cloth of gold and silver only in their kirtles and lining of their garments, and knights' wives to wear cloth of silver in their kirtles only.

Embroideries of gold or silver, passment, lace or any other lace of gold or silver, or mixed with gold or silver; cowls attires or other garnishings for the head, trimmed with pearls, under the degree of a baron's eldest son's wife, except barons' daughters, the wives of the Knights of the Order of the Garter or of Privy

Councilors, the ladies and gentlemen of the Privy Chamber, the Maidens of Honour, and such whose husbands may dispend £100 by the year for term of life in possession above all charges.

Satin in kirtles; damask, tufted taffeta, plain taffeta, grosgrain in gowns, under the degree of a gentleman's wife bearing arms, except gentlewomen attendant upon knights' wives of the like or higher degree, and such whose husbands or themselves may dispend £40 by the year for term of life in possession above all charges.

Gentlewomen attendant upon duchesses, marquises, countesses may wear in their liveries given by their mistresses as the wives of those that may dispend £100 by the year and are so valued *ut supra.*

Gentlewomen attendant upon viscount's wives and barons' wives may wear in their liveries as the daughters of those who may dispend 300 marks the year, and as the wives of those that may dispend £40, valued *ut supra.*

None shall wear any velvet, tufted taffeta, satin, or any gold or silver in their petticoats, except knights' daughters and such as may be matched with them in the former article, who shall not wear a guard of silk upon their petticoats.

Velvet, tufted taffeta, satin nor any gold or silver in any cloak or safeguard except the wives of barons, knights of the order, or councilors, ladies and gentlemen of the privy chamber and bed chamber, and the maidens of honour, and all degrees above them.

Damask, taffeta, or other silk in any cloak or safeguard, except knights' wives and the degrees and persons above mentioned.

No person under the degree above specified shall wear any guard or welt of silk upon any petticoat, cloak or safeguard.

All which articles, clauses and premises her majesty straightly commandeth to be from henceforth exactly and duly observed in all points; and the parties offending to be further punished as violators and contemners of her royal and princely commandment by this her highness' proclamation expressed and published.

4.45 Elizabethan gardens

There had been enormous changes in the nature and quality of gardens in the course of the sixteenth century. Thomas Platter, a Swiss who visited England when he was twenty-five, gives some indication of the intricacy and sophistication of the gardens at the now destroyed Nonsuch Palace.

On Sunday September 26th I and my party drove by coach through the borough of Tooting to the royal place at Nonsuch, which is situated some twelve miles from London.

At the entrance to the gardens is a grove named after Diana, the goddess. From there we came to a rock out of which natural water flows into a basin, and on this was carved with great skill and realism, the story of how the three goddesses took their bath naked, and sprayed Actaeon with water, causing antlers to grow on his head, and turning him into a deer, so that his own hounds afterwards tore him to pieces. Further on there was a small vaulted temple containing a fine marble table, with inscriptions engraved on it.

We next entered an arbour or pavilion, where the Queen sits whilst the hunt is going on in the park, and from where she can see the game go past. Then through a wood in the garden with fine, long straight alleys through it, designed in this fashion. In the very densest part of the wood in this area a great many trees are uprooted and cleared to a width of some eighteen to twenty feet, along a straight course, so that there is a continuous vista from beginning to end. And here and there they are partitioned off, on either side to form courts for playing ball-games in the shade, rather like tennis courts.

Thence we came to a maze or labyrinth surrounded by high shrubberies to prevent anyone passing through or over them. In the pleasure gardens are charming terraces and all kinds of animals, dogs, hares and the like cut out of the shrubbery, so that from a distance one could take them for the real thing.

At Hampton Court he noted

A fine large fountain, made of white marble, surrounded by marvellous water-works with which one may spray any ladies or others standing there, and soak them. At the entrance to the garden I noticed numerous patches where square cavities had been dug out, as though for paving stones, and some of the spaces filled up with red brick dust, others with white sand, and others grassed over, so that the whole area looked like a chess-board. The hedges and surrounds were of hawthorn, bush firs, ivy, roses, juniper, holly, English or common elm, box and other shrubs, giving a very pleasant and lively effect. There were great varieties of topiary work, men and women, centaurs, sirens, serving-maids with baskets, French lilies and delicate crenallations all round, made from dry twigs bound together. All this evergreen, these shrubs, and rosemary bushes were shaped all true to life, and so cleverly and amusingly interwoven, mixed up with each other as they grew, and then trimmed and arranged to create a pictorial effect that their equal would be difficult to find.

> Two years earlier in his essay 'Of Gardens' Francis Bacon had put forward plans for a garden which are at variance with that described by Platter at Nonsuch.

For gardens, (speaking of those which are indeed prince-like, as we have done of buildings) the contents ought to be not well under thirty acres of ground, and to be divided into three parts; a green in the entrance, a heath or desert in the going out, and the main garden in the midst, besides alleys on both sides. And I like well that four acres of ground be assigned to the green, six to the heath, four and four to either side, and twelve to the main garden. The green hath two pleasures; the one because nothing is more pleasant to the eye than green grass kept finely shorn, the other because it will give you a fair alley in the midst, by which you can go in front upon a stately hedge which is to enclose the garden. But because the alley will be long, and in great heat of the year or day, you ought not to buy the shade in the garden by going in the sun thorough the green, therefore you are on either side the green to plant a covert alley, upon carpenter's work, about twelve foot in height, by which you may go in shade into the garden. As for the making of knots or figures with divers coloured earths, that they may lie under the windows of the house on that side which the garden stands, they be but toys; you may see as good sights many times in tarts. The garden is best to be square, encompassed on all the four sides, with a stately arched hedge. The arches to be upon pillars of carpenters' work, and upon the upper hedge, over every arch, a little turret with a belly, enough to receive a cage of birds, and over every space between the arches, some other little figure, with broad plates of rounded coloured glass, gilt for the sun to play on. But this hedge I intend to be raised upon a bank, not steep, but gently slope, of some six foot, set all with flowers. Also I understand that this square of garden should not be on the whole breadth of the ground, but to leave on either side ground enough for diversity of alleys, unto which the two covert alleys of the green may deliver you. But there must be no alleys with hedges at either end of this great enclosure; not at the hitherend, for letting your prospect upon this fair hedge from the green; nor at the further end, for letting your prospect from the hedge, through the arches upon the heath.

For the ordering of the ground within the great hedge I leave it to variety of device, advising nevertheless, that whatsoever form you cast it in, first it be not too busy or full of work. Wherein I, for my part do not like images cut out in juniper or other garden stuff; they be for children. Little, low hedges, round like welts, with some pretty pyramids I like well and in some places fair columns upon pillars of carpenters' work. I would also have the alleys spacious and fair. You may have closer alleys upon the side grounds, but none in the main garden. I wish also, in the very middle, a fair mount with three ascents and alleys enough for four to walk abreast, which I would have to be perfect circles, without any bulwarks or embossments, and the whole mount to be thirty foot high.

For fountains, they are a great beauty and refreshment, but pools mar all, and make the garden unwholesome and full of flies and frogs. Fountains I intend to be of two natures; the one that sprinkleth or spouteth water; the other a fair receipt of water, of some thirty or forty foot square, but without fish or slime or mud. For the first the ornaments of images, gilt or of marble, which are in use, do well; but the main matter is, so to convey the water, as it never stay either in the bowls or in the cistern; that the water be never by rest be discoloured green or red or the like, or gather any mossiness or putrefaction. Besides that, it is to be cleaned every day by hand. Also some steps up to it, and some fine pavement about it, doth well. As for the other kind of fountain, which we may call a bathing pool, it may admit much curiosity and beauty, where with we shall not trouble ourselves, as that the bottom be finely paved with images; the sides likewise, and withal embellished with coloured glass, and such things of lustre, encompassed also fine rails of low statuas. But the main point is the same we mentioned in the former kind of fountain, which is that the water be in perpetual motion, fed by a water higher than the pool, and delivered into it by fair spouts, and then discharged away underground by some equality of bores, that it stay little. And for fine devices of arching water without spilling it, and raising it in several forms (of feathers, drinking glasses, canopies and the like) they be pretty things to look on, but nothing to health and sweetness . . .

For the main garden, I do not deny but there should be some fair alleys ranged on both sides with fruit trees, and some pretty tufts of fruit trees, and arbours with seats set in some decent order, but these by no means to be set too thick, but to leave the main garden so as it be not close, but the air open and free. For as for shade, I would have you rest upon the alleys on the side grounds, there to walk, if you be disposed, in the heat of the year or day, but to make account that the main garden is for the more temperate parts of the year, and in the heat of summer, for the morning and evening, or overcast days.

For aviaries, I like them not, except they be of that largeness that they may be turfed, and have living plants and bushes set in them, that the birds may have more scope and natural nesting, and that no foulness appear on the floor of the aviary.

4.46 Engraved portraits forbidden

The hand of the Elizabethan state lay heavily on the lives and activities of its citizens. On 30 August 1600 the Privy Council issued the following warning, instigated in part at least by the fact that an engraved portrait of the Earl of Essex had achieved a great success, a fact not a little displeasing to the Queen.

There is of late times a use brought up to engrave in brass the picture of noblemen and other persons, and then to sell them in paper, set forth oftentimes with verses and other circumstances not fit to be used. Because this custom doth grow common, and it is indeed not meet such setting forth of any pictures but of Her Majesty should be permitted (if the same be well done) the Council have given direction that hereafter no personage of any nobleman or other person shall be ingraven and put to sale publicly, and those prints already made shall be called in, unless the Archbishop of Canterbury shall think fit to allow them.

(*Acts of the Privy Council*, vol. xxx, p. 619)

5. Kings and courts

A new gentility under the Stuarts

5.1 Hall furnishings, 1603

An inventory of the furnishings of Hengrave in Suffolk, reprinted in John Gage's *Hengrave* (1822) records the typical contents of a moderately large Jacobean hall.

In the HALL.
Three square boards with fast frames to them.
Two joyned coobards mayde fast to the wainskote.
One long table for a sholven borde with a fast frame to it.
One other long table with tressels to it.
One piece of wood carved with the Queen's arms.
Ten joyned formes for the square borde.
One long forme, not of joyner's work.
One great branch of copper which hangs in the midst of the hall
    to serve for lights.
Four copper-plate candlesticks, iii of them being grate and one
    littel, which hangs upon the skreine by ye pantrye.
One cradel of iron for the chimneye to burne seacole with.
One fier shovel made like a grate to sift the seacole with.
One other fier shovel and one payre of tonges.
In ye Great Chamber.
Arras.
Carpets.
Cushions.
Thirty-two stools joyned.
Four chayers.
Curtains.
One joyned cooboard.
One square borde.
Longe joyned borde and extension peece.
Two longe footstooles under above.
One payer of tables.
One sevenfold and one fourfold skreenes.

One great copper sesteurne to stand at the cooboard.

Two payre andryones.

Two payer creepers [small andirons].

Four copper branches for lights.

Two fier sholves, two payer tongues and one fier forke.

In ye GALLERIE at ye TOWER.

One billiarde borde with two stayves to it of bone and two of
wood and 4 balls.

5.2 The Masque of Blackness, 1605

Despite their ephemerality, masques were nodal points of painting,
architecture, design, costume, music and theatre, and attracted
talent from many areas. In his *Vindication of Stone-Heng Restored*,
John Webb, the pupil and disciple of Inigo Jones commented 'What
of his masques, for the delight and pleasure of all those several
great Princes, since that for variety of scenes, machines, habits and
well-ordering of them in the judgement of all foreign embassadors
and strangers, they exceeded whatever of that kind were presented
in any other court of Christendom beside.' Ben Jonson, the script
writer of many of them, wrote down an account of the design of
The Queene's Masque of Blacknesse by Inigo Jones inspired by James
I's wife Anne of Denmark, presented on Twelfth Night in 1605.

First for the scene was drawn a landtschap consisting of small
woods, and here and there a small void place filled with huntings;
which falling, an artificial sea was seen to shoot forth, as if it
flowed to the land, raised with waves which seemed to move, and
in some places the billows to break as imitating that orderly
disorder which is common in nature. In front of this sea were
placed six tritons in moving and sprightly actions, their upper parts
human, save that their hairs were blue, as partaking of the sea
colour; their desinent parts fish, mounted above their heads and all
varied in disposition. Behind these a pair of sea-maids, for song,
were as conspicuously seated, between which two great sea-
horses, as big as life, put forth themselves. The Masquers were
placed in a great concave shell, like mother-of-pearl, curiously
made to move on those waters, and rise with the billow; the top
thereof was stuck with a cheveron of lights, which, indented to the
proportion of the shell, struck a glorious beam upon them as they
were seated one above the other. On sides of the shell did swim
six huge monsters, varied in their shapes and dispositions, bearing
on their backs the twelve torch-bearers. These thus presented, the

scene behind seemed a vast sea, and united with this that flowed forth, from the teermination or horizon of which (being the level of the stage which was placed in the upper part of the Hall) was drawn by the lines of prospective, the whole work shooting downwards from the eye; which decorum made it the more conspicuous, and caught the eye afar off with a wandering beauty; to which was added an obscure and cloudy night piece that made the whole set off. So much for the bodily part, which was of Master Inigo Jones's design and art.

5.3 A mosaic picture and others

Anxious to promote their careers at home, and to curry favour with the powerful, English diplomats abroad were assiduous in obtaining works of art, and carrying out similar cultural commissions for their patrons. In 1608 Sir Henry Wotton, from his Venetian embassy in the Canareggio, wrote to the Earl of Salisbury.

Venice; On Good Friday [April 4th] 1608.

I must give your Lordship humble thanks, apart from the rest of my great obligations, for your picture [by John de Critz] wherewith it hath pleased you to honour me, which I now expect here within a few days, having been long since shipped from thence. And when it cometh I shall be bold to put it into another material [mosaic]. I would likewise beseech your Lordship (if it might so please you) to send me your Coat armour in the true colours, with the mantling and crest; for I have thought that being done here in mosaic, it may afterwards be very fitly placed in the front of your buildings over the portal, wherein shall be observed here such breadth and height as you will direct. And I assure your Lordship, I have seen the same in this country stand with great decency and dignity. This your Lordship may send in one of your packets. I promised by Captain Pinner to send your Lordship some drafts of architecture, for which I am, as God help me, ashamed not yet having been able to make them ready, out of which impatience in the meantime I have ventured to entertain your Lordship with two or three poor things (for I will break none of your commandments) that are sent in a ship called the *Martha* of London, whose master is one Sammon. There is a picture of this famous Duke [the Doge Leonardo Dinato] done truly and naturally, but roughly *alla Vene-*

tiana, and therefore to be set at some good distance from the sight. There is also a figure (I take it) of Prometheus devoured by the eagle, done by Giacobo Palma in concurrence with Titiano, which for the emulation between two painters (both of no small name) I dare almost to say to be worthy of a corner in one of your Lordship's galleries. I have added to these a map of Italy (the country where by your favour I have received my first credit) distinguished not by provinces, but according to the estates and governments. They shall be brought to your Lordship by one Harry Cogan, an old and honest servant of mine, whom, since the placing of Rouland Woodward with my Lord of London, I have taken again into my small uses at home. And your Lordship may, in the conveyings of your packets, or other commandments unto me trust him very confidently, being both careful and (as far as I can judge) discreet,

Your Lordship's humble and obliged servant many ways,
HENRY WOTTON.

> Almost a year later the mosaic was finished and Wotton wrote to the Earl:

Venice, the 24th *of April* 1609.

Style of the place.
Right Honorable and my very good Lord,
I will present unto his Majesty no other occurrence by this post. In the rest of this sheet I will take the boldness to advertise your Lordship that having caused here your picture to be made in mosaic, as the best present I could conceive for my Lord of Cramborn your son, in humble acknowledgement of my own great obligations towards your noble person and memory, and having long expected an opportunity to transport the same into England by sea, I have this week adventured it on a ship called the *Thomas* of London, bound directly homewards, whereof the master, one Gardiner, whom, that he might take the better care thereof I have here delivered by intercession of the State of some difficulty wherein he stood. His vessel doth not exceed 100 ton, but she is a well-conditioned ship, and himself hitherto fortunate in his voyages. The picture is made precisely according to the draught of that wherewith your Lordship, upon my humble bequest, did honour me; I mean as nearly as the natural colours of the stone can approach to artificial, and so near indeed, as I must confess unto

your Lordship hath much exceeded my own expectations. Only there is added a year more unto your Lordship's age, and to your title *Gran Tesauriere d'Inghulterra*, the rest being likewise in Italian, for the workman would by no mean give his consent (nor I neither) to the French superscription. It is directed to your Lordship in this time of my Lord of Cramborn's absence, whom I have advertised thereof by the way of Lyons; and it is the workman's special suit and remembrance that it may be set in his true light, and at a little more height from the eye than a coloured picture would require. I will hearken after the success of it on the way, that it should chance to miscarry (which I hope it will not) yet I may cause another to be made by the same hand and pattern. And so, having discharged this small duty towards your Lordship, which mine own conscience and sense of your favours imposed upon myself, I must humbly rest, as I am bound, Your Lordship's always to serve and honour you,

HENRY WOTTON.

(*The Life and Letters of Sir Henry Wotton*, ed. Logan Pearsall Smith, Oxford 1907, vol. I, pp. 419–20 & 452–53)

5.4 Arts and manufactures

Encouraged by Henry, Prince of Wales, and the Duke of Buckingham, James I began to take an interest in the idea of setting up in England a tapestry works similar to that which Henry IV had established in Paris. He therefore obtained a copy of the contract made in France between the king and the Flemish weavers. An advisory committee was set up, which reported on the plan for such a tapestry works in England as proposed by Sir Francis Crane.

His Majesty, knowing in his great wisdom that the arts and manufactures do add both ornament and wealth to those countries and commonwealths where they do most flourish, and being therefore desirous to encourage industry in that kind by all means possible within these his own realms and dominions, and to entertain all such laudable projects and inventions as may tend anyway to that end. Amongst the rest he hath been pleased of late to cast his princely cogitation upon that excellent art of making tapestry, and finding that our neighbouring countries (who have not the means to maintain the said manufacture which his majesty's dominions have) have attained already to so great a perfection therein, is not without hopes that the same may be established also in this kingdom, with as good success at least as in any other place whatsoever. But for as much as so great a work, before it be undertaken, requireth consideration touching the manner and means how to settle the same. His majesty continuing a gracious opinion of your [i.e. Crane's] sufficiency and judgement, but the experience he hath had of you in other services, is pleased that this project also shall be referred to you, to be first moulded and framed as you in your discretion, upon mature advice shall conceive to be most expedient for the advancement of the work, to which you are forthwith to apply yourself, and with as much convenient expedition as you may, to make a report to this board, of which you may think meet to be recommended to his majesty by way of opinion wherein the better to prepare your judgements (but not as a rule whereby to guide them) we have sent you a copy of an edict made by the late French king when this art was by himself established in France, from which you may take some light and make use of it, so far as may stand with the condition of this time and place. And so:

The privileges and conditions on which Sir Francis Crane doth undertake to do his majesty service in bringing over and establishing the manufacture of all sorts of tapestries in England, and only there.

That towards the pensions he shall give the charges of building and fitting of houses to the work and all other charges incident thereunto, his majesty will be pleased according to his promise to give him the benefit of four baronets [to be sold]. And one of them may be permitted to pass, though he be of Dutch descent, in respect of the service that the state shall herein receive from that nation, he being otherwise a very rich man, and already knighted.

That for the space of twenty years he may only have the privilege to make all sorts of tapestries, wherein those may be excepted that make already, so as within six months of the grant, they repair to the Lords Commissioners, and having made profession of the use of their trade, do take a testimonial from their Lordships to warrant the same. Otherwise not to work but under his privilege.

That the tapestries may be made customs free for certain years.

That such of the principal masters he may draw over (when he may desire it for them) may be naturalised.

In regard of these favours and privileges, if it be his majesty's pleasure that this art be taught here, and he do think it fit, the City of London, out of the hospitals that are in it (in which a great number of boys are kept at the public expense) appoint every year a certain number to be taught, Sir Francis Crane will be bound by the Patent to take these boys for seven years as apprentices, and will teach them the art, the City taking order only during this time for their maintenance. And if they will appoint rooms for it either in the hospitals or anywhere else within the city, he will be bound they shall be taught there, and will furnish the whole stock that shall set them all on work.

(From a manuscript in the National Art Library, Victoria & Albert Museum)

5.5 Gravity and licence

The ideals of contrast between gravity in public forms and licence in private imaginings which underlay so much artistic activity in the sixteenth and seventeenth centuries are admirably expressed by Inigo Jones, in the lines he wrote in his copy of Palladio's *Quattro Libri dell'Archittetura*.

Friday ye 20 January 1614. In all invention of caprocious ornaments one must first design the ground, and the thing plain, as it is for use, and on that vary and adorn it. For as outwardly every wise man caryeth a gravity in public places where there is nothing else looked for, yet inwardly hath his imaginacy set on fire, and sometimes licentiously flying out, as nature herself doth, sometimes stravagantly, to delight, amaze us, sometimes move us to laughter, sometimes to contemplation and horror, so in architecture, the outward ornaments ought to be solid, proportionable, according to the rules, masculine and inaffected. Where within the chimeras used by the ancients the varied and composed ornaments, both of the house itself and the moveables within it are most commendable!

5.6 Trade in Venetian glass

The buying and selling of rarities by the well-to-do was not confined to paintings and the like. On 1 February 1615 that middle-class gentleman of comparative leisure, John Chamberlain, wrote to Alice Carleton, the sister of his friend Dudley in Venice.

Yesterday by your brother Williams I received your letter of the 16th of January but I cannot follow your advice therein to send the glasses you sent me, for I have not one left within three days after they came into my hands, having disposed of them all as soon as maybe.

I brought the Lady Winwood and the Lady Fanshawe to see in one room and in one view above eight hundred dozen of Venetian glasses that came all in the same ship as mine, whereby you may see that this town is fully furnished with that commodity, and no great estimation to be made of them unless they be somewhat extraordinary and rare.

One thing I will entreat more, if it may be had; that you would procure half a dozen such looking glasses as you sent me, which are so well liked of that my Lady Winwood hath been in hand with me twice or thrice, and no longer ago than yesternight, to get her so many to furnish both her houses.

5.7 An application

In March 1616 William Smith wrote to Thomas Howard Earl of Arundel asking for a job. He eventually got one, as the Earl's agent in Rome, where he made some interesting purchases of paintings and sculptures. In 1636 he was killed whilst acting as Arundel's trumpeter on his Viennese embassy.

Right Honourable and my singular good Lord,

Remembering the great love and affection which your Honour beareth to the mystery of painting (which I profes) appearing unto me at your Honour's being in Brussels some five years past, when I showed unto your Honour the paintings of the Duke of Askott, I make bold at this time, having seen the best workmanship in France, Germany and Italy, and being at this instant in Rome, with a purpose, notwithstanding to return to England shortly, after my seven years' travel for the bettering of my knowledge, to make tender of myself and service unto your Lordship as that noble personage whom I most honour. In the mystery I am sure I can do something, but of myself will say nothing, saving that during my two years' continuance in France, I wrought for many of the Princes, and for the Queen herself. Since which time, I have spent other two years in Rome, where I shall remain, meeting here with the best works that ever my eyes beheld, for surely they exceed all other Nations, and are without compare. I have also been employed by the Cardinals and others in work after the China fashion, which is much effected here.

All which I make bold to intimate at this time to this end only, to let your Honour know some part of my ability, and my desire to be accounted one of your Lordship's servants. And that I will be ready if your Honour hath any occasion to use paintings, or Statues in stone or metal, to show as well the readiness of my affection as the best of my skill. And did I but know that your Lordship did affect any special pieces that are to be had in these parts, I would procure the same (if I could) or a true copy thereof. If your good Lordship be pleased to signify your pleasure unto my good cousin, Mr Page one of the Clerks of his Majesty's kitchen, I will not fail but give attendance upon your Honour at my first coming,

Your Lordship's most humble servant,

WILLIAM SMITH.

5.8 Rubens does a deal

Like many artists of his time, Rubens was an active dealer and collector, and in both roles he came into contact with the Jacobean court, as this correspondence with that active diplomatic entrepreneur, Sir Dudley Carleton, shows.

To Sir Dudley Carleton   Antwerp, April 28, 1618
Most excellent Sir:

By the advice of my agent, I have learned that Your Excellency is very much inclined to make some bargain with me concerning your antiquities; and it has made me hope well of this business, to see that you go about it seriously, having told him the exact price that they cost you. In regard to this, I wish to place complete trust in your knightly word. I am willing also to believe that you made such purchases with all judgement and prudence, although high personages, in buying or selling, are sometimes likely to have a certain disadvantage, because many people are willing to compute the price of goods by the rank of the purchaser – a practice to which I am very averse. Your Excellency may be assured that I shall put prices on my pictures, just as if I were negotiating to sell them for cash; and in this I beg you to rely upon the word of an honest man. I find that at present I have in the house the flower of my stock, particularly some pictures which I have kept for my own enjoyment; some I have even repurchased for more than I had sold them to others. But the whole shall be at the service of Your Excellency, because I like brief negotiations, where each party gives and receives his share at once. To tell the truth, I am so burdened with commissions, both public and private, that for some years to come I cannot commit myself. Nevertheless, in case we agree as I hope, I will not fail to finish as soon as possible all those pictures that are not yet entirely completed, even though named in the list here attached. [In margin: The greater part are finished]. Those that are finished I would send immediately to Your Excellency. In short, if Your Excellency will resolve to place as much trust in me as I do in you, the matter is settled. I am content to offer Your Excellency of the pictures by my hand, enumerated below, to the value of 6,000 florins, at current cash prices, for all those antiquities in Your Excellency's house, of which I have not yet seen the list, nor do I even know the number, but in everything I trust your word. Those pictures which are finished I will consign immediately to Your Excellency, and for the others that remain in my hands to finish, I will furnish good security to Your Excellency, and finish them as soon as possible. Meanwhile I submit to whatever Your Excellency shall conclude with Mr Frans Pieterssen, my agent, and await your decision, while I commend myself with a true heart to the good graces of Your Excellency, and kiss your hands with reverence.

From Your Excellency's most affectionate servant.
Peter Paul Rubens

To Sir Dudley Carleton   Antwerp, May 12, 1618,
Most Excellent Sir:
Your very welcome letter of the 8th instant reached me yesterday evening, by which I learned that Your Excellency has had in part a change of thought, in wishing to have pictures for only half the value of the marbles, and for the other half tapestries or cash. However, I shall not find the former except by means of the latter. This change seems to result from a scarcity of pictures on my list, since Your Excellency has taken only the originals, with which I am perfectly satisfied. Yet Your Excellency must not think that the others are mere copies, for they are so well retouched by my hand that they are hardly to be distinguished from originals. Nevertheless, they are rated at a much lower price. I do not wish to influence Your Excellency by fine words, because if you persist in your first idea, I could still furnish pure originals up to this amount. But to speak frankly, I imagine that you haven't the desire for such a quantity of pictures. The reason I would deal more willingly in pictures is clear: although they do not exceed their just price in the list, yet they cost me, so to speak, nothing. For everyone is more liberal with the fruits that grow in his own

garden than with those he must buy in the market. Besides, I have
spent this year some thousands of florins on my estate, and I should
not like, for a whim, to exceed the limits of good economy. In fact,
I am not a prince, *sed qui manducat laborem manuum suarum*[1] I should
like to infer that if Your Excellency should wish to have pictures
for the full value of the sum, whether originals or well-retouched
copies (which show more for their price), I would treat you liber-
ally, and always refer the price to the arbitration of any discerning
person. If, however, you are determined to have some tapestries,
I am content to give you tapestries to your satisfaction, to the
amount of 2,000 florins and 4,000 florins in pictures; that is, 3,000
florins for the originals already chosen by Your Excellency – the
Prometheus, the Daniel, the Leopards, the Leda, the St Peter and
the St Sebastian – while for the remaining 1,000 florins you may
choose from the other pictures on our list. Or else I will pledge
myself to give you, for that sum, such originals by my hand as you
will consider satisfactory. If you will believe me, you will take that
Hunt which is on the list, which I will make as good as the one
Your Excellency already has by my hand. They would match each
other perfectly, that one showing tigers and European hunters, and
this one lions and Moorish and Turkish riders, very exotic. I rate
this piece at 600 florins, and there remain, then, 400 florins. As a
supplement the Susanna would be appropriate, similarly finished
by my hand to your satisfaction; and finally, for the last 100 florins
I should add some other trifle by my hand, to complete the 4,000
florins.

I hope that Your Excellency will be satisfied with this arrangement, which seems so reasonable, considering that I accepted your
first offer willingly, and that this change comes from Your Excellency and not from me. I certainly could not increase my offer, for
many reasons. Therefore, will Your Excellency be good enough
to inform me, as soon as possible, as to your decision. And in case
you are willing to accept my offer, you could, at your convenience,
before your departure for England, consign the marbles to Mr
Frans Pieterssen. I will do the same with the pictures which are
ready, and send the rest in a few days.

As for the tapestries, I can be of great help to this merchant
friend of yours, for I have had great experience with the tapestry-
makers of Brussels, through the many commissions which come

---

1. 'But one who lives by the work of his hands' (Psalm 128, 52).

to me from Italy and elsewhere for similar works. I myself have made some very handsome cartoons at the request of certain Genoese gentlemen, and which are now being worked; and, to tell the truth, if one wishes to have exquisite things, they must be made to order. In this I will gladly take care that Your Excellency is well served, although I defer to your opinion.

In closing, I kiss Your Excellency's hands with all my heart and remain, *in omnem eventum nostri negotii*,[2] always your most devoted servant. Mr Frans Pieterssen has not yet sent me the list of your marbles, and I should also like, in case we come to an agreement, that list with the names which you write me that you have found.

Peter Paul Rubens

I beg Your Excellency that if the matter is settled, you will proceed to obtain free passage for these marbles; and if you still have the wooden cases in which they were sent from Italy, these will not be useless to you, but of great convenience to me for this journey.

5.9 Commendable and useful

Written for young William Howard, son of the connoisseur Earl of Arundel, Thomas Peacham's *The Compleat Gentleman*, first published in 1622, became almost instantly popular to a generation, which had recently acquired new wealth, and was anxious to know the proprieties. It was republished in 1627, 1634 and 1661 (significantly the year after the Restoration), and maintained its popularity until the end of the century. Its comments on drawing are especially significant.

Since Aristotle numbereth *graphice*, generally taken for whatever is done with the pen or pencil (as writing, fair drawing, limning and painting) among those his generous practices of youth in a well-governed commonwealth, I am bound also to give it you in charge for your exercise at leisure, it being a quality most commendable and so many ways useful to a gentleman. For should you, if necessity required, be employed for your country's service in following the war, you can describe no plot, manner of fortification, form of *battalia*, situation of town, castle, fort, haven, island, course of river, passage through wood, marsh, over rock, mountain etc. (which a discreet general doth not always commit to the eye of another) without the help of the same. In all mathematical demon-

---

2. 'Whatever the outcome of our negotiations.'

strations nothing is more required in our travel in foreign regions.
It bringeth home with us from the furthest part of the world in our
bosoms whatever is rare and worthy of observance, as the general
map of the country, the rivers, harbours, havens, promontories,
etc., within the landscape of fair hills, fruitful valleys, the forms
and colours of all fruits, several beauties of their flowers; of
medicineable simples never before seen or heard of; the orient
colours and lively pictures of their birds, the shape of their beasts,
fishes, worms, flies etc. It presents our eyes with their complexion,
manner and their attire. It shows us the rites of their religion, their
houses, their weapons and manner of war. Besides it preserveth the
memory of a dearest friend or mistress. And since it is only the
imitation of the surface of nature, by it as in a book of golden and
rare-limned letters, the chief end of it, we read a continual lecture
of the wisdom of the Almighty Creator by beholding, even in the
feather of a peacock, a miracle, as Aristotle saith.

And that you should not esteem basely of the practice thereof,
let me tell you that in ancient times, painting was admitted into
the first place among the liberal arts, and throughout all Greece
taught only to the children of noblemen in the schools, and altogether forbidden to be taught to servants or slaves.

Neither was it the exercise of nobility among the ancients only,
but of late days and in our times we see it practised by the greatest
Princes of Europe without prejudice to their honours. Francis 1st
King of France was very excellent with his pencil, and the virtuous
Margaret of Navarre, besides her excellent vein in poesy, could
draw and limn excellently. The like is reported of Emmanuel,
Duke of Savoy.

Nor can I overpass the ingenuity and excellency of many nobles
and gentlemen of our own nation herein, of whom I know many,
but none in my opinion who deserveth more respect and admir-
ation for his skill and practice therein than Master Nathaniel Bacon
of Brome in Suffolk (younger son to the bountiful-minded Sir
Nicholas Bacon, knight and eldest baronet) not inferior in my
judgement to our skilfullest masters.

Painting is a quality I love, I confess, and admire in others,
because ever naturally from a child I have been addicted to the
practice thereof. Yet when I was young I have been cruelly beaten
by ill and ignorant schoolmasters, when I have been taking in white
or black the countenance of someone (which I could do at thirteen
or fourteen years of age) beside the map of any town, according
to geometrical proportions, as I did of Cambridge when I was of

Trinity College [a junior sophister] yet could they never beat it out of me.

5.10 'Well-seen in statue-craft

Peacham also has also advice to give about the essential gift of appreciating antique statues, understandably in view of his connexion with the Earl of Arundel, whose collection of them was probably the greatest ever amassed in England.

It is not enough for a gentleman to behold these statues with a vulgar eye, but he must be able to distinguish them, and tell who and what they be. To do this there must be four parts; First by general learning in history and poetry, whereby we are taught to know Jupiter by his thunderbolt, Mars by his armour, Neptune by his trident, Apollo by his harp, Mercury by his wings on his cap and feet, or by his caduceus, and so generally of most of the deities. Some mortals are also known by their cognizances, as Laocoön by his snakes stinging him to death, Cleopatra by a viper, Cicero by his wart, and a great many more.

But because all statues have not such properties and badges, there is a second way to discern them, and that is by their coins. For if you look upon them sideways and consider well their half-faces, as all coins show them, you will easily know them. For this is certain (which also witnesseth the exquisite diligence of ancient works) that all the faces of any one person, whether on old coins or stones, in greater or less volume, are all alike. In so much as if you bring an old rusty coin to any reasonable antiquary, if he can see but a nose on it or a piece of the face, he will give you a shrewd guess at him, though none of the inscription is to be seen.

A third, and very good way to distinguish them is by the book of collection of all the principal statues that are now to be seen at Rome, printed there with the title *Icones Statuarum quae hodie visuntur Romae.*

The fourth and last help, and without which the rest are weak, is to visit them in company of such as are learned in them, and by their help to grow familiar with them, and so practice their acquaintance.

Now besides the pleasure of seeing and conversing with these old heroes (whose mere presence, without any further consideration, reared on their several pedestals, and ranked decently either *sub dio* [in the open air] where they show best, or in a stately gallery, cannot but take any eye that can but see) the profit of knowing them redounds to all poets, painters and architects, and generally to such as may have occasion to employ any of these, and by consequent to all gentlemen. To poets, for the presentation of comedies, tragedies, masques, shows or any learned scene what-soever, the properties whereof can neither be appointed, nor judged of but by such as are well-seen in statue-craft. To painters for the picturing of some exquisite arm, leg, torso, or wreathing of the body, or any other rare posture whether smooth or forced.

Besides, 'rounds' (so painters call statues and their fragments) may be had when the life cannot, and have the patience to stand when the life will not. And this is a maxim among artists of this kind, that a round is better to draw by and comes nearer the life than any flat or painting whatsoever. And if a painter will meddle with history, then are old statues to him the only life itself. I call Rubens to witness, the best story painter of these times, whether his knowledge in this kind has been his only making. But his statues before named, and his works do testify for him. Yea, while he is at work, he useth to have some good historian or poet read to him, which is rare in men of his profession, yet absolutely necessary. And as for architects, they have great use of statues for ornaments, for gates, friezes and cornices for tombs and divers other buildings.

And therefore I may justly conclude that the study of statues is profitable for all ingenuous gentlemen, who are the only men that employ poets, painters aad architects, if they be not all these them-selves. And if they be not able to judge of their works, they deserve to be cozened.

5.11 Enlarging a great chamber

Typical of the cost and the mechanics of building in the early seventeenth century is a 'Computation for Reparations' in connexion with the Great Chamber at Petworth in 1619, amongst the household papers of the 9th Earl of Northumberland.

Articles agreed uppon with the mason for repayringe the Greate Chamber at Pettworth.

First your Lordshipp is to provide soe much lyme, sand and stone as shall be necessarily required towards the finishinge of the sayde worke.

Secondly the mason is to sett upp the scaffoldes, and to take downe the whole wall between the head of the upper windowes and the battlement, to take off the ruff-caste of the whole wall, and to take downe the windowes withowt demaunding therefore anie allowance.

And for the residewe of the worke to be donne by him, your Lordship is to paie him according to the rates hereafter mencioned vizt. for everye rodd of ruff wall to be newe built from the grownde, contaynyne in thicknes from the foote of the fowndacion to the water table.[1] three foote, and from the water table to the corbell table[2] two foote, well wrought upp and joyned with the olde wall now standinge, two shillings; for hewing and settinge the ashler 3d. of the foote; for mowldinge, hewinge and placinge of the water table, cornishe, corbell table and battlement vj the foote; for takinge upp of soe much of the Horsham stone, and placinge ytt againe as shall be needfull xxs.; and for hewinge and settynge of the windowe stuff vd. the foote.

For all wych he is to be paid accordinge unto theis rates, and accordinge to trewe measure and not otherwyse from tyme to tyme as the worke shall goe forward.

The whole charge of the mason's worke will come to abowt 44li. I have agreed with Dee for all the carpenter's worke for vij l.; the smith's and glazier's work will comme to somme 4li.; the ruff stone wil be digged in the Liths and the ashler stone at Byworth Quarrey, your Lordship to paye for digginge, and the stones to be carryed by your Lordship's tenaunts. The lyme wilbe sent in from Sutton att vs. the loade, your Lordship fydynge woode to burne ytt; the chardge of the lyme wilbe iij li The sand will cost little.

5.12 Doting on new fashions

Peacham in his *Compleat Gentleman* (1622) was concerned with the great variations which were taking place in sartorial fashions, and addressed himself to the probem in a chapter entitled 'Of Following the Fashion'.

---

1. water table: a horizontal projecting ledge set along the side of a wall to throw off the rain.
2. corbell table: a projecting course resting on a series of ledges or corbels projecting from a wall.

I never knew any wholly affected to follow fashion to have been in any way useful to the commonwealth, except that way Aristotle affirmeth the prodigal man to be, by scattering his money about to the benefit of many – tailors, seamstresses, silkmen etc. Neither ever I knew any man esteemed the better or the wiser for his bravery, but among simple people. Now this thing we call fashion is so much hunted and pursued after like a thief with hue and cry, that our tailors dog it into France, even to the very door. It reigns commonly like an epidemical disease, first infecting the court, then the city, after the country, from the countess to the chambermaid, who rather than that she will want her curled locks will turn them up with a hot pair of tongs instead of the irons. The fashion, like an higher orb, hath the revolution commonly every hundred year, when the same comes into request again; which I saw once in Antwerp handsomely described by an he- and she-fool turning a wheel about, with hats, hose and doublets in the fashion fastened round about it, which when they were below started to mount up again, as we see them. For example, in the time of King Henry VII the slashed doublets now used were in request. Only the coats of the King's Guard keep the same form they did since they were first given to them. After that the Flemish fashion in the time of King Henry VIIIth came in request – of straight doublets, huge breeches let out with codpieces and puffs. In Queen Mary's time the Spanish was much in use. In Queen Elizabeth's time there were the great-bellied doublets, wide saucy sleeves that would be in every dish before their master, and buttons as big as tablemen [pieces used in a board game], or the lesser sort of Sandwich turnips, with huge ruffs that stood like cartwheels about their necks, and round breeches, not unlike St Omer onions, where to the long stocking without garter was joined, which then was the Earl of Leicester's fashion, and their's who had the handsomest leg. The women wore straight-bodied gowns, with narrow sleeves drawn out with lawn or fine cambric in puff, with high bolstered wings, little ruffs edged with gold or black silk. And maids wore cauls of gold, now quite out of use. Chains of gold were then of lords, knights, and gentlemen commonly worn, but a chain of gold now (to so high a rate is gold raised) is as much as some of them are worth.

The like variety hath been in hats, which have been but of late years. Henry the Fourth is commonly portrayed with a hood on his head such as the liveries of the city wear on their shoulders. Henry the Sixth, the Seventh, and Eighth wore only caps, King Philip in England wore commonly a somewhat high velvet cap with a white feather. After came in hats of all fashions, some with crowns so high, that, beholding them far off, you would have thought that you had discovered the Tenerife. Those close to the head like barber's basins, with narrow brims, we were at that time beholden to Cadiz in Spain for. After that came up those with square crowns and brims almost as broad as a brewer's mashvat or a reasonable upper stone of a mustard quern, which among my other epigrams gave me occasion of this:

> Soranzo's broad-brimmed hat I oft compare
> To the vast compass of the heavenly sphere:
> His head, the earth's globe fixed under it,
> Whose centre is his wondrous little wit.

No less variety hath been in hatbands, the cypress being now quite out of use save among some few of the graver sort.

Wherefore the Spaniard and Dutch are much to be commended, who for some hundreds of years never altered their fashion, but have always kept one and the same . . .

I have much wondered why our English above other nations should so much dote upon new fashions, but more I wonder at our want of wit that we cannot invent them ourselves, but, when one is grown stale, run presently over into France to seek out a new, making that noble and flourishing kingdom the magazine of our fooleries. And for this purpose many of our tailors lie ledger there, and ladies post over their gentleman-ushers to accouter them and themselves as you see. Hence came your slashed doublets (as if the wearers were cut out to be carbonadoed upon the coals) and your half shirts; picadillies, now out of request; your long breeches, narrow towards the knees like a pair of smith's bellows; the spangled garters pendant to the shoe; your perfumed perukes or periwigs to show us that lost hair may be had again for money; with a thousand such fooleries unknown to our manly forefathers.

5.13 Paintings for the Duke

George Villiers, Duke of Buckingham, was an omnivorous collector of paintings, and builder of houses, whose main rival in the acquisition of works of art was, as Thomas Roe pointed out, Thomas Howard, Earl of Arundel. Buckingham's agent was the industrious and persuasive Balthasar Gerbier, two letters from whom give some indication of the range of his activities.

Boulogne, 17 November 1624

I mentioned in my former letter by Sir James Arthur Long the large and rare paintings in the possession of a person called President Chevallier, who has also some antique heads in marble and bronze, the whole neither to be sold nor to be given away without some scheme, but I have sworn to myself, as I did about the Prelate of Venice, that we must have them or I lack invention, for as they are the ornament of a handsome house in France, they must be the jewels at York House.[1] These paintings and these heads, five thousand pounds sterling, in tapestry, rich with gold and silver and silk, and made after a pattern by Raphael, and one hundred and fifty thousand francs in cash, which make fifteen thousand pounds sterling, are within the centre and circumference of this business. I fear the long recital of it will make your Excellency as weary as I am vexed at sea, that prevents my seeing your blessed countenance.

This is the matter. The very day that I had given my last letter to Sir James Arthur Long, a stranger came to see me, who had heard that I was in the employ of the Duke of Buckingham, and who, as I very well remarked, had taken notice of the pictures which I had been looking for; he addressed me in these words; The marriage [of Charles, Prince of Wales] concluded, people were now anxious only for the arrival of the Duke of Buckingham, whose virtue and popularity in a time so extraordinary could not fail of acquiring for him the power of doing good service to whom he would; that if it were in the will and favour of the Duke, to show it to one who cast the anchor of his hopes upon his arrival, that not only would he present him with all the pictures I had seen, but also 50,000 francs worth of Raphael tapestry, and a present of 150,000 francs besides.

I answered him in this manner.

'That though a servant of the Duke of Buckingham, my passion did not transport me to say more of him than all the world to whom he was known allowed, that nothing could more incline him to act virtuously than the love of virtue itself, and that as he was devoted to worthy and exalted things, he was an enemy of all that was base and low, more especially avoiding the having his eye or his hand in the direction of lines which are not perpendicular that

---

1. Buckingham had three houses in London: York or Buckingham House in the Strand was the one he used for state occasions.

is to say medling with any affair unjust or contemptible, much less would he be concerned in anything mercenary [*despite this disclaimer Gerbier then goes on to give details of the action the Duke is being asked to undertake in return for the bribe*] If it please your Excellency these pictures will come into our hands with the rest. The tapestries are on the way from Antwerp to Paris, and for the other sum they promise, as I have said fifteen thousand pounds sterling. During the time I have been in Paris, I have not passed one hour without searching after some rarity, and I should have stayed there but four days, had it not been as I thought, very necessary that I should find out all there is in Paris; and I never could have thought they had so many rare things in France, all of which are to come into your hands at your happy arrival. I beg your Excellency yet to read the other sheet, and you will see there are three rare pictures of Michelangelo and Raphael. It is because, my lord, since my last I have found, at the house of the Bishop of Paris, three of the most rare pictures that can be. The first is a St Francis, a good sized painting from the hand of the Cavalier Ballion, as good as Michelangelo Carazoago [Caravaggio], and the other a picture of Our Lady by Raphael, which is repainted by some devil who, I trust was hanged; but still it is so lovely and the drawing is so fine that it is worth a thousand crowns. There is another picture of Michel Angelo Buonarotti; but that should be seen kneeling, for it is a Crucifixion with the Virgin and St John – the most divine thing in the world. I have been such an idolator as to kiss it three times, for there is nothing that can be so perfect. It is a miniature. I have a hundred thousand things to say, but I offend too much in trespassing upon your patience. I have met with a most beautiful piece of Tintoret, of a Danaë, a naked figure the most beautiful, that flint as cold as ice might fall in love with it. I have given twenty crowns in hand; it costs with another head of Titian, sixty pounds sterling. I have given also twenty crowns in hand for the Gorgon's head; it cost two hundred crowns. I have not yet paid for them, because I was not willing to draw bills until I knew how much I should employ in Paris. But, my Lord, after your Excellency shall have made a large collection, I beg of you to attack Mons. de Montmorency, for he has the most beautiful statues that can be spoken of, that is Two Slaves by Michelangelo, and some others. He is so liberal that he will not refuse them. I beg of you to mention it to Mons. de Fiat, for perhaps he has some friends about him. I hope your Excellency will carry away some fine things from France.

Three months later Gerbier wrote again, from London a letter which is of interest not only because it shows the range of the commissions which he undertook for the Duke, but because of its spirited defence of collecting works of art. In the event, when the collection was sold by Parliament in 1649, Gerbier's prognostications about its investment value were fully realised.

Sometimes, when I am contemplating the treasure of rarities which your Excellency has in so short a time amassed, I cannot but feel astonishment in the midst of my joy, for out of all the amateurs and princes and Kings, there is not one who has collected in forty years as many as your Excellency has collected in five. Let enemies and people ignorant of paintings say what they will, they cannot deny that pictures are noble ornaments, a delightful amusement, and histories that one may read without fatigue, which neither eat beef, nor drink greedily, nor feed on oats (as this horse that Mr Graymes has given me will do, and for which therefore I take the liberty of begging your Excellency that I may have an allowance of oats). Our pictures, if they were to be sold a century after our death, would sell for good cash and for more than three times what they cost. I wish I could only live a century, if they were sold, in order to be able to say to those facetious folk who say 'it is monny cast away for bobbles and shadows'. I know they will be pictures still when those ignorants will be lesser than 'shadows'. So much for them . . . To conclude if your Excellency will only give me time to mine quietly I will fill Newhall with paintings, so that foreigners will come there in procession, but we must proceed very quietly. Tuesday the paving the cabinet with marble begins, which will be the grandest thing in the kingdom, but it will be at least three weeks before it is finished. I am very desirous of your presence, but I should be glad not to see you for three weeks, for we are whiting the ceilings, which had not been whitewashed before, so we have got scaffolding everywhere. I should like all to be clean before your arrival, and that all should be done before I set out for France. Madame has not given orders about the furniture of Persian cloth of gold, nor for matting the other apartments; that should be done in time, for new mats for a month or so have an ill smell. Half of our Dutch mats are come. Mr Crow will have the dress with pearl ornaments made at Boulogne; the patterns I send, the larger is not made to my fancy. My design was for the compartments to be small, and the flowers too; which might be changed in the working, and be made as small as one pleased. The one is for the inside, the other for the outside. This is only a little paper lost. There is the name of the Prince and of Madame, and the roses and lilies combined; that is for the inside of the mantle. It would cost near on twelve hundred pounds sterling.

5.14 'Old idolls'

Thomas Howard, Earl of Arundel, was not only a collector of paintings, but of Graeco-Roman statuary – the remnants of his once great collection are in the Ashmolean Museum – and his chaplain William Petty scoured the Middle East for him. He was greatly assisted by Sir Thomas Roe, the English ambassador at Constantinople, who in October 1625 wrote to Arundel giving news of Petty's mishaps.

Hee had gotten many things, going to Ephesus by sea, hee made shipwracke in a greate storme on the coast of Asia, and, savinge his own life lost both all his collection of that voyadge, and his commans and letters [of credit] by me procured; desiring mee to send him others, or else that he can proceed no further. Hee was putt in prison for a spy, having lost in the sea all his testimonyes, but was released by the witness of Turks that knew him. From thence he recovered Scio, where he furnished himself againe, and is gone to the place where he left his boate to fish for the marbles in the hope to find them, and from thence to Ephesus, and this is the last news I heard of him.

In the following March Roe wrote again to Arundel recounting some of his own problems in the search for statues.

My Lord,

My last letters brought your lordship the advice of Mr Pettyes' shippewracke and losses upon the coast of Asya, returning from Samos; his commands and letters of recommendation, and his labours there perished. The first I presently renewed, and sent them to Smyrna; and the other I thinke he hath by great industry recovered. It shall suffice me to say in grosse, that though hee will not boaste to mee, yett I am informed hee hath gotten many things rare and antient. Ther never was a man so fitted to an employment that encounters all accidents with so unwearied patience; eates with Greakes on their worst daies, lyes with fishermen on plancks, at the best is all things to all men, that he may obteyne his ends, which are your lordship's service. He has gone to Athenes, whither also I have sent, and from thence promiseth to visit me in this citye, where I shall bee glad to entertayne him, and to know the history of his labours.

I have in my endaevour bad success by ignorance of those I am forced to employ, who send me heavy stones at great chardge, that proove new images, wher I seeke old idolls; for such also were the Roman statues of their Emperors. From Angory I had half a woman, brought 18 dayes by lande upon change of mules, which wants a hand, a nose, a lip and is so deformed shee makes mee remember an hospital. Yet the malicious Turkes brought trouble on the buyers by a false command, accusing them of great wealth stolen out of the castle. It hath cost mee mony to punish them, and that is all I have for my labor. I have sent three servints togither to Tassas, Cavalla, Philippi, and all the coast of Thrace; followed Mr Petty to Pergamo, and Troy; am digging in Asya, and to fulfill the proverbe, digging of all stones. Somewhat I hope to gett, to save my creditt; but I dare not write to his grace until I am in possession, so often I have beene by Greekish promise deceived.

Those on Port Aurea stand up, ready to fall, in spight of all my arts and offers, the tymes are so dangerous that I dare not veanture to entreague others, but there is an opportunity attended to make them stoope. The glory of taking them from the Gate of Constantinople inciteth mee farther than any bewtye I see in ruines, that only showe there was once bewtye; good emblemes of one that had beene a handsome woman, if an old woman were not a better; yet few love them.

When I have made my collection, I will not forgett that I was engaged by your Lordship's commands, as I am sure your Lordship will not grudge mee to performe the service I owe the Duke of Buckingham, between whom and your Lordship, if ther had beene a union, ther had beene nothing difficult to us both here, and many things much cheaper. So humbly kyssing your Lordship's hands, I commit you to the heavenly protection,

> Your Lordship's most ready servant,
> Tho. Roe.
> Constantinople 28 March old stile.

5.15 A great deal

The purchase by Charles I of the major part of the collection of the Duke of Mantua was the largest art transaction which had ever taken place, and brought to England an unrivalled collection of works of art. Many people were involved in the business, but, although the main credit must go to Nicholas Lanier, Master of the King's Music, Daniel Nys was also involved, and was remarkably forthcoming about his activities as these letters show.

Daniel Nys to Endymion Porter.   *Venice April 17 1628.*

Illustrious Sir and most esteemed Patron:

Signior Lanier, who is the bearer of this letter, has used every care and diligence to repair and trim up the pictures procured from the young Duke of Mantua, and has caused them to be encased and conveyed, by the ship *Margaret*, in a way in which His Majesty will be greatly pleased to see them, and he will understand from him the course which I have undertaken to obtain them. Since I came into the world I have made various contracts, but never a more difficult one than this, and which has succeeded so happilly. In the first place the City of Mantua, and then all the Princes of Christendom, both great and small, were struck with astonishment that we could persuade Duke Vicenzo to dispose of them. The people of Mantua made so much noise about it, that if Duke Vicenzo could have had them back again, he would readily have paid double, and his people would have been willing to supply the money. The Prince of Guastallo preferred half the gain, I believe, to make them a present to the Emperor [Rudolph II, who was also an avid collector]. The Grand Duke of Tuscany, and the same of Genoa have done the same. It seems as though some fatality had favoured me, not for myself, but for the sake of him for whom I negotiated, I mean the King of Britain. Pray God they may arrive safe in port and that His Majesty may receive a lasting enjoyment from them. In treating for them I used every artifice to obtain them at a modest price; as, had it been known that I was acting for His Majesty, they would have demanded so much more. At present I am in treaty at Rome to procure the picture of St Catherine of Correggio and hope to succeed. These wars against Monferrat are the cause of the Duke of Nevers pledging many of his jewels, but I doubt whether he will dispose of the marble statues, the list of which you have had before. In case His Majesty should desire to have them, will you please to let me know, so that others may not carry them off, and I will then do all I can to procure them to the best advantage. Moreover I beg you will be pleased to assure His Majesty that I will speedily give him advice of all that is fine that may fall into my hands, in order that he may become the master of it, having entirely dedicated myself to his service, in all that he may judge me worthy of Sigr Lanier departed this evening with two pictures of Correggio, the finest in the world, and which alone are worth the money paid for the whole. God grant him a favourable voyage. I have provided him on all sides with letters of credit. And so ending, I recommend myself to your good favour, and beg you will retain me in His Majesty's favour.

Venice May 12th 1628.

Most Illustrious Sir,

It is now the 12th of May. This serves to confirm the departure of Sig. Lanier, from whom I have letters from Bergamo of 2nd of May. He departed via the Grisons for Basle in good health, and with fine horses, God accompanying him throughout. He carries with him two paintings of Correggio in tempera, and one of Raffaelle, the finest pictures in the world, and well worth the money paid for the whole, both on account of their rarity and exquisite beauty. The ship *Margaret* must now be far advanced on her voyage. I have not as yet heard that she has arrived at London, so that His Majesty may see so many beautiful and exquisite pictures. Among them is the Madonna of Raffaele del Cannozzo, for which the Duke of Mantua gave a Marquisate worth 50,000 scudi, and the late Duke of Florence would have given the Duke of Mantua 25,000 ducatoni in ready money; the man who negotiated the matter is still alive. Then there are the twelve Emperors of Titian, a large picture of Andrea del Sarto, a picture of Michelangelo di Caravaggio; other pictures of Titian, Correggio, Giulio Romano, Tintoretto and Guido Reni, all of the greatest beauty. In short, so glorious and wonderful a collection that the like will never again be met with; they are truly worthy of so great a king as His Majesty of Great Britain. In this negotiation I have been aided by Divine Assistance, without which success would have been impossible. To Him then be the glory.

5.16 A contract for a stately tomb

Nothing was left to chance or hazard in the commissioning of works of art, and even though most of the specifications must have been added by the designer, it is clear that the patron was also involved in the process. In 1630 Nicholas Stone recorded in his *Notebooks* (Walpole Society, vol. 7, 1919) 'I made a tombe for Ser

Charles Moreson and his ladie and sett it up in the Chencell of
Watford in Harfordshere for the which I was well payd unto me
£400.' The contract for the tomb has survived at Cassiobury.

Articles of Agreement, made the 3d day of March 1628, between
Dame Mary Morrison of Kashbury [Cassiobury] in the Parrish of
Watford, late Wife of Sir Charles Morrison Knt and Bart and
Nicholas Stone of the Parrish of St Martin-in-the-Fields in the
County of Middlesex, Carver and Tombe Maker.

Imprimis, the said Nicholas Stone, for himself, his executors etc.
doth covenant etc. to and with the said Dame Mary Morrison, her
executors etc by theis presents, that he, the said Nicholas Stone,
his executors etc. shall and will at his, or their owne proper costs
and charges, artificially make, frame, carve, erect, sett up and finish
one faire and staightly tombe or monument in memorial of the said
Sir Charles Morrison deceased; to be placed and sett upp in a
chapell of the said Dame Mary Morrison, adjoyneing to the chaun-
cell of the parrish church of Watford. The which said tombe or
monument shall consist or be made of white marble, touchstone
and allabaster, and to containe in the whole 14 foote in breadth and
16 foote in height from the ground. The severall parts whereof shall
consist and contayne as followeth; that is to say, the stepp of the
said tombe to be of Kentish stone or Portland stone 6 inches deep;
upon which stepp is to be raised a basement of allabaster, 1 foote
in height, to be fairly moulded and wrought and on the said basement to raise the main body of the tombe in manner of an altar,
three foote in height, to consist of good allabaster, and at each
corner a pedestall of touch or black marble, one foote square, at
the top of which pedestalls shall be placed a capitall of white
marble, and betweene the said pedestalls shall make one faire table
of touch or black marble, to containe two foote in breadth and four
foote and a half in length, which mayne body or altar is to be
covered over with a table or ledger stone of touch or black marble,
fairly wrought, polished and glayzed, to containe seven foote and
three ynches in length and two foote and a halfe in breadth, to be
all of one firme stone. And shall make one other fayre ledger or
table, of touch stone or black marble, alsoe of seven foote and three
ynches in length and two foote in breadth, to be raysed up in height
six inches above the other table, to the end it maye give a better
prospect or viewe of the statue or picture of the said Sir Charles
Morrison, which is thereon to be playced. Which said statue or
picture is to be royally and artificially carved, pollished, glazed, and

made of good, pure white marble, in compleat armour, with sword
and spurrs, according to the life, to consist of six foote in length
of one entire peece of stone, and shall make a picture or statue, for
and of the said worthy lady, to be laid on the table-stone, first
before herein expressed, to consist of good and pure white marble,
carved and artificially wrought, polished glazed and made to the
life, in such abillaments, ornaments and jewells, as he shall receave
directions for, which statue shall containe six foote in length, or
neere thereabouts, all of one entire peece of marble. And at the
West end of the said Monument shall raise a kind of basement of
allabaster, fairly wrought and moulded and inricht with two tables
of touchstone or black marble, the same basement to consist of two
and a half foote in height and three foote in length, on which is
to be placed the statue or portraighture of Mrs Elizabeth Capell,
daughter of the said Sir Charles Morrison and Lady Mary, the same
statue to contayne four foote in height, kneelinge; and at the East
end of the said Monument, shall raise another basement in like
kinde, wrought, moulded and enriched, as aforesaid, whereon shall
be placed the statues or pictures of the two sons deceased of the
said Sir Charles and Lady Mary; the eldest of which sonns to be
made three foote in height, kneeling, with his cloake and sword;
the other to be two foote in height, kneeling with a coate; all three
to be made of pure white allbaster, fairly wrought, carved and
polished. And shall, at the fower corners of the aforesaid monument rayse and place fower pillars of touchstone or black marble,
to containe in height with their bayses and capitalls six foote and
a halfe; the bases of the same pillars to be of white marble, and the
same to be finely wraught, pollished and glazed, and their capitalls
to be fairly carved in a composative manner with festons of wreaths
and flowers, betweene which four fower pillers behind the statues
on the wall side is to be placed one fair table of touchstone or black
marble for inscriptions, which table shall contayne three foote in
length and four foote and a halfe in height, enclosed with a
compartment of allabaster, fairly wraught, and on the topp of the
said fower pillers shall raise two arches of allabaster, fairely
wraught and carved with flowers and other enrichments; which
arches shall come forth from the wall, and plancher, cover and
overshadowe the two statues of marble that lye underneath; under
which arches shall make an archtrave and freeze, enriched with
cherubines' heads and black marble and other enrichings, and on
topp of these arches shall make a cornishe which is to break up with
two frontispeeces on the foreside and one on the West end, and an

other at the East end, between which two frontispieces on the fore side, is to be placed the arms of the said Sir Charles and the said Dame Mary, empaled in one party scutcheon of good allabaster, fairly carved with festoons of leaves and flowers and other scrolles, compartment wayes, and on the corner of the said cornish, upon two pedestalls, shall place the creast of the arms belonging to the said Sir Charles and the said Dame Mary and shall carve and put in the proper metalls and cullors, their several arms, and shall grave and guild such inscriptions as shall be in due tyme delivered unto him, and shall finish the saide stately tombe according to the fore-said expression and signified by a designe or drafte thereof drawne by the said Nicholas Stone, approved and signed by Dame Mary on or before the last daye of May which shall be in the yeare of Our Lord God 1630.

5.17 A memory to outlive our lives

Attitudes to death were very different in the seventeenth century from our own, and indeed throughout history the quest for immortality had been one of the major incentives to the production of works of art. One of the most memorable results of this concern is Donne's monument in St Paul's. In 1631 Nicholas Stone recorded 'Humphrey Mayor finisht the statue for Dr Donne's monument, £8', and later noted his own payment for the whole work, 'I made a tombe for Dr Donne and sette it up in St Paul's, London for the which I was payed by Dr Mountford the sum of £120. I took £60 in plate in part of payment'! Izaak Walton in his life of Donne provides the background to the work.

It is observed that a desire of glory or commendation is rooted in the very nature of man; and that those of the severest and most mortified lives, though they may become so humble as to banish self-flattery, and such weeds as naturally grow there, yet they have not been able to kill this desire of glory, but that like our radical heat, it will both live and die with us; and many think it should do so; and we want not sacred examples to justify the desire of having our memory to outlast our lives, which I mention because Dr Donne, by the persuasion of Dr Fox easily yielded at this very time to have a monument made of him but Dr Fox undertook not to persuade him how or what monument it should be; that was left to Dr Donne himself.

A monument being resolved upon, Dr Donne sent for a carver

to make him in wood the figure of an urn, giving him directions for the compass and height of it, and to bring with it a board, of the just height of his body. These being got, then without delay a choice painter was got to be in readiness to draw his picture, which was taken as followeth. Several charcoal fires being first made in his large study, he brought with him into that place his winding sheet in his hand, and having put off all his clothes, had this sheet put on him, and so tied with knots at his head and feet, and his hands so placed as dead bodies are usually fitted to be shrouded, and put into their coffin or grave. Upon this urn he thus stood, with his eyes shut, and with so much of the sheet turned aside as might show his lean, pale and death-like face, which was turned towards the east from whence he expected the second coming of his and our Saviour, Jesus Christ. In this posture he was drawn at his just height, and when the picture was fully finished, he caused it to be set by his bedside, where it continued, and became his hourly object till his death, and was then given to his dearest friend and executor Dr Henry King, then Chief Residentiary of St Paul's, who caused him to be thus carved in one entire piece of white marble, as it now stands in that church.

And now having brought him through the many labyrinths and perplexities of a various life, even to the gates of death and the grave, my desire is he may rest till I have told my Reader that I have seen many pictures of him in several habits, and at several ages, and in several postures; and I now mention this because I have seen one picture of him drawn by a curious hand at his age of eighteen, with his sword, and what other adornments might then suit with the present fashions of youth, and the giddy gaieties of that age; and his Motto then was –

How much shall I be changed,

Before I am changed!

5.18 A bad bargain, 1630

Round about 1625 Charles I bought from Sir Francis Crane a set of tapestries made by the latter's factory at Mortlake, on the subject of *Vulcan and Venus*, for the immense sum of £12,000. In 1630 Dru Burton, the Auditor-General, claimed that the king had been grossly overcharged for them and other works. No account was taken of this 'discovery' though Burton was dismissed from his post. It does reveal however a good deal about the nature of Crane's business dealing and the costs of tapestry-making.

To the King's Majestie.
A discoverie of the great gaine made by the manufacture of the
tapestrie. It may please your Majestie. The first suits of tapestrie
of the storie of *Vulcan and Venus*, which is the foundation of all the
good Tapestries made in England, wherein there were but 16
ounces of gold, the whole suit consisting of nine pieces coritaining
479 ells, 1 stick ⅝ Flemish (the materials workmanship and all other
charges being included) cost the undertaker by just account £905
8s. 1½d., which comes to 37s.10d. the Flemish ell or thereabouts,
and will bee made good by particulars beyond contradiction, was
sold to ye Majestie, being then Prince, for £2,000 as containing 500
ells Flemish at £4 the ell, the most part of the monie being
imprested before the worke was finished, whereby was clearly
gained to the undertaker of that manufacture £1094 11s. 10½d.
[Marginal note against above paragraph] 'The accompt of
£905.8s.1½d. was made by Burton, according to Philip de Maecht's
books, being Manager and Director of the Tapestries. The £2,000
was payed by Mr Cunningham upon three privie seals dated
15 Jan 1620 £500; 17 May 1621 £500; 17 March 1621 £1,000 =
£2,000'.

  There were since made and delivered, as by Your Majesties'
Letters Patent of the 10th of May may appeare, three suites of gold
tapestry (which cannot well bee but the former storie of *Vulcan* and
were sold at 6. the ell for £9,000, though the patent neither expres-
seth the storie nor price nor how they were disposed of. For £3,000
whereof the undertaker was satisfied by £500 impressed to him the
10th December 1623 and 2,500 by making five Sergeants at Law.
And for the £1,000 remaining your Majestie granted him an
annuitie of £1,000 p. annum for ten yeares. If that £6,000 and
reasonable consideration for the forbearance were not before payd,
which annuitie for that terme will more than satisfie the £6,000 and
Use upon Use for the forbearance at 8 per cent per annum by more
than £1,661.

  Which three suits could not cost more in proportion than the
former (the gold only excepted) for the workmanship admitted of
small difference, and the silk and yarne were then as cheap or
cheaper bought with readie money than at the first. And if there
bee allowed four ounces of gold to every Flemish ell (which is four
times as much as was thought convenient at first) and is as much
as there is silk in an ell, and may be discerned by eye to be lesse.
The price of the ell, which still keepes but one dimension cannot
come to be above 30s. per medium for there may bee more store

of gold in the borders to give lustre to the work, yet the storie within the borders hath not so much, and where there is most gold there is need of silk and worstead, so that by this computation of the charge thereof, which is conceived to bee made very large, there is clearly gained by the last three suites £4,500 and £1,661 7s. 6d. more if the annuitie bee paied for the full terme. To which if £1,094 11s. 10½d. the cleare gaine of the first suite be added, there hath and will bee gotten by the 4 suites delivered before the patent £7,255 odd monie. Whereby it appears that the manufacture, being so profitable, needed no support. Notwithstanding, by the same patente your Majestie hath granted £1,000 a yeare for ten yeares by way of contribution to uphold the worke. And if any tapestrie hath been sold at the same rate since the Patent, there is so much the more gained from them; and if there have been none, the undertaker by the gaines and support money hath cleared by this Christmasse 1629 £12,255 besides what hath beene gotten by sundie suites before made and solde here, and others exported and £5,000 which he shall receive by £1,000 a yeare hereafter. So that the gaine of that manufacture may be thought to have exceeded anie other in the Kingdom, and that with little or no adventure or hazard, and if it have no more examination or comptrolling put upon it than it hath hitherto, may grow to be exhorbitant especially if any greate workes (such as that of the Apostles) bee to bee made. But if some sworne officer that understandes these workes be appointed by yr Majestie (as is usual in such undertakings wherein yr Majestie hath interest) to keepe books of comptrolling put upon it of comptrolling with the undertaker and Mr Workeman of the Tapestries of all the tapissers wages, materials, charges and payments, which concern the tapistries made for yr Majestie, and of the true measure of the same then should your Majestie pay no more for them than they truly coste and the undertaker rest sartisfied with the £1,000 a yeare gained by your Princely gift and contribution, which with that which hath beene and may be gained by the Tapestries sold to others may be thought sufficient.

Besides, by that course, if at any tyme hereafter your Majestie shall bee pleased to take the manufacture into your own handes your Majestie may with £1600 a yeare or therabouts quarterly imprested and punctually payd have such a suite of Tapestrie mayde for it as hath stood your Majestie in £3,000 the rather in regard your Majestie hath given £1,000 a good while since for the building and furnishing of a House for the making of tapestries. [In margin] 'In April 1627'

Particular interest attaches to the actual cost of making the *Vulcan and Venus* set since it shows how the distribution of work was broken down, and how high were the wages of those involved.

The first Suite of Tapistrye of the *Storye of Vulcan and Venus* contayning 9 pieces was begun the 16 of September 1620 and ended the 5 of June 1622. The whole tyme of the mayking thereof being one yeare and 266 days.

The nine pieces contayning 479 ells 1⅝ sticks cost for the common worke at 17s. the ell   £407 5s. 1½d.

Stick equals one sixteenth of an ell

5.19 Patching up St Paul's

The largely Gothic structure of St Paul's was in a bad state of preservation by the 1620s, complicated by the fact that it also supported the church of St Gregory. On 28 May 1631 the Commissioners for Pious Uses directed a warrant to Inigo Jones to survey the church of St Gregory and come to a decision about the effects it might be having on the cathedral. He replied on 14 June.

According to yor L'ps order I have viewed St Gregorie's church neere St Paul's and doe finde that the said church being in some danger of ruyne, by reason of an Arch wych was decayed, and much of the timbers perished, the parishioners are now repayring of the same.

As for the neerness of the Situacion Joyning to the walls of St Pauls, I conceave it in no way hurtfull to the foundacion of or walls of the said church nor stopping of any lights; they intending to cover with lead the said church wch before was tiled, and so to leave the roof flatt and lower.

Touching the taking away the beauty of the aspect of St Paules when it shall bee repaired and the howses demolished, it butteth on an auncient tower called the Lollards' Tower the wch is answered on the other side with another tower unto wych my lo. Bishopp's hall doth adoine; And I do conceave that neyther of them are any hinderance to the beauty of the aspect of the said church, neither can I find any more convenient part thereabouts for the saide church of St Gregorie to stand in than where it now doth.

Lastly, I, finding a vault now digging for burialls (as the p'shioners say) close to the foundacion of St Paules' church, have forbidden them the proceeding therein, and ordered them to fill the earth in again and make their vault – if they will have it – on the other side, wch they are willing to doe.

All wch I humbly leave to your Lo'ps further consideration,
INIGO JONES

> But then, as now town planning had its problems. The parishioners of St Gregory's petitioned the Privy Council, claiming that 'divers skilful workmen' had certified that the vault would do no harm. The Privy Council rejected their plea and ordered them to stop. This they refused and the Commissioners for Pious Uses instructed Jones in January 1632 to stop them. On 25 February he replied:

May it please yr. lordpps according to yr orders of the 13th of January 1631 I went unto the church of St Gregorye's nere unto St Paule's London to vewe a vaulte wch was formerly begunne to be digged by the pshioners there for the Buriall of the Dead, wch I find to be stopped up accordinge to an order made by yr Lords at the Counsell Table, I also find that the sayd parishoners have made a new vaulte wch goeth outwharte the church from the South of St Paules towards the strete near to Lollards' Tower; 50 foote in length and 14 foote in breadth or thereabouts. And this I caused two sufficiente workmen of His Mats. to viewe and search. And they found that in digginge they had bared 3 settings from the South side of the cathedrall church And St Paules, and upon the East and South side of Lollards Tower 5 foote deepe from the fixte settinge of above the ground, the wch although I cannot say there is any present danger to ye church or tower by digginge the sayd vaulte, yet in my opinion I hold it not fitte that the foundation of soe greate and noble a worke should be underwroughte upon any occasion whatsoeer, seeinge the parishoners might have digged their vaulte towards their churchyard, and not have come nere to the walles of the sayd churche or the tower.

All wch I leave to your Lordps consideracion,
INIGO JONES.

5.20 Art from Madrid

Howard of Arundel's contacts were everywhere. On 7 August 1631 Sir Arthur Hopton, the English ambassador in Madrid, write to him about his dealings with Jan Battista Crescentio, who played to the Spanish court the same role that Inigo Jones played to that of James I.

May it please your Lordship,
By this bearer Hen. Davis I received your Lordship's of the 11th. of May together with your Lordship's directions concerning matters of Art, wherein I will punctually follow your Lordship's order in doeing nothing without the advice of the Marques de la Torre (who is the Cavallero Crescentio, whom your Lordship mentions in your letter) and doeing soe, I shall humbly desire your Lordship to accept of my desire to doe your Lordship service, and not to lay the success to my charge if anything shall happen not to your Lordship's expectation, which I should be sorry for.

The Marquess remembers all the tokens of your Lordship's being at his house at Rome, and confesseth that hee at that time tooke your Lordship for a Principall Gentleman, but if he had then understood of your Lordship's quality, hee would have served your Lordship with whatever was in the city, And now I finde him very ready to do your Lordship all service.

I have receaved uppon the bill of exchange that your Lordship sent me 4,000 Reals in silver.

Uppon making known to the Marquess your Lordship's purpose, he carryed me presently to a paynter's house, and bought these Drawings (which he esteemes to be a good bargaine) which I send by this bearer Davis packed upp according to his own direction. Within a few days after hee sent for mee, and told mee that (uppon a chance) hee was offered certain pictures of great valew, and tould mee that hee hath knowne one of them to have been sould for more than was demanded for three; and with them were to be sold two peeces of *paesi* [bucolic scenes] of Brugle [Bruegel] which he is much taken with, and because they were not to bee had but altogether, I was in some doubt, but observing by your Lordship's letter that you would be contented to laye out the whole sum of your bill and something more, if the Marquess should choose peeces to such a valew, I resolved not to lett them passe, and soe have bought them, and have sent them safe packed up to Bilbao to bee convayed to your Lordship.

The pieces are one of Lionardo da Vinci the beheading of St John the Baptist, which is the principal peece and was brought from Rome by the Conde of Lemos when he came from being Vice-King of Naples. The second is a Passion of Our Saviour by Tintorett. The third is of our Lady with the Saviour in her arms, and St Joseph standing by her, and on her other side St John the Baptist. They are much esteemed here, and the Marquesse assures me they will give your Lordship great contentment.

This inclosed note will give your Lordship an accoumpt of how your money is laid out, and of the overplus that remains due to me, which I beseech your lordship to command to bee paid to Mr Drake, a mercer at the Three Nuns in Cheapside.

The twoe pictures of the life of Ticiano [Titian] are in the possession of the Marquess of Lleganes, and are past recovery.

The picture of Sir Thomas More is in Rome, in the Cardinal Crescentio's house & is nott to be had at any price, as the Marques tells me.

I have been often called upon for the Primer your Lordship speaks of, but will not part with it till I hear from your Lordship, and do not send it nowe because the Marquess likes it not, yet confesseth it to bee a very laborious peece, it will not be had anything under 100 ducats. While I am writing this, the owner comes and tells mee that he cannot leeve it with mee beyond about two monthes, in which time I desire to know your Lordship's resolution.

The gentleman that is the owner of the booke drawn by Leonardo di Vinci hath been of late taken from his house by order from the Inquisition whoe, after some time of restraint at Toledo, was permitted to goe live in Sevill where hee now is. All the dilligence that I can use therein is to procure to have advice when either by his death or otherwise his goodes are to be sould, wherein I shall be very watchful.

I know not whether there be many things of art (worthy your Lordship's haveing) to bee sould in this place, but I observe there are very few buyers of such things, soe that if the choice the Marques has now made for your Lordship shall encourage your Lordship to goe any further with him, your Lordship may command a credit for money to lye here with Peter Ricauts, correspondent, which being alwaies ready wee may better serve your Lordship.

The pictures are sent to Bilbao and are consigned to Mr Robert Oxwicke, a merchant in London, upon whose accompt the ship is here. God almighty blesse your Lordship, according to the prayers of

> Your lordship's humble servant,
> ART. HOPTON.

For the Right honorable, the Earle of Arundell

For drawings	0660 Reals silver.
For a Case of Satten and a cover	0008 Reals silver.

For three pictures	2800 Reals silver.
For 2 little peeces of Brughel	1000 Reals silver
For the Custome of the pictures for taking out an order out of ye Council of Hazienda to precent opening them on the way and for rewards for such as took pains therein	0320 Reals silver.
To a servant of the Marques de la Torres	0028 Reals silver.
To a carpenter according to his bill annexed	0249 Reals brasse.
The carriage of the pictures to Bilbao	0200 Reals brasse.
	5265

Of this received	4000 Reals silver.
Remains due to me	1265.
The exchange	0064.
Some total	1329.
In English money is	£003 30 4s. 0d.

5.21 Setting up an organ

On 26 July 1631 Edward Paler of Thoraldby in Yorkshire was fined £1,000 for the crime of incest with his niece. With admirable promptitude, the Dean and Chapter of the Minster petitioned the King to grant this fine to them 'for repaireing the ruines of the said church and for setting up an organ'. The detailed costs of this throw considerable light on the wealth of material and the amount of craftsmanship involved in such a construction.

Articles of agreement indented, made, concluded and agreed upon the one and twentieth day of March, *anno domini* 1632, between the right worshippful John Scot, doctor of divinitie, Deane of the Cathedrall and Metropoliticall Church of St Peter of Yorke, Phinees Hudson, doctor of divinitie, chancellor and canon residentiary of the said Church; George Stanhope, doctor of divinitie, precentor and canon residentiary of the same church, and Henry Wickham, doctor of divinitie, archdeacon of Yorke and canon residentiary of the said church, of the one party, and Robert Dallam, citizen and blacksmith of London, of the other party, touchinge the makeinge of a great organ for the said Church as followeth.

The names and numbers of the stoppes or setts of pipes for the said great organ to be new made, every stoppe containinge fiftie-one pipes, the said great organ conteigning eight stoppes.

In primis, two open diapasons of tynn to stand in sight, many of them to be chased, £80. Item, one diapason stopp of wood £10. Item two principalls of tynn £24. Item one twelft to the diapason £8. Item, one small principall of tynn £6. Item one recorder to the said small principall £6. Item one, two and twentieth [presumably pipes] £5. Item, the great sound board with conveyances, windchestes, carryages and conduits of lead, £40. Item the rowler board, carryages and keyes £20.

The names and numbers of stoppes of pipes for the chaire organ, every stopp containinge five stoppes.

In primis, one diapason of wood £10. Item one principall of tynn to stand in sight, many of them to be chased £12. Item one flute of wood £8. Item, one small principall of tynn £5. Item one recorder of tynn unison to the voice £8. Item, the sound board, windchest, draweing stoppes, conveyances and conduits £30. Item rowler board, carriages and keyes £10. Item the three bellowes with winde trunckes and iron workes and other thinges agreed thereto £15. Summe totall £297.

It is agreed by and betweene the parties above said, and the said Robert Dallam doth covenant, promise and grant for him, his executors and administrators, to and with the saide Deane and canons residentiary above named, by these presents that he the said Robert Dallam, his executors and administrators shall and will well and sufficiently and workemanlike, new make and finish the said organs in every the particulars before mencioned accordinge to the true intent and meaninge thereof, before the feast of the nativitie of Saint John Baptist which shall be in the yeare of Our Lord 1634. In consideracion of which worke undertaken to be done as aforesaid, the said Deane and Canons residentiary above named have paid unto the said Robert Dallam in hand £100; and doe promise to paye unto him the residue of the said summe of £297, as soone as the said worke shall be finished, and for the more speedie finishinge of the said work the said Dean and residentiaries are pleased to appointe the said Robert Dallam some convenient roome neare unto the said Cathedrall Church to woorke in, and further the said Deane and residentiaries doe promise to pay to the said Robert Dallam towards the expence of himself and servants in comminge from London hither abouyt the saide worke, the summe of £5. In witnes whereof the parties above said to these present articles indented have interchangeablly sett their hands and saeles the daye and yeare above first written.

Two years later John Ranson the Cathedral Chamberlain set out the details of the total expenditure of the fine, which also included £50 for Sir George Radcliffe 'His majesties' atturney in the North', £100 for the court which originally imposed the fine, and £223 8s. 4d. which the Archbishop himself had spent in London on communion plate, cloth of gold and other liturgical accessories.

Paid to William Slater and Daniell Beacocke, painters, upon agreement, by articles, for colouringe and guildinge the screene behind the altar, £24. To Edwarde Horsley for joyninge in the same worke and supplying the wantes of the first undetakers, £5. To Doctor Stanhope, June 8th 1633, which he had paid to Edwarde Horsley for worke done by him in the quire, 20s. More, paid to the saide Edwarde Horsley, Nov. 1633 upon his note for worke done about the screene and alter, 51s. Paid March 2 1632 for eight bookes contaieinge 200 leaves of gold for guilding the screene, at 8s. a hundred 16s. For five bookes 10s. Paid the 14th of March, 1632 foure bookes of gold at 2s. 6d. a booke, 8s. 8d.[?]. Paid, March 31 1633 to Mr Ralph Hindmars, clerke of the workes, which he had payd to a joyner upon his note, for worke done aboute the tables for the commandements and the screene, and for baordes and other materialls used about the same worke £5 10s. 6d. Paid to Robert Metcalfe, joyner, 20 Feb, 1632 for worke done about the said tables and screene, 2s. 6d. More to him, May 11th 1633 upon his note, 9s. 8d. Paid Aprill 13th 1633 to William Wilson, joyner, for worke done at the screene 29s. 3d. Paid May 10th 1633 to Mr Ralph Hindmars, for worke done at the screene by the joyner, plummer and smythe for deales etc. £16 18s. 11d. Paid 11th May 1633 to Mr doctor stanhope which he gave to one of my lord Grace's servants for his paines in giveeinge some directions for the cloathes about the alter, 5s. Paid May 30th 1633 for six pounds of flurry for coloureinge the screene, 3s. summa. £59 4s. 5d. Paid to Mr Robert Dallom of London, blacksmith upon articles with him for makeinge the organ £302. Paid to him when the organ was finished £5. Paid to Richard Feilder, carpenter, upon articles with him, for making the organ loft, £30. Paid to him which he disbursed for leadinge xi loades of tymber to the Church for the said lofte 29s. 6d. Paid Jany. 2nd 1633 to the said Richard Feilder by Mr doctoer Stanhope's appointment, for worke done at the organ loft, more than was covenanted by him viz. for carveing the arches and pendants, 40s. More, paid 29th March 1634, for worke done by him at the organe loft, more than covenant £4 3s. 4d. Paid August 1, 1633, to two labourers for bringing furdeales from Mr Becke's in Thursday markett to the Minster 3s. 4d. Paid to Richard Feilder which he disbursed for leadinge three wayne loads of tymber from Langwith 7s. 6d. Paid 25 September 1633 to Mr Dallom for [undecipherable] of deales bought of Mr Becke £5 10s. To Chr. Richardson, carver, for himselfe and his man, for their charges in comeinge from Durham hither, and bringing their tooles with them, 13s. 4d. Paid to the said Chr. for himself and his man for workeinge at the organ case, at the rate of 20s. a weeke for 52 weekes, viz. the first beginninge the 22nd September 1633, and the last endinge the 18th October, 1634 £52. To him more for worke 20s. 8d. Given to him at his goeinge away the 20th November 1634 by Mr doctor Stanhope's appointment 40s. To Francis Harrison joyner for making the canopy over the organ £6. Paid to him for makinge the gallery aboute the chaire organ, £5. Paide to him for workinge by day about the organ loft and font viz. for cxxxix days and half a day £13 19s. Paid to him for saweinge two deals for the organist's cupboard 6d. Given to him at his goeing away 20s. To William Wilson, joyner upon agreement, for worke and stuffe about the organ case, £46. Paid July 26th 1634 to the said William Wilson for nailes etc. used about the gallery, 53s. 4d. Paid to him for sealing bordes and other things used about the organ loft £3 10s. Paid to him for latte nails 2s. Paid to him for boards etc. and worke done at the funt and canopie over the organ, 22s. 4d. Paide to him for makeinge pyramides for the toppes of the organ, and for other work about the same 9s. Paid 3 May 1634 to Paull Ellerbecke, carpenter for one daye's work 14d. Paid 10 May 1634 to two joyners for worke done about one of the pillars under the organ, 112s. 6d. Paid to Mr Becke, merchant, for 60 deales for the canopy over the organ (whereof 40 were whole and 20 slitt) £3 5s. Paid 11 February 1633 to Mr Robert Dallom which he disbursed for planckes, stoothes [thin spars of wood for use with plaster etc. to make dividing walls] and railes for the canopie over the organ £3 5s. 8d. Paid 21 July 1634 to him for deales for the canopie viz. tenn slitt deales and two whole deales 14s. 6d. Paid to Thomas Haggas and Michael Hindle masons for workeing at severall times at the pillars adjoyning about the organ 35s. Paid May 9th 1634 to Mr Henry Mangy, locksmith, for work done about the organ 35s.; Paid May 9th 1634 to Chr. Mangy, locksmith for iron work about the scaffolds and the canopy over the organ 17s. 8d. Paid October 31 to the said Henry Mangy for worke about the organ 12s. 6d. Paid to Edward Turner, labourer, for working 92 days £3 1s. 4d. To Wm. Mason, labourer for three days 18d. Paid December 11

1633, for the loane of two pulleyes for the organ worke 18d. Paid 8 March 1633 for 300 of tenn penny nailes used about the canopie, 2s. 6d. For two seckes of lyme 15d. For a secke of lyme, 8d. For nailes for scaffoldinge 5d. For 12lbs of candles bought for the use of Chr. Richardson the carver 5s. 7d. Paid 8th of October for borrowing of certaine powles at the Manner and carrying them home again 6s. 8d. To Wm. Davey, pinner, for nailes 2s. 9d. To Mr Babb painter, for work done about the organ £100. Paid 21st of December 1633 to Mr Robert Dallom which he disbursed for collors, callicoe and other things used by Mr Babb and the carver 26s. 6d. To John Powell sevant to Mr Babb, at his goeing up to London, 20s. Paid to Mr Babb, for work done at the font, and the diall of the clocke £10. Paid Dec. 24 1634 to the saide John Powell for painteinge the railes about the font & stuffe used about the same worke £5 16s. 7d. Paid Jan. 9 1634 to Edward Mangy for iron work about the same worke £5 16s. 7d. Paid Jan. 9 1634 to Edward Mangy for iron work about the font £2 1s. Summe of all payments and allowances aforesaid £101 6s. 11d.

5.22 'The privie bardge'

Skill and craftsmanship were deployed in all kinds of fields. In April 1630 John Dessent, His Majesty's Sergeant-Painter sent in the following bill to the Privy Purse.

For repairing, refreshing, washing and varnishing the whole boddye of H.M. pryvie Bardge, and mending with fine goold and faire cullers manye and divers parts thereof as about the Chair of State, the dores and most part of the anticks about the windows, which weare spoyled and deafaced; the two figures at the entrance being most newe cullered, and painted the Mercury and the Lyon, which was fyxed in the Stearne likewyse being new painted and gilt, the tow bardge also being new painted wher it was defaced, the Tafferels in many parts being new gilt and starred with fine Biso which are to be sett on the top of the Bardge, the two figures Justice and Fortitude most agayne being new painted and gilt, the Border and outside of the Bulk being new layde with fine whit, and toused [teased] over with greene, according as the custom here-tofore as also the owards belonging to the Tow Bardge being in number 36 new painted and cullered.

Som £38 13s. 4d.

5.23 Carpenters or joiners?

The problem of the delimiting lines between carpenters and joiners had been rumbling on since the Middle Ages. On 25 September 1632 a Committee appointed by the Lord Mayor and Aldermen of the City of London, which had been set up finally to decide on the issue delivered a judgement which incidentally throws considerable light on how woodwork was evaluated at the time.

That these works next following do properly belong to the Joyners:

1. Item Imprimis. All sorts of Bedsteads whatsoever (onlie except Boarded bedsteads and nayled together).
2. Item all sorts of Chayres and Stooles wych are made with mortesses or tenants.
3. Item all tables of Wainscoate, Wallnutt or other Stuffe glewed with frames mortresses or tennants.
4. Item all sortes of formes framed made of boards with the sides pinned or glewed.
5. Item all sorts of Chests being framed, dufftailed, pynned or Glewed.
6. Item all sorts of Cabinetts or Boxes dufftailed, pynned, joyned or glewed.
7. Item all Sorte of Cupboards framed dufftailed, pynned, glewed, or joyned.
8. Item all Sorte of presses for weareing apparell, Mercers, Silkmen Haberdashers, Gouldsmiths, Millenors or Napkin presses being pannelled, dufftailed, pynned, or Glued.
9. Item all Sorts of Wainscott and sealing of houses and setling made by the use of two Iages.
10. Item all sorts of Shopp windowes that are made for Ornament or beautie which cannot be made without glew.
11. Item all Sorts of Doors, framed pannelled or Glewed.
12. Item all hatches framed or Glewed.
13. Item all pewes, pulpitts and seates with the deskes belonging to them Panelled, or Glewed.
14. Item all Sorts of frames upon Stalls being Framed or Glewed.
15. Item all frames for pictures, Latesses for Scrivenors, or the Like.
16. Item all lyning of Walls for Wainscott.
17. Item all signe boards of Wainscott or carved.
18. Item all worke, whatsover invented, or that hereafter shall be invented, made by one or two iages with the use of all manner of nayles.

19. All carved workes either raised or Cutt through or sunck in with the ground being taken out being wrought and cutt with carving Tooles without the use of Plaines.
20. That all Coffines made of Wainscott but if they bee made of other woode wee conceive fitt that the makeing thereof by left indifferent either to the Joyners or the Carpenters.

And these works following doe properly belong to the Carpenter.

1. Item. Imprimis all Drapers Tables, all Tables for Tavernes, Victuallers, Chandlers Compting House tables made of Deale, Ealme, Oake, Beeche or other woode nayled together, without Glue, except all sorts of Tables either nayled, framed or glewed, being moveable.
2. Item all Sesterne stools, washing stooles, bucking stooles and all other Stooles whatsoever, that are to be headed with Oake, Elme, Beeche, or Deale and footed with square and rounde feete: Except all framed Stooles glued or pinned.
3. Item all sortes of Frames made of Elme, Oake, beeche, or deale heads with Square or round feete, or with Feete of Boards or plankes with sides of boards to be nayled or boarded so as they bee not turned feet.
4. Item the Laying of all flowers of Elme or Oake, except such floores of Elme or Oake as are grobed, which we conceive properly to belong to the Joyners, and if the Floore be of Deale, we conceive Fitt that the workmaster be left at Liberty to make choyce whether he will have a Carpenter or Joyner to lay the same.
5. Item the dividing of warehouses and Chambers, and other roomes unwainscotted and unpanelled with slit or whole deales, or any other materialls, Wainscott excepted and except all particions grooved, glued, battened, or framed.
6. Item the Shelving of all Roomes unwainscotted and unpanelled with Seates and bracketts, except worke in Studdies which we conceive to be left indifferently to both Companies.
7. Item all Signe Boards not made of Wainscott not gelded or carved.
8. Item we conceive fitt that the setting up of all Pillars or balasters for lights in a particion of what wood soever if the particion be made by the Carpenters doe belong to them, but if the particion bee of the Joyners making then do belong to them.
9. Item all galleries in Churches and other places unless of wainscott or pannelled or carved.

10. Item the shelving in a Kitchin with Racks for Spitts and other racks for hanging upp of furniture except all peeles.
11. Item the laying of plates and floores for pewes in Churches if they be Laid with Oake or Elme but if with deale then the workmaster to be at his choice whether he will have a Carpenter or a Joyner to lay them.
12. Item all frames of Screenes for Halles or other Roomes not made of wainscott glewed carved or pannelled.
13. Item And lastly wee think fitt that the Iage be indifferently used by the Carpenters so as they use the same in the making and perfecting such worke only as before expressed to belong unto them and not otherwise all which we leave to grave Judgements of this Honourable Court.

Martin Lumley, Hugh Hammersley, James Cambell, Nicholas Rainton, Thomas Moulson, Martin Bond, William Hollingshead.

(Edward Basil Jupp, (*An Historical Account of the Worshipful Company of Carpenters*, London 1848, pp. 148–50)

5.24 The furnishings of a noble household

On 6 December 1632 four of his servants drew up an inventory of 'the goods, chattels, plate, lynnen, carpetts, hangings, beddinge and household stuffe of the right honourable Henry, Lord Peircie [Percy] late Earle of Northumberland'. It provides an illuminating picture of the contents of a great house – in this instance Petworth in Sussex, one of the several Percy residences. The following extracts are selective.

IN THE WITHDRAWEING CHAMBER. Item five peeces of imagerie hangings; one Persian carpet for the court cupborde; one Turkey foote carpet; two great elbow cheyres, twelve high stooles, seaven longe cushions, all of velvet fringed with silke and silver fringe, and covered with cases of yellow cotton, one drawing table; one court cupboarde; one payre of brasse andyrons, tonges and fireshovell with brasses, and one yron backe. (Total £79)

IN THE GREENE BEDD CHAMBER. Item six peeces of hanginges imagery, the story of Hester; one bed of mingled colour perpetuanie gray, vizt. five curtaines, headcloth, double vallence, fower sleeves, one counterpoint, all laced with a broade mingled colour lace of silke; five taffetie curtains sarcenet ashecolour; one feather bedd and boulster; one downe pillowe; one pair of fustian blanketts; one pair of woolen blanketts; one holland quilt; one canvas mattresse; two greene cloth carpets; two backe chairs; foure greene stooles fringed with greene silke fringe; one square table; one court cupboarde; one payre of brass andyrons, tonges and fyreshovell with brasses, and one yron backe. (Total £73 10s.)

IN THE PRESSE AT THE SIDE OF THE WARDROBE. Item three longe cushions of blacke velvet, laced with silver lace; two lardge windowe curtaines of greene baysel; one old greene cloth carpett with silk fringe; two paires of fustian blanketts, one paire of them olde; three of the best sorte of woolen blanketts; one lardge crimson rugg, old and stayned, belonginge to the yellowe printed saye bedd; two olde greene ruggs; one peece of the finest sort of hangings, herbagrie; one old peece of herbagrie with half-moones; one peece suitable to the hangings in the new buildings; two peeces of forrest worke; five peeces of hanginges bought of Sir Joecelyn Peircie; eighteen peeces of verders; five old peeces of olde hangings, ymagery upon a table neere to the presse of divers suites[1] (Total; £88 15s.)

IN HIS LORDSHIPPS CHAMBER: Item, hangings of forrest worke, six peeces, one stammell bedd with a broade silke lace of crimson and ashe collour, vizt. five curtaines, testerne, headcloth, balls and sleeves, double valliance called and fringed, one counterpoint; one elbowe chayre, foure high stooles and two lowe stooles, twoe carpetts, all suiteable to the bedde; fyve ynner curtaines of crimson taffita sarcenet; one downe bedd and boulster; one paire of fustian and one paire of woollen blanketts; two holland quilts, whereof one of them ould; one canvass mattresse; one bedsted, the pillers covered and the bottom of lathe; one ould foote carpett; one paire of brass andyrons, shovell and tounges with brasses; one yron backe; redd bayes cases for the stoole and chayres; one paire of snuffers; one paire of bellowes; one chamber pott; one table, and one court cupboard. (Total £125 6s.)

IN THE LOWER GALLERY IN THE NEW BUILDING. Item fourteene peeces of hangings of herbadgery with half moones; seaven Turkey worke stooles; two greene carpetts; one lardge mapp of the world;[2] two wainscott tables; one paire of brasse andyrons, fire shovell and tongues with brasses, and one yron backe. (Total £42 16s.)

IN THE DYNEING PARLOUR. Item twelve items of hangings of herbadgerie with halfe moones; eleven Turkie worke stooles; two

---

1 Possibly a cassone–type piece of furniture.
2 Probably the 'Leconfield World Map' which was sold at the Petworth sale in 1928, but is now in the possession of the Duke of Northumberland.

greeche back chairs; two leathern stooles; one foote carpet of Turkie worke; one frame of a cooche bottomed with girthweb; one round table; one side table; one court cupboard; one pewter cysterne; one payre of playeinge tables with ivorie men; andyrons of cast yron; one paire of snuffers; one baise curtaine and curtaine rodd. (Total £54 9s.)

IN THE LIBRARY. Item chests of bookes of all sorts, fiftie two, and to fill twelve small chests besides; one cuppboarde with mathematicall instruments; one large globe[3] and two small ones; pictures, videlicet twelve Turkes, twenty foure Emperours, Hercules' laboures twelve, of all other sorts of pictures twenty eight; three dozen of wainscott stooles; two large pictures of St Lawrence and the Maccabees; one ovall table; one other table with a foulding frame; two little wainscott tables; one nedstede corde and matt; one very large globe, whyte, not perfitted; two yrons in the chimney; one yron backe and two curtain rods. (Total £581 3s.)

5.25 Various purchases ·

Nicholas Stone Junior kept a careful account of his money on his trip to Italy in 1638, and his accounts record his daily purchases in Florence and Rome. Some are of a sartorial nature, 'for a payre of showes 7 iulios 5 biocs' but others are of a more cultural nature, and suggest the interests of a young man of artistic inclinations in Italy. (Walpole Society, vol. vii, 1919).

Florence.
From Sept. 22 1638.
The booke of prints of the show upon the water entertainment of the Great Duke's mother in the year 1608. 1 liver 5 cratts.
a paper book to draw in, and paper, 3 livers.
the prints of the masque att the marrage of this Duke Ferdinano, 1 liver.
11 loose paper or prints   2 livers 8 cratts.
for a drawing of a horse   1 liver 4 cratts.
The booke of Euclid Geometrie   3 livers, 4 cratts.
the booke of the ruines of Rome   4 livers.

---

3. This is still at Petworth.

Rome.
October 1638.
for a quire of gray drawing paper 1 iulio 5 biocs.
for a paper and red cholke   2 iulios.
for blake chalke   2 biocs.
for a cloth for my picture to be painted on   7 biocs.
November 9th
for prints of Spanioletta   7 iulios.
for a print of Ralphyell   4 biocs.
April 1639.
for two feete and one hand caste in plaister of the Grekes Venus.
4 iulios. for two plaister heads of Venus and Cicero 7 biocs.
June 30.
according to my father's direction in his letter I bought the booke
of Archytecture of Domenico Fontana to be sent for England for
Mr Kinsman being very scarcely to be found; cost 25 iulios.
August 8.
for paper 19 sheets   1 bioc.
August 29th
for baking of a modell of the Satyre Martius 3 biocs.
Sept. 10.
for 4 prints of archytecture   2 biocs.
Sept. 14th
for 2 bookes of temples antike   1 iulio 4 biocs.
Sept. 26th
for baking a clay moddle of a woman 1 bioc.
for a booke of the fountaines of Rome 3 crownes.
for seven prints and a little booke of sights of gardens 3 crowns.
October 19th
for Archytecture of Vitruvius 1 crown 8 juilii.
December 27th
For a plaister head 4 julii.
February 10th
for a plaister figure representing a Bacchus moulded from the
antique which stands in Marquesse Iustinianus Pallace 6 crowns.
March 20th 1640.
for a place to stand to see the Jew burnt in Campo Fiora 1 julii.
June 11th
To the Garda Roba of Medices [Villa Medici] 6 julii; to an old
woman for opening the door 3 julii.
July 17th
For prints of Alberta Dura 5 julii.

August 24th
for two plaister heads, one of Venus, the other of Cicero 7 julii.
for a plaister leg moulded from the antique 4 juilii.
for a Baccus in plaister 6 crowns.
for lute strings to send to Ligorne 2 crowns.
for some prints of Alberta Dura the passion 5 julii.
for 113 small peeces of severall sorts of marbles to send for England
according to my father's orders.

5.26 Charles I as a connoisseur

> The king's interest in paintings was not merely an acquisitive lust,
> and Richard Atkyns, in his *The Original and Growth of Painting; how
> Gentlemen may and some do know the Mystery of Arts* (1667) recounted
> the following story.

This excellent Prince, hearing of some rare painted Heads, amongst
other pictures sent from Rome, sent Sir James Palmer to bring
them to Whitehall where there were present divers Picture Drawers
and Painters. He asked them all of whose hand that was? Some
guessed at it; others were of another opinion, but none was posi-
tive. At last said the King, 'This is of such a man's hand, I know
it as well as if I had seen him draw it, but is there just one man's
hand in the picture?.' None could discern whether there was or not,
but most concluded there was but one hand. Said the King, 'I am
sure that two hands have worked at it, for I know the hand that
drew the heads, but the hand that did the rest I have never seen
before.' Upon this a Gentleman that had been in Rome about ten
years before, that he saw this very picture with the heads unfinisht
at that time, and he heard his brother, who had staid there some
years after him, say that the Widow of the artist who painted it,
wanting money got the best painter she could to finish it, and make
it saleable. This is a strong proof of the King's Judicious skill in
so critical a point of art.

5.27 The Golden Gate for England?

Sir Thomas Roe saw part of his duties as English Ambassador in
Constantinople as endeavouring to secure for one or other of his
patrons and customers such as Howard of Arundel and the Duke
of Buckingham, as many of the treasures of that city as he could
lay hands on. One of his most ambitious schemes was to acquire

the celebrated statues of the Golden Gate, supposed to have been
erected to commemorate the victory of Theodosius over Maximus
(AD 388). In a letter to Buckingham, Roe described his activities
in this direction, emphasising by implication, the vogue for
classical sculptures amongst those able to afford them and illuminating his own standards.

Wee have searched all this cytte, and found nothing but upon one
gate, called antiently *Porta Aurea*, built by Constantine, bewtified
with two mighty pillars, and upon the sides and over yt, twelve
tables of fyne marble, cutt into hystoryes, some of very great
relevo, sett into the wall, with small pillars as supporters. Most of
the figures are equall, some above the life, some less. They are, in
my eye extreamly decayed, but Mr Petty doth so prayse them, as
he has not seene much better in the great and costlye collections
of Italye. Your grace, for better enformation, may view his letters
to the earle of Arundell, how he hath allowed them. There are of
them but sixe that are worth the taking downe, the others beeing
flatt Gothish bodies, layme, and of later tymes, sett up only to fill
place of the other sixe. Two, in my opinion (though Mr Petty likes
them) want much of excellence, great, but brute, and, as I conjec-
ture, are some storye of Hercules, not mentioned in his labors.

The fower, to which I have most affection, are fuller of woorke.
The one is, as we comment, an Endymion carelessly sleeping by
his sheepe; Luna descending from the sckye, with a torch in her
hand, representing night, and a Cupid hovering in the ayre, to
signify her love. This last gentleman is much misused, and wee can
only know him; the other two want some parts, and the faces
battered; but the general proportions are both brave and sweete.

The next is a hystorye I understand not, eyther of some race or
game; in the middest is a horse, a young man running nayked by
yt, and reaching to pull another off. Some other figures ther are,
which I remember not; but it hath beene a peice of great bewtye
and art; the relivo so high that they are almost statues, and doe but
seeme to stick to the ground; some legges and other parts, standing
holow off, are broken and lost; yet, in the whole it hath a show
of rare antyqyty.

The third is a Pegasus, with the Nimphes or Muses; one
representing the famous Pirenne powring out water. These figures
are manie, but less than half the life, as I judge them; not so much
defaced, standing hygh, and to a vulgar eye like mine of most grace
and pleasure.

The last is a Satyre, sckipping between a Hercules or a wilde man, and a woman which she seemes to avoid; the one hath a whip in his hand, the other a pott of water held behind her. These are above the life, and rather grate and stately than delightfull, but generally they have suffered much violence, both by weather and spight.

Yet they are so well esteemed by this gentleman that I will endevor to gett them. Promise to obteyne them I cannot, because they stand upon the ancient gate, the most conspycuous of the cittye, though now mured up, beeing the entrance by the castel called the Seaven Towers, and never opened since the Greek emperors lost yt.[1] To offer to steale them, no man dares to deface the cheefe scate of the grand signor, to procure them by fayvour is more impossible, such envy they beare to us. There is then onlie one waye left; by corruption of some churchman to dislike them, as agaynst their lawe, and under that pretence to tayke them downe to bee brought into some pryvate place, from whence, after the matter is cold and unsuspected, they may be conveyed. I have practised this for the foure and am offered to have it done for 600 crownes. To send them home, chested and freight, with some other bribes att the water syde, may cost 100 more. This is a great price, and yet I rather despayre of obteyning them.
Constantinople 1/11 May 1625

> (Samuel Richardson, *Negotiations of Sir Thomas Roe in his Embassy to the Ottoman Porte*, London 1740, p. 386)

5.28 Learned in antiquities

The extent to which antiquarianism, in all its meanings, had been accepted in Stuart England is suggested by Thomas Nabbe's *The Bride* of 1640.

Friend. You are learned in antiquities?
Horten. A little, sir,
I should Affect them more, were not tradition
One of the best assurances to show
They are the things we think them. What more proofs,
Except perhaps a little circumstance
Have we for this or that to be a piece
Of Delphos' ruins? Or the marble statues

---

1 There was a belief that when the Christians eventually retook Constantinople, they would enter by this gate.

Made Athens more glorious when she was supposed
To have more images of men than men?
A weather-beaten stone with an inscription
That is not legible, but through an optic,
Tells us its age.
For Antiquity I do not store up any under Greecean.
Your Roman antiquities are but modern toys
Compared to them. Besides, they are so counterfeit
With mouldings, 'tis scarce possible to find
Any but copies. My trial's such
Of anything I doubt, all the imposters
That ever made antiquity ridiculous
Cannot deceive me. If I light upon
Ought that's above my skill, I have recourse
To those whose judgement at the second view
(If not the first) will tell me what Philosopher's
That eyeless, noseless, mouthless fellow is.

6 The Civil War and after

Puritanism and affluence

6.1 Parliamentary iconoclasm

The zeal against imagery which was part of the Puritan ethos had political and religious origins, and was imposed on the nation by an Ordinance passed by Parliament in 1643.

That before the first of November all altars and tables of stone shall be utterly taken way and demolished, and all communion tables removed from the east end of every church, chapel, or place of public worship, and be set in some other fit and convenient place or places of the body of the church or chapel; and all rails whatsoever which have been erected near to, or before, or about any altar or communion table in any of the said churches or chapels, shall before the said day be taken away, and the ground of every such church or chapel or other place of public prayer, which has been within these twenty years raised for any altar or communion table to stand upon, shall before the said day, be laid down and levelled as it was before; and all tapers, candle-sticks and basins shall before the said day be removed, and taken away from the communion table, in every church, chapel, or place of public prayer, and not be used again afterwards.

And all crucifixes, images and pictures, of any one or more persons of the Trinity, or of the Virgin Mary, and all other images and pictures of saints, or superstitious inscriptions in or upon any of the said churches, or other places belonging to the said churches, or churchyards, or in any other open place shall before the said first of November be taken away and defaced by the proper officers that have care of such churches. And it is further ordained that the walls, windows, grounds, and other places that shall be broken, impaired, or altered by any of the means aforesaid, shall be made up and repaired in good and sufficient manner in all and every said parish churches, chapels or places of public prayer belonging to the parish, by the church-wardens for the time being, and in any cathedral or collegiate church or chapel, by the dean, or sub-deans, and in the Inns of Court by the benchers Land readers of the same, at the cost and charges of all and every such person or persons, body politics or corporations to whom the charge of repairs does usually belong, upon penalty of forty shillings to the use of the poor, for the space of twenty days after such default; and if such default be made after December 1st, the justice of the peace of the county or city shall have power to perform it. Providing that this Ordinance shall not extend to any image picture, or coat of arms in glass, stone, or otherwise in any church, chapel or churchyard set up by, or engraved for a monument of any king, prince or nobleman, or other dead person who has not commonly been reputed or taken for a saint.

6.2 'To be taken away and defaced'

How this Ordinance was put into practice can be seen from the fact that on 19 December, 1643 the Earl of Manchester, commander of the Parliamentary Forces, issued a commission to William Dowsing Gent. in the following terms.

Whereas by an ordinance of the Lords and Commons assembled in Parliament bearing date the 28th of August last, it is amongst other things ordained yt. all Crucifixes, Crosses & all Images of any one or more psons of the Trinity, or of the Virgin Marye, & all other images & pictures of Saints & superstitious inscriptions in or upon all & every Churches or Chapells or other place of publique prayer, Churchyards or other places of publique praier belonginge, or in any other open place shall be before November last be taken away and defaced, as by the said Ordinance more at large appeareth. And whereas many such Crosses, Crucifixes, other superstitious images and pictures are still continued within the associated Counties in manifest contempt of the sd. Ordinance, these are therefore to will and require you forthwith to make your repaier to the several associated counties & put the sd. Ordinance in execution in every particular, hereby requiring all Mayors, Sheriffs, Bayliffs, Constables head boroughs & all other his Majesties Officers and lovelinge subjects to be ayding and assisting you, whereof they may not faile at their peril. Given under my hand and seale this 19th of December 1643.

Manchester.

To Willm. Dowsing Gent.
& to such as hee shall appoint.

> (*Proceedings of the Suffolk Institute of Archaeology*, vol. vi, 1888)

> Dowsing not only carried out his mission with a zeal bordering on psychosis, but kept a journal in which he recorded his activities. Typical are the following entries, the first describing the activities of one of his deputies Francis Jessup, the second his own.

GORLESTON. In the chancel, as it is called, we took up twenty brazen inscriptions, *Ora Pro Nobis* etc.; broke twelve apostles carved in wood, and cherubims, a Lamb with a cross, and took up four superstitious inscriptions in brass in the North chancel, *Jesu filii Dei miserere mei* etc.; broke in pieces the rails, and broke down twenty two popish images of angels and saints. We did deface the font and a cross on the font; and took up a brass inscription there with *Cuius ainmae propitietur Deus*, and 'Pray for ye soule' in English. We took up thirty superstitious brasses. Ordered Moses with his rod and Aaron with his mitre to be taken down. Ordered 18 angels off the roof, and cherubims to be taken down, and nineteen pictures on the windows. The organ I brake; and we brake seven popish pictures in the windows – one of Christ, one of Saint Andrew, another of Saint James etc. We ordered the steps to be levelled by the parson of the town, and brake the inscription *My flesh is meat indeed, and my blood is drink indeed.* I gave orders to break in pieces the carved work, which I have seen done. There were six superstitious pictures, one crucifix, and the Virgin Mary with the infant Jesus in her arms, and Christ lying in a manger, and the three kings coming to Christ with presents, and three bishops with their mitres and their crosier staffs, and eighteen Jesuses written in capital letters which we gave orders to do out. A picture of St George, and many others which I remember not, with divers pictures in the windows, which we could not reach, neither would they lend us ladders, so we left a warrant with the Constable to do it in fourteen days. We brake down a pot of holy water, St Andrew with his cross, and St Catherine with her wheel, and we took down the cover of the font, and a triangle for the Trinity, a superstitious picture of St Peter and his keys, an eagle and a lion with wings. In Bacon's isle was a friar with shaven crown, praying to God in these words *Miserere mei* etc. which we brake down. We brake a holy water font in the chancel. We rent to pieces a hood and surplices. In the chancel was Peter pictured in the windows, with his heels upwards and John the Baptist and twenty more superstitious figures, which we brake and I H S the Jesuits' badge, in the chancel windows. In Bacon's isle twelve superstitious pictures of angels and crosses, and a holy water font and brasses with superstitious inscriptions. And in the cross alley we took up brazen figures and inscriptions *Ora pro Nobis*. We brake down a cross on the steeple, and three stone crosses in the chancel, and a stone cross in the porch. UFFORD. In the chancel we brake down an angel; 3 *Orate pro anima* in the glass, and the Trinity in a triangle, and Twelve Cherubims on the roof of the church, and nigh a hundred JESU MARIAS in capital letters, and the steps to be levelled. And we brake down the Organ Cases and gave them to the Poor. In the church there was on the roof, above 100 JESUS MARIA in great capital letters, and a crosier staff to be brake down in glass, and above 20 Stars on the roof. There is a Glorious cover over the Font, like a Pope's triple crown, with a Pelican on the Top, picking its Breast, all gilt over with Gold. And we were kept out of Church above 2 hours, and neither Churchwardens William Brown nor Roger Small that were enjoined these things above three months before had not done them in May, and I sent one of them to see it done, and they would not let him have the key. And now neither the Churchwardens nor William Brown, nor the Constable James Tolklove and William Gardener the Sexton would not let us have the key in two hours time. New Churchwardens Thomas Stanard, Thomas Stroud, and Samuel Cadham of the same town said 'I sent men to rifle the church', and Will Brown the old Churchwarden, said 'I went about to pull down the church, and had carried away part of the church.'

Dowsing's experiences at Gorleston and Ufford suggested that not everybody accepted happily the destruction of so much of the legacy of the past. In 1646 the author of *Querela Cantabrigiensis, or a Remonstrance by way of Apology for the banished Members of the late flourishing University of Cambridge by some of the said sufferers* (Oxford 1646) complained:

And one who calls himself John [sic] Dowsing and by virtue of a pretended commission goes about the Country like a Bedlam breaking glasse windowes, having battered and beaten downe all our painted glasse, not onlie in our Chapples, but (contrary to order) in our publique schools, College Halls, Libraryes and Chambers, mistaking perhaps the liberall Arts for Saints (which they intend in time to pull down too) and having (against an Order) defaced and digged up the floors of our Chappells, many of which had lien so for two or three hundred years together not regarding the dust of our founders and predecessors, who likely were buried there, compelled us by armed Souldiers to pay 40s. a college for not mending what he had spoyled and defaced or forthwith to go to prison. We shall need to use no more instances than these two to show that neither place, person, nor thing hath any reverence or respect among them.

6.3 Caring for pictures

It is symptomatic of the real interest Charles I had in paintings – even though they were portraits with a family interest – that when he escaped in 1647 (albeit for a short time) from his Parliamentary captors, he left the following note for one of them.

11 November 1647

COLONEL WHALEY

I have been so civilly used by you and Major Huntingdon that I cannot but by this parting farewell acknowledge it under my hand, as also to desire the continuance of your courtesy, by your protecting of my household stuffe and moveables of all sorts, which I leave behind me in this house [Hampton Court] that they be neither spoiled or embesled; only there are three pictures here which are not mine that I desire you to restore; to wit my wives picture in blew, sitting in a chair you must send to Mistris Kirke; my eldest daughter's picture copied by Belcam to the Countess of Anglesey, and my lady Stannop's picture to Cary Rawley [Carew Raleigh]. There is a fourth which I had almost forgot, it is the original of my eldest daughter (it hangs in this chamber over the board next to the chimney) which you must send to Lady Aubigny. So being confident that you wish my preservation and restitution, I rest,
Your friend CHARLES R.
PS I assure you it was not the letter you shewed me today that made me take this resolution, nor any advertisement of that kinde. But I confess that I am loath to be made a close prisoner under pretence of securing my life. I had almost forgot to desire you to send the black grew bitch to the Duke of Richmond.

6.4 Histories

Round about 1648 Edward Norgate wrote his *Miniatura or The Art of Limning* which exists in various MS editions in the Bodleian, the British Library and elsewhere, and was first edited and published by Martin Hardie in 1919 (Oxford, Clarendon Press). It is full of practical and theoretical information about painting.

Histories in Lymning are strangers in England till of late Yeares it pleased a most excellent King to command the copieing of some of his owne peeces, of Titian, to be translated into English Lymning, which indeed were excellently performed by his Servant, Mr Peter Olivier.

And I verely beleeve that all excessive comendation given by Giorgio Vasari in his prolixe *Historie Delle Vite dei piu Excellenti Pittori* to don Julio Clovio, an Italian Lymner, might with much more truth and reason have been given to this our Countreyman, whose abilities in that Art are infinitely superiour to the other. Now it is possible in their sleight washing way to express that excellent colouring which we see frequently in Titian and his excellent Imitation.

Of whose hand there remaines a peece of Lymning, being the History of the buriall of our Saviour Christ begun by Mr Isaac Olivier the father, but by that royall comand finisht by the Sonne, of which, for the rare art, Invention Colouring and Neatness may be said as Giorgio Vassari speakes of Don Jovio Clovio, *onde possian dire che habbia superato in questogdi antichie moderni e che sia stato a tempi nostri un nuovo Michel Angelo.* In Lymning of Histories there is requirable more study of designe, more varietie of Colouring, more Art and invention, and more patience and diligence than in any picture by the Life, which is the work of a few dayes onely, whereas the Madonna of Mr Isaac Olivier's Lymning cost him two yeares, as he himself told me. For where in one and the same peece there are many Figures, and those of differing complexions and ages, wherein the passions of the mind as well as the lyneaments of the body are to be exprest, there must bee in the workman a prompt and ready hand, and Invention (easier to tell than to teach) well read in story, and something of the Poet (whereof they say painting is a silent species) besides the observance and Imitation of those excellent Italian Masters in this Art soe much and celebrated by the Virtuosi. Of this kind is Raphael, da Vinci, Perin del Vago, Don Julio Clovio, and many others too long to repeate, whose works, if they came in your way cannot but be of singular use for the attainment of a laudable proficiencie in this kind of painting, which methinks differs from picture by the Life as much as a Poet from an Historian, or, if you please Ariosto from Phillip de Commines. The one doth truly and plainly *narrare rem gestam*, tells very honestly what he said and did, the other describes such a Ruggiero or Orlando as hee could wish it to be. Yet let not your imitation of others prejudice your own Genius, which perhaps may find out ways better for you than those of other mens' making.

However do not affect the extravagant humer of those our late Dutch Masters that soe powder their workes with blewish, greenish and purple shadowes, never to be seene in the Life, nor anywhere else, for any good or wise workman to ymitate. Nor are our Italians free from this affectation. Old Bassano, in his time and way an excellent master, yet was he soe affected as to stuff his peeces with pots, pans, tubs, kettles, Cats and Dogs that his great Hystorye of the Deluge in St James seems rather a confused or disordered Kitchin than Noah's Flood, nor can you find water enough in all that Deluge to drowne his Dog.

But to leave this digression, I conceave there are fower kinds of Colouring generally to be used in story viz. of young Infants, of faire Virgins, women of middle age, and old men and women of salow, leane and lether Complexions; and in every one of these the judicious workman will vary his Colouring according to the severall Complexions, and not like Horatio Getilesco, whose gray freemason Colouring is all of a temper, and must serve for all complexions, sexes, ages or whatsoever.

Infants, being of a soft, tender and thin Complexion, the Crimson and fine colourred blood appearing through the skin almost transparent, is best exprest by White, Lake and a little Min, the shadows thin, faint and subtile; the Cheekes, Lipps, Fingers, elbows and knees dasht with a soft tincture of Red more discernable in those than in any other parts of the body. To speak particularly of the severall shadowes requisite in this worke would be a long and large peece of impertinency. It may be referred to your judicious observance of what hath bene said before.

Their Draperies and Lynnens to be made fine and faint, without those hard and strong touches, as are for those of men. In like manner and with little difference are Virgins and young women to be made, their muscles, arteries and other eminenties of their bodyes easily appearing and gently exprest with sweetness of shadowes sutable for that sex.

The browne and ruddy Complexion of mens' Bodyes is made with a little White, English and burnt oaker, and a little Min; the deeper shdows with Cologne Earth, Pinke and lake, and the Mezzo Tinto as was before mentioned – onely in this of Historie you have leave and roome to expresse the freedom of Invention in the varietie of coluring, not onely of Faces and Complexions but of Habits, Perspective and Lanscape, ruines and such like additionall Ornaments, to illustrate the story you endeavor to expresse.

An excellent shadowe for old men's bodies is Pinck, Lake and Cologne Earth; in the deepest, lake pinke and a touch of Ivory, which will make an excellent glowing shadow. The expression of the severall wrinkles and furrowes in the face, hand &c of people extreamly aged, with their dark and shady eyes and melancholly aspect will afford you subject enough wherein to show your Invention and spirit, specially if it sute with the story that those salow complexioned people I speak on be seconded and set off by others of the other sexe of beauty and perfection.

For draperies and apparrelling your personages, I doe not find that the best painters have been anything carefull to sute draperies to the age or yeeres of the represented, but rather the Contrary, which the Dutch call *schilderachtich*, or painter-like, and what they think may best illustrate their worke.

To vest St Peter in yellow and blew (frequently done almost everywhere) may better shew the painters faire Colours than sound Judgement. The Blessed Virgin is most commonly represented in purple and Azure; St John by Elshaimer and others, in greene and scarlet (I mean the Evangelist, for the baptist is never without his hairie hide) the Lamb with Agnus Dei. The rest of the Apostles, though never so venrable, you will find vested in greene, purple, azure, or as you please Mr Painter. For making these draperies there are two wayes, viz, the Itallion way, which is to work in the apparrell and foldings in a washing manner without a ground, working in with the point of the pencill with stips, pricks or punches, as it were a graine in the work, yet soe when all is done you shall see the parchment quit through the Colour, which is but a slight and single old device. The better and more sollid way certainely is the English; that is to lay a full ground of substantiall Colour flat and faire, so that you may both highten and deepen upon it. For example, if your Drapery must be blew, lay the ground faire Bise, smooth and even, deepen it with Lake and Indico, and let the hightning be faire white, with which you may lightly touch the extremities of the light places, letting the blew ground appeare between the light and the shadow, which will make your worke shew with greater roundness and luster than any other way. The same course you are to take with all Draperies of what colour soever, laying a flat Mezzo tinto and hightening and deepening thereon, ever remembring that your light and shadow be never reconcild nor meete together, but let the middle colour ever appeare.

6.5 'A fair renown'

Henry Stone, son of Nicholas the sculptor, studied painting abroad, made copies of works by Van Dyck and others, and displayed those qualities of mind and ability recorded by his brother on a tablet in St Martin-in-the-Fields' churchyard. It has subsequently disappeared, but was recorded by George Vertue early in the eighteenth century.

To the memory of Henry Stone of Long Acre, painter and Statuary, who haveing passed the greatest part of 37 years in Holland, France and Italy, acheaved a fair Renown for his Excellency in Artes and Languages and departed this Life on the 24 day of August An.D. 1653, and Lyeth buried near the Pulpit in this church.
His friends bewail him thus:

> Could arts appease inexorable fate,
> Thou had'st survived this untimely date;
> Or could our votes have taken place, the sun
> Had not been set thus at its glorious noon;
> Thou shouldst have lived such statues to have shown,
> As Michael Angelo might have wished his own;
> And still thy most unerring pencil might,
> Have raised his admiration and delight,
> That the beholders should inquiring stand
> Whether was Nature's of the Artist's hand.
> But thy too early death we now deplore,
> There was not art that thou couldst live to more,
> Nor could thy memory by age be lost,
> If not preserved by this pious cost;
> Thy name's a monument that will surpass,
> The Parian marble or Corinthian brass.

John Stone, to perfect his Fraternal affection, erected this Monument.

6.6 'An ingenious wife'

Between 1671 and 1681 Charles Beale kept a series of memoranda
books, containing in the words of Vertue, a friend of whose had
bought them from a book stall in the 1720s, 'many affairs of business and family accounts &c but the most remarkable is the daily
imployments of his most ingenious wife Mrs Beale concerning her
painting and drawing from the life, or from famous paintings'. The
following extracts give some idea of the nature of the art world
of late seventeenth-century London, its preoccupations and its
attitudes.

20 April 1672. Mr Lely was here meaning, I think, to see Mrs Beale
and her workes, with Mr Gibson and Mr Skipwith and
commended very much her coppy that she had made after Sir
Anthony Van Dyke's own picture, also her coppy after Our
Saviour praying in the garden &c after Antonio Da Corregio. Her
copy in little after Endimion Porter his lady and 3 sons, he
commended extraordinarily and said (to use his own words) it was
painted like Van Dyke himself in littel and that it was the best
coppy he ever saw after Van Dyke. Also he liked very well her two
Coppyes in great of Mr Porter's littel son Phil. Both he and
Mr Gibson commended her other workes.

Mr Lely told me at the same time as he was most studiously
looking at my Bishop's portrait of Van Dykes after I chanced to
ask him how Sir Anthony could possibly divise to finish, in one
day, a face that was so exceedingly full of work & wrought up to
so extraordinary a perfection. I believe, said he, he painted it over
14 times. And upon that he took occasion to speake of Mr Laniere's
picture by Sir Anthony Van Dyke which, said he, Mr Laniere
himself told me, he satt seaven entire dayes for it and that he
painted upon it all those seaven dayes, both morning and afternoon
& only intermitted the time they were at dinner. He said likewise
that tho' Mr Laniere sat so often & so long for his picture yet he
was not permitted so much as once to see it, till he had perfectly
finisht ye face to his own satisfaction. This was the pycture which
being showed to king Charles ye first caused him to give order that
V. Dyke should sent for over into England.

19 April 1672. My dearest painted over ye 3rd time a side face; this
Mr Flatman liked very well.

Mrs Beal's price for pictures from the like; a head £5; half length
£10.

24 April 1672. My most worthy friend Dr Tillotson sat to Mr Lely

for his picture for me. He drew it first in chalk, rudely and afterwards in colours, and rubbed upon that a littel colour very thin in
places for the shadows and laid a touch of light upon the height-
ening of the forehead. He had it done in an hour's time.

June 5 1674. Dr Tillotson sat about three houres to Mr Lely[1] for
him to lay in a dead Colour of his picture for me. He, apprehending the colour of the Cloth upon which he painted was too
light, before he began to lay on the flesh colour he glazed the whole
place where the face and haire were drawn in colour over thin with
cullens earth and a little bonn black, as he told us, made thin with
varnish.

July 22. Mrs Beal painted her own picture.

1 August. Dr Tillotson sat to Mr Lely about three houres for the
picture he is doing for me. This is ye 4th time, and I believe he
will paint it (at least touch it) over again.

His manner in the painting of this picture this time especially
seemed strangely different both to myself and my dearest heart
from his manner of painting the former pictures he did for us. This
wee thought was a more conceiled misterious, scanty way of
painting than the manner he used formerly, wich wee thought was
a far more open & free, and much more was to be observed and
gained from the seeing him painting then my heart with her most
carefull marking learn from his painting.

Delivered to Mr Lely I ounce of ultramarine at £2 10s. od an
ounce towards payment for Dr Tillotson's picture.

Sept. 30th. I carried my two boys Charles & Batt. to Mr Lely's &
shewd them all his pictures, his rare collections.

Oct. 1. I went again to Mr Lely's and shewd Mr William Bonnett
the same excellent picturers. This person was a learner there.

I have paid Mr Lely towards the pictures of Col. Brooke
Bridges & Dr Tillotson, which he is doing for me, by severall
parcells of Lake, of my own making which he sent for 20 August
1671, and Ultramarine and money £13 12s.

Received this yeare for pictures done by my dearest heart
£202 5s.

Aug. 1674. Mr Lely dead-coloured my son Charles' picture. Took

---

1. The Beales, as became apparent from the entry for January 1677/8 commissioned
Lely to paint pictures in their own house, so that they could study his techniques
(Walpole Society).

a drawing upon paper after an Indian gown which he had put on his back, in order to the finishing of the drapery of it.

November. Borrowed of Wm. Chiffinch Esq., eleaven of His Majestie's Italian drawings.

1674. Received this yeare for pictures done by my dearest £216 5s.

4 June 1677. Mr Commer ye painter being at our house told my dearest as a Secret that he used black chalk ground in oil instead of blew black, and found it much better and more innocent Colour

January 1677/8. Mr Lely came to see Mrs Beale's paintings, several of them he much commended, and upon observation said Mrs Beale was very much improved in her painting. No doubt this was due to much practice and study such as by this time she had had, and the coppys from severall of Van Dyke's paintings and Lely's, besides the opportunity of seeing Mr Lely paint several pictures from the life. Both her sons Batt. and Charles learnt to draw & paint.

Mrs Beale painted Sir William Turner's picture from head to foot for our worthy friend Mr Knolleyes. He gave it to be set up in the hall at Bridewell, Sir William having been president in the year he was Lord Mayor of London.

16 February 1676/7. I gave Mr Manby 2 ounces of very good Lake of my own makeing & 1 oz. ½ pink in consideration of the Land-skip he did in the Countess of Clare's picture.

Borrowed six Italian drawings out of the King's collection for my sons to practise by.

1677. This year Mrs Beal had great business, amongst people of quality, as well as others, and the account cast up at the end of the year for her paintings done mostly from the life, money received £429.

13 January 1680/81. The King's half-length which I borrowed of Sir Peter Lely was sent back to his executors to Sir Peter Lely's house.

1681. My wives' pictures this year amounted to £209 17s.6d.

6.7 Tapestry exports

British tapestry achieved a considerable reputation abroad in the seventeenth century, and an inventory of Louis XIV's furnishings *c*. 1675 recorded no less than some 140 pieces including the following, some of them probably sold by royalists during the Civil War.

A set of high-loom tapestries of wool and silk enhanced with gold of English making representing part of the *Acts of the Apostles*, designed by Raphael in a border having a column wound round with branches of vine and a boy at the foot climbing to grasp bunches of grapes. In the upper border are a coronet and arms with the Order of the Garter of an English lord.

A set of tapestries of wool and silk enhanced with gold of English making, designed by Raphael, representing the story of *Vulcan* in a tawny border with branches, six medallions of gilded bronze colour, and a blue oval sustained by two angels in the middle of the border at the top, and in the middle at the foot a shield in grisaille.

One piece of tapestry of silk and wool of English making, enhanced with gold, designed by Albert Dürer, representing *The Feast given to our Saviour by Simon the Leper.*

A set of tapestries in wool and silk of English making, representing in Gothic figures *The Triumphs of Petrarch* in six pieces, furnished with bands of linen in a border with a blue ground and ornamented with angels, grotesques, festoons of flowers and trophies of arms, with three inscriptions in Latin verse.

A set of tapestries in wool and silk of English making, partly Gothic and partly in the style of Lucas van Leyden and Albert Dürer in design, composed of pieces of different sorts, representing something of the *History of King Priam*, leaves, flowers, grapes and other fruit on a brown background.

A set of high loom tapestries of English making of wool and silk designed in the manner of Lucas van Leyden representing *The History of Joseph* in a border of small flowers, fruits and foliage on a brown ground at the top and in the corners.

A set of high loom tapestries of wool of ancient English making, with Gothic figures representing *The History of King Ahaseurus* explained by inscriptions on a red ground at the top and bottom of each piece without border. Formerly in six torn pieces which have been cut and made into 7 pieces.

6.8 Small statues

By the middle of the seventeenth century a fashion had grown up for small statues for domestic use. One of the main producers of this kind of ware was the Florentine Francesco Fanelli, who spent most of his working life in London, and about whom Vertue wrote the following note (*Notebooks*, vol. iv).

Fanelli, the Florentine sculptor, who livd and dyd in England made many small statues, models, and cast them in brass, which he sold to many persons that were curious to sett on tables, cupboards, shelves, by way of ornament. Many were bought by William Duke of Newcastle and left at Welbeck where the Earl of Oxford found them. This Fanelli had a particular genius for these works and was much esteemed in K. Charles I time, and afterwards. Many of these statues I have seen at Lord Oxford's, namely:
2 Horses standing, one a capriol; a horse full gallop; a horse ambling; a Cupid on horseback; a Turk on horseback; a Centaur with a woman; a horse eating, standing; St George on horseback, the dragon dead; another St George combatant with the dragon.

6.9 A Yorkshireman in Florence, 1657

Foreign travel was becoming an accepted part of a cultivated man's education, and the process was given an added impetus by the Civil War and its aftermath, which forced many who, whilst being royalists did not want to compromise themselves, to take evasive action by going abroad. Typical of these was the twenty-year-old John Reresby of Thybergh Hall in the West Riding, who had recently come down from Cambridge. He set off in 1654, and having dawdled through France and Switzerland, arrived in Florence in April 1657. His observations on the Palazzo Pitti reveal the kind of attitude which must have informed many such travellers. His concern with prices is not without interest (*The Memoirs and Travels of Sir John Reresby Bart*, London 1813).

The palaces are numerous; the first and best is that of the Grand Duke, built by one Pitti, a burgher of Florence, to outvie one Strozzi, another wealthy citizen, who had before erected the then best in town, but so inferior to this, that the middle court would contain the other palace, and its windows carry proportion to the doors of that of Strozzi. But the founder, ruining himself by such expense, was forced when finished to sell it to the Great Duke's predecessors, who since, by enlarging it at both ends, have certainly made it the finest in Europe. The outside is of freestone, wrought after the Tuscan manner; the stones of a vast size; the front of the house is three hundred paces long. On one side of the court lies a square loadstone four yards about, every way; on the other a large fountain, well stored with fish.

The first storey, besides others, hath four and twenty chambers on a floor in a right line, as large as ordinary halls, the doors opening so directly upon one another, that you have an easy perspective from the first to the last; these contain the whole length of the house, of three hundred paces as before mentioned.

The furniture was but ordinary; the season beginning to grow hot, the walls were but covered with sarsnet, or bare. The guard-robe was well provided with rich furniture; the hangings for one apartment were wrought in pearls; the beds, chairs and stools embroidered with gold, drawn into small wire. These cost five thousand crowns; all the pictures in the house, but especially those in the upper rooms, are of great value, drawn by hands of the most knowing men in that art of all ages.

The statues are both excellent and numerous, many of them made by Michael Angelo, the most famous of our modern carvers.

The lower rooms, all wrought with mosaic, are very spacious, and so cool, by reason of the holes in the floors through which the air breathes out of the caves below, that the Great Duke makes choice of them in the greatest heats for his apartments.

In some by chambers we saw several mathematical instruments; one demonstrating the perpetual motion, another that either by land or sea, if you see the fire of a cannon, or hear the report, and desire to know at what distance it is from you, it infallibly shows it, as they say, to a quarter of a mile, by the knocking of a leaden plummet, fastened by a string against the wood of the instrument; with many others.

The gardens on the left hand are inclosed from the rest, where grow all sorts of flowers, according to the season.

At the end are two grottos or aqueducts, the water springing out of several pipes at once.

On another side is a mount, from whence within the compass of this large garden, appear hills, valleys, walks open and covered, fountains, water-works casting up streams into the air in various shapes, groves, mazes, wildernesses, hedges of myrtle and cypress, lemon and orange trees, and all sorts of greens.

From the Duke's palace is a secret passage or gallery of half a mile long, which brings you to the Palazzo Vecchio, or the Old

Palace, so called because therein all the consultations and assemblies were made whilst Florence continued a Commonwealth. There we saw many spacious rooms, in one of which is kept the Duke's plate, contained in twelve large cupboards; there is one service of massy gold; a saddle given by the Emperor to the Great Duke, all embroidered with pearls and diamonds; rich Turkish saddles, the stirrups of massy gold; Turkish knives of great value (for their bravery in Turkey consists much in a pair of rich knives). In another room was the altar in making, which when finished is intended for St Lawrence's chapel; it is all covered with several coloured stones of great value, inlaid with plates of gold as broad as a man's finger, with fair crystal pillars. In the middle is represented Christ and the twelve apostles at the Passover. It is not finished by much, and the charge of what is done said to amount to three millions, if you believe them.

This palace adjoins to the Duke's gallery, so famous for the possession of all rarities that either his or his predecessors' interest or treasure could procure; it is supported on great pillars of stone; underneath are the courts of justice.

In the gallery hang the pictures of the most famous princes, both of Europe and of other parts of the world; there are many old Roman statues, and one of Cupid, in touchstone.

In the first room joining to the said gallery is a table of paragona or touchstone, inlaid with precious stones of all colours, representing divers sorts of flies, birds and flowers, to the life, valued at five thousand crowns; an amber candlestick with large branches of coral, as it grows naturally; a cupboard of divers things, turned in ivory, by the most knowing of that art in Germany; a fine landscape in needlework, with divers other pictures and landscapes, and little statues, carved in a black sort of stone, and of hideous shape, which were heathenish idols.

The second room, as the former, hung with landscapes, and other pictures of value, affords you the sight of two pillars on each side the door, of oriental transparent marble; a table in which is the draught of the town of Leghorn, in precious stones, ships and galleys in the harbour, which cost twelve thousand crowns; an ebony cabinet beset with jewels.

In the third are a couple of globes, of a greater circumference than an ordinary millstone; the statues of the Caesars in a fine carved wooden frame [Bas-reliefs].

The fourth, besides many little statues and pictures different from those of the former rooms, has a table made by the present

Duke of touchstone, set with rubies, emeralds, pearls and some diamonds, joined together to represent flowers and birds in their natural colours; it is esteemed worth one hundred thousand crowns; most incomparable statues of men and other creatures in brass, with an artificial rock of mother-of-pearl; a man's head, cut out in a Turkey stone; a nail, half of it converted out of iron into gold by the philosopher's stone; a cabinet of ebony, covered with agates, emeralds and amethysts, within it the passion of our Saviour, and the twelve apostles is excellently figured in yellow and white amber; it cost two hundred thousand pounds; two cupboards of all sorts of glasses and agate cups, inlaid with gold; in fine the whole room is valued at two millions of crowns.

In the fifth room is the armoury of the Grand Duke, where are all descriptions of arms for men and horses, richly gilt, as well as those in use amongst us as in other nations, both now and in former ages. There you see Turkish darts, targets, rich scymatars and knives, with all their rich equipage for themselves and horses; Hannibal's headpiece, weighing but seven pounds, and yet musket-proof; 'tis made of Corinthian brass; Charlemagne's sword; the King of China's vest; a scarlet gown of parrots' feathers, worn by the women of quality in India; two sceptres of agate; Turkish and Persian swords, with pistols in the hilts; an Italian lock; the skin of a horse presented to the Great Duke by the Duke of Lorraine; his mane is yet there to be seen of three ells and a half long; a loadstone, which takes up sixty pounds of iron, and a long fowling piece, curiously carved, the barrel of gold.

As Italy has produced more knowing men in the arts of architecture, carving in stone and wood, and limning, than other nations; so there is no city which has so abounded in them as Florence, where artists, to gratify their foundress, have each of them beautified her with some extraordinary piece or other, whence she is called Fiorenza Bella, or Beautiful Florence.

6.10 The taste of Pepys

Samuel Pepys was deeply interested in painting; when he died he possessed 61 pictures, of which 33 were portraits. He was an avid collector of prints, leaving his collection to Magdalene College, Cambridge, as part of his library. He was interested in, and had an eye for architecture. His judgements, expressed in what he imagined would ever remain an arcane language, were spontaneous, and sincere. He was also a typical man of his time. Despite

the general accessibility of his *Diary*, especially in the superb edition
edited by Robert Latham and William Matthews, it is impossible
to document the tastes of late Stuart England without reference to
his reactions.

February 27th 1660. Mr Blayton and I took horse, and straight to
Saffron Walden where at the White Hart, we set up our horses and
told the maister of the house to show us Audley End House; who
took us on foot through the park, and so to the house, where the
housekeeper showed us all the house, in which the stateliness of
the ceilings, chimney pieces, and form of the whole was exceedingly worth seeing. He took us into the cellar where we drank most
admirable drink.

May 19th 1660. Went to Scheveling . . . Here I met with Mr Pinkny
and his sons, and with them went to The Hague in our way
lighting and going to see a woman that makes pretty rock-work
[miniature grottoes] in shells &c which, could I have carried safe,
I would have bought some of. At The Hague we went to buy some
pictures, where I saw a painting done upon woolen cloth, drawn
as if there were a curtain over it, which was very pleasant, but dear.
Another pretty piece of painting I saw, of which there was a great
wager laid by young Pinkny and I whether it was a principal or
a copy; but not knowing how to decide it, it was broke off, and
I got the old man to lay out as much as my piece of gold came to;
and so saved my money, which had been 24sh. loss I fear.

November 19th 1660. After dinner I went by water to London to the
Globe in Cornehill, and there did chose two pictures to hang up
in my house [probably from John Cade, a stationer], which my
wife did not like when I came home, and so sent the picture of
Paris back.

February 8th 1664. So to Cades the stationers, and there did look
upon some pictures which he promised to give me the buying of,
but I found he would have played the Jacke with me; but at last
he did proffer me what I expected, and I have laid aside 10 or 12 l.
worth, and will think of it, but I am loath to lay out so much money
on them.

August 8th 1664. So home to dinner, and after dinner to hang up
my fine pictures in my dining-room, which makes it very pretty.

March 23rd 1666. I out by six a clock by appointment to Hales's,
where we fell to my picture pretty hard, and it comes on a very
fine picture, and very merry; pleasant discourse we had all the
morning while he was painting. Anon comes my wife, and Mercer

and little Tooker. And having done with me, we all to a picture-drawer's hard by, Hale carrying me to see some landskip of a man's doing, but I did not like any of them, save only a piece of fruit which was indeed very fine.

April 18th 1666. Allen and I to Mr Lillys the painters, and there saw the heads, some finished, and all begun of the Flagmen [flag-officers] in the late great fight with the Duke of Yorke against the Dutch. The Duke hath them done to hang in his chamber, and very finely they are done indeed.

June 18th 1666. Thence to Hales's to see how my father's picture goes on, which pleases me mighty well, though I find again, as I did in Mrs Pierce's, that a picture may have more of likeness in the first or second working than it shall have when finished; though this is very well and to my full content; but so it is. And, contrarily, mine was not so like at the first, second or third sitting as it was afterwards.

June 20th 1666. Thence to Faythorne the picture dealer, and there chose two or three good Cutts to try to Vernish. And so to Hales to see my father's picture, which is now near finished, and is very good.

December 16th 1666. Lay long talking with my wife in bed. Then up with great content, and to my chamber to set right a picture or two, Lovett having sent me yesterday Santa Clara's head, which is very fine. And now my closet is so full-stored and so fine as I would never desire to have it better.

December 21st 1666. So home to dinner, and spent the whole afternoon in putting some things, pictures especially, in order and pasting my Lady Castelmayne's print on a frame, which I have made handsome, and is a fine piece.

August 10th 1668. So away to Cooper's, where I spent the whole afternoon with my wife and girl, seeing him make an end of her picture, which he did to my great content, though not so great, I confess, as I expected, being not satisfied with the greatness of the resemblance, nor in the blue garment; but it is most certainly a rare piece of work as to the painting. He hath 30 l for his work, and the crystal and gold case comes to 8l. 3s. 4d. which I sent him this night that I might be out of debt.

January 22nd 1669. Up and with W. Hewer to White-hall, and there attended the Duke of York; and thence to the Exchange, in the way calling at several places on occasions relating to my feast tomorrow, on which my mind is now set – as how to get a new looking-glass for my dining room, and some pewter and good wine against tomorrow. And so home and had the looking-glass set up; cost me 6l. 7s. 6d. And here at the Change met with Mr Dancre, the famous landscape painter, with whom I was on Wednesday; and he took measure of my panels in my dining-room, where in the four I intend to have the four houses of the King, White-Hall, Hampton-Court, Greenwich and Windsor.[1]

January 23rd 1669. After dinner my Lords to cards, and the rest of us sitting about and talking and looking on my books and pictures, and my wife's drawings which they commend mightily.

February 1st 1669. So meeting Mr Povey he and I away to Dancres to speak something touching the pictures I am getting him to make for me. And thence he carried me to Mr Streeters, the famous history painter over the way, whom I have often heard of, but never did see him before; and there I found him and Dr Wren and several virtuosos looking upon the paintings which he is making for the new Theatre at Oxford; and indeed they look as though they would be very fine, and the rest thinks better than those of Rubens in the Banqueting House at Whitehall, but I do not fully think so – but they will certainly be very noble, and I am mightily pleased to have the fortune to see this man and his works, which is very famous, and he is a very civil little man, and lame, but lives very handsomely. So thence to Lord Bellasses, and meet him within; my business only to see a chimney-piece of Dancre's the glaring of the light, which I must have done within my room, and indeed it is pretty, but I must confess I do think it is not altogether so beautiful as the oyle pictures; but I will have some of one and some of the other.

March 3rd. Thence to Dancres the painter's, and there saw my picture of Greenwich finished to my very good content, though the manner of distemper doth make the figures not so pleasing as in oyle.

April 11th 1669. After dinner my wife and I out by coach, and Balty with us, to Loton, the landskip-drawer, a Dutchman living in St James's Market, but there saw no good pictures, but by accident he did direct us to a painter that was then in the house with him, a Dutchman newly come over, one Everelst, who took us to his lodging, close by, and did show us a little flower-pot of his own doing, the finest thing that ever I think I saw in my life – the drops of dew hanging on the leaves, so as I was forced again and again

---

1. On 31st March Pepys decided to have a view of Rome instead of the picture of Greenwich.

to put my finger to it to feel whether my eyes were deceived or not. He doth ask £70 for it. I had the vanity to bid him 20l. but a better picture I never saw in my whole life, and it is worth going 20 miles to see.

6.11 Plasterers versus painters

> In the tightly demarcated world of the guilds, controversies were always arising about activities which involved more than one craft. Gold-beaters were involved in painting and book-binding; plasterers used colours. In 1664 the Painter-Stainers' Company put a bill before Parliament to regulate their relationship with the latter, in which it was stated that the Plaisterers were allowed to lay colours 'plain as necessary about the seilings of rooms and such like . . . the Plaisterers being altogether unskilful in that art, which tends towards the scandal and disgrace of the Art of Painting within our English Nation'. Due to the opposition of the Plaisterers the Bill did not pass, and the Painter-Stainers had in the meantime produced these significant arguments against their opponents.

We challendge far from beyond the first scale of plastering, and their trade of plaistering that cullors originallie, and especiallie, do and ought to belong to Payntors and Steynours, which were sometime two companies, and united in the year I of Edward IV, and that cullors are proper to their art, being mingled or tempered with oyle or size, and laid on with brush or pencil, for no payntors can be without cullors.

And the Plaisterers in the begynning did not use paynting or culloring, but have lately intruded themselves into that mysterie. And the Paynters' facultie was to cullor posts, teymber, windows and such like, and the Steynors' cloth. Wherefore it pleased your Majestie of your prerogative by your Highness' letters patent the Paynters encorporacion to forbid all (after the manner of paynting) to laie cullors in London, the liberties and suburbs, except they have been apprenticed to a Paynter by the space of seven years at the least.

The Paynters desire that the Acte may passe for them for they hold that all cullors and culloring belong to them, being mixed and tempered and laid on as aforesaid, and especiallie for that the Plaisterers have intruded themselves into that arte and do go about by all meanes to depryve them of all these workes, as well laid in oyle and sise, suggesting their masters did use the like.

It is moste untrue that by lawe it is free for any artificer to use cullor in oyle or sise, as is alledged, for the statute saith that none shall use any manual occupacion but that which he hath been apprenticed to by the space of seven yeares. Paynting and culloring is a manual occupacion; therefore everyone that hath not been apprenticed to that by this space of seven yeares, ought not to use it as the Plaisterers do. And that the Plaisterers did use it beyond the memorie of man is utterlie untrue, and therefore your Majestie for the better establishing that in the Paynters hath appropriated the same to them as proper to their art, forbidding others to use it as above said, and no Company but the Plaisterers do use it. The countrie is at libertie, for the Acte is but to extend to London, the liberties and suburbs.

The Paynters do not worke until the Plaisterers have done, neither do they work upon scaffolds, but upon lathers [ladders] and will perform also their work before the Plaisterers shall make their scaffolds, and therefore there shall be no chardge to builders as the Plaisterers suggest. For in the King's houses and all other stately buildings lathers were used by the Paynters, and not scaffold, and therefore they abuse the House with their untrue and false suggestions.

Now they will worke for xvid. a daie, but before they would not worke under xxd. and xviiid., and yet the Paynter shall better deserve xviiid. the daie than the Plaisterer, for the Plaisterer doth fill up the chink carfes of the tymber with lyme and searde, which the Payntor doth with oyle and cullors, and so it is more bewtifull and more dureable.

> In a further document the Painter-Stainers described themselves in greater detail.

The Paynter-Steynors are incorporated, in which corporation all persons are forbidden to paint (except gentlemen for their pleasure) but such as have been apprenticed and brought up with a Painter-Steynor for seven years (23 Eliz.) The Payntor-Steynors are in number above 400 householders within and about the City of London, besides their families, the greater part not attaining to the perfection of workmanship, have usually lived on the grosser part of the sence as painting upon timber, stone, iron and such like, which the Plaisterers now intruding into the said science of painting, have utterly taken awaie; but our Bill now exhibited is only to restrain them from oyl cullors . . .

It is to be noted that in every house throughout the Realm the Plaistere is set on work, and the Paynter not in one house amidst a hundred, and also it is to be lamented that when the grosser works of painting be taken away, men that grow in years and have been workmen, their sight waxing dim, and their hands beginning to shake, they have no work to get their living by, but only by painting with those flat colours, which relieveth not only the aged, but all such poor men as have not the capacity to attain to workmanship.

6.12 Wren in France

In July 1665 Christopher Wren made his only visit abroad, to France. In the preceding month he had written to Ralph Bathurst, President of Trinity College, Oxford, for whom he was designing an extension to the college, that he would appeal for guidance 'to Mons. Mansard, or Signor Bernini, both of whom I shall see in Paris within the fortnight'. The visit clearly made a great impression on him, and his reactions are recorded in *Parentalia*, compiled by his sons, and published in 1750.

In the year 1665 Mr Wren took a Journey to Paris, where at that Time all Arts flourish'd in a higher Degree than had ever been known before in France, and where there was a general Congress of the most celebrated masters in every Profession, encourag'd by royal Munificence, and the Influence of the great Cardinal Mazarine. How he spent his Time in that Place will in Part appear from a short Account he gave by Letter to a particular Friend, wherein he returns Thanks for his Recommendations of him to the Earl of St Albans, who in the Journey and ever since had us'd him with all Kindness and Indulgence imagineable, and made good his Character of him as one of the best Men in the World. He then proceeds to the following Particulars; I have, says he, busied myself in surveying the most esteem'd Fabrics of Paris, & the Country around; the Louvre for a while was my daily Object, where no less than 1000 Hands are constantly employ'd in the Works; some in laying mighty Foundations, some in raising the Stories, Columns, Entablements &c with vast Stones by great and useful Engines; others in carving Inlaying of Marbles, Plaistering, Painting, Gilding &c Which altogether make a School of Architecture, the best probably at this Day in Europe. The College of the Four Nations is usually Admir'd, but the Artist has purposely set it ill-favouredly, that he might show his Wit in struggling with an inconvenient Situation.

An Academy of Painters, Sculptors, Architects and the chief

Artificers of the Louvre, meet every first and last Saturday of the Month. Mons. Colbert, chief Superintendant, comes to the Works of the Louvre, every Wednesday, and, if Business hinders not, Thursday. The Workmen are paid every Sunday duly. Mons. Abbé Charles introduc'd me to the Acquaintance of Bernini, who shew'd me his Designs of the Louvre, and of the King's Statue. Abbé Bruno keeps the curious rareties of the Duke of Orleans' library, well filled with excellent Intaglios, Medals, Books of Plants, and Fowls in Miniature. Abbé Burdello keeps an Academy at his House for Philosophy every Monday Afternoon. But I must not think to describe Paris, and the numerous Observables there in the compass of a short Letter.

The King's Houses I could not miss; Fontainebleau has a stately Wildness and Vastness, suitable to the Desert it stands in. The antique Mass of the Castle of St Germains & the hanging Gardens are delightfully surprising (I mean to any Man of Judgement) for the Pleasures below vanish away in the Breath that is taken ascending. The palace, or if you please the Cabinet of Versailles, call'd me twice to view it; the Mixtures of Brick, Stone, blue Tile and Gold make it look like a rich Livery; Not an Inch within but is crouded with little Curiosities and Ornaments; the Women, as they make here the Language and Fashions, and meddle with Politicks and Philosophy, so sway also in Architecture; Works of Filgrand and little Knacks are in great Vogue; but Building certainly ought to have an Attribute of Eternal, and therefore the only Thing uncapable of New Fashions. The masculine Furniture of Palais Mazarine pleas'd me very much better, where there is a great and noble Collection of antique statues and Bustos (many of Porphyry) good Basso-relievos, excellent Pictures of the Great Masters, fine Arras, true Mosaiks, besides Pierres de Rapprt in Compartiments and Pavements; Vases on Porcelain painted by Raphael, and infinite other Rarities, the best of which now furnish the glorious Appartment of the Queen Mother at the Louvre, which I saw many Times.

After the incomparable villas of Vaux and Maisons, I shall but name Ruel, Courances, Chilly, Essoane, St Maur, St Mande, Issy, Meudon, Rincy, Chantilly, Verneul, Lioncour, all of which, & I might add many others, I have survey'd, and, that I might not lose the Impressions of them, I shall bring you almost all France on paper, which I found by some way or other ready design'd to my Hand, in which I have spent both Labour and some Money. Bernini's Design of the Louvre I would have given my Skin for, but the old reserv'd Italian gave me but a few Minutes' View; it was five little Designs on Paper, for which he has receiv'd as many thousand Pistoles. I had only Time to copy it in my Fancy and Memory; I shall be able by Discourse and a Crayon to give you a tolerable Account of it. I have purchased a great deal of *Taille-Douce*, that I might give our Countrymen Examples of Ornaments and Grotesks, in which the Italians themselves confess the French to excel. I hope that I shall give you a very good Account of all the Artists in France; my Business now is to pry into Trades and Arts, I put myself into all Shapes to humour them; 'tis a Comedy to me, and tho' sometimes expenceful, I am loth yet to leave it'.

6.13 A merchant's tastes

The increasing wealth and self-confidence of the mercantile class were beginning to assert themselves in terms of collecting *objects d'art* and furnishings, often of an exotic nature. Typical of these was Evelyn's friend Bohun, a visit to whom he recorded in his *Diary*.

August 31st 1671. After evening service to see a neighbour, one Mr Bohun, related to my son's late tutor of that name, a rich Spanish merchant, living in a neat place which he has adorned with many curiosities, especially several carvings of Mr Gibbons, and some pictures by Streeter.
July 30th 1672. Went to visit our good neighbour Mr Bohun [Lea, Kent] whose house is a cabinet of all elegancies, especially Indian. In the hall are contrivancies of Japanese screens instead of wainscot, and there is an excellent pendule clock inclosed in the curious flower-work of Mr Gibbons in the middle of the vestibule. The landscapes of the screens represent the manner of living and country of the Chinese. But above all his lady's cabinet is adorned on the fret, celing and chimney piece with Mr Gibbons' best carvings. There are also some of Streeter's best paintings, and many rich curiosities of gold and silver as growing in the mines. The gardens are exactly kept, and the whole place very agreeable and well watered. The owners are good neighbours, and Mr Bohun has also built and endowed a hospital for eight poor people, with a pretty chapel, and every possible accomodation.

6.14 Daily concerns

Architect, scientist, eccentric, hypochondriac, secretary of the Royal Society, Gresham Professor of Geometry, Surveyor of

London, Robert Hooke (1635–1703) typified a certain kind of seventeenth-century man. And, like Pepys, he kept a diary. Largely concerned with the state of his bowels and similar matters, it lacks a great deal of the human interest of that of his endearing contemporary, but its often laconic entries relevant to the fine arts probably typify the kind of degree of involvement shared by many of his contemporaries.

1672

February 21st. Bought 4 landskips for 30sh. of Upholstere in Lothbury.

1673

April 9th. Brought from Arundell Library 3 volumes of Vasari of the Lives of the painters, Cesari Ripa of Iconologia, Rubens' Life etc.

September 16th. Mr Sibber [Cibber, the sculptor] gave me a picture of Toby and his fish.

1674

January 7th. Paid Fenwick for 12 chairs at 13sh. and Smyrna carpet £5 5s.

February 17th. Saw Mr Dwight's English china. Dr Willis, his head. A little boy, a hauke in his fist. Severall little Jarrs of severall colours, all exceeding hard as flint. Very light, of very good shape. The performance admirable, and outdoing any European potter.

April 3rd. Wat Dole shewed me a plate of his doing in metzotinto. I thought it had been done in Sir Chr. Wren's way, but it proved to be done by squeezing a file on it with a presse. I suppose it may be much better done by Sir Chr. Wren's powder.

May 16th. Back to Mr Knipe's at Little Chelsey. Saw his oyster shell windows [a kind of transparent porcelain]. He told me that a chinois told him that porcellane was made of the same claye of which our Tobacco pipes are made, and that for the preparing thereof they used to mix it with water in a tub, and by putting in the bark of a certaine plant fermented it in tubbs close stopped. Then scummed off the finer part from the top and wrought it in vessels. He was always champing scurvy grasse like the indian betele.

June 29th. Invented the way of printing with the common press pictures made with Pins. An invention of Great Use.

December 22nd. At picture shop Globe Exchange. At Pitz, saw *Hortus Estinensis* which hast 368 plates of plants. Inprised at £9. Well worth it at 3d. a leaf.

1675

August 5th. Delivered in the bill of the Painter. Painting pales in white once is worth 4d. Guilding with Gold 2d. per leaf. Painting in oylc 3d. a time; veining 2d., 3d. or 4d. per yard; painting over a balcony 4sh.

1676

January 18th. Smoked with Sir Christopher. With him in his coach to Bloomsberry. He told me of the man at Prince Rupert's painting pictures in white marble. His way is thus. He first soaked the stone in oil of [indecipherable] then mixed his severall colours which were all juices of plantes inspissated and mixed with an other oyle, then painted on the stone cold, as with distemper, then evaporated away the first oyle by burying the stone in hot sand. He had no goode black. His best was burnt grease.

April 29th. At Faithornes. Saw the Raphere [Raphael] of St Paul. Saw outcry of pictures at Sommersett House.

July 20th. At home. Mr Knox here. Showed him picture box. He lent me *L'Art de Peinture* de C. A. Fresnoy, second edition A Paris 1673.

1677

June 10th. I made a table of my prints. 7sh. of St Peters; 10sh. Tarrpipans Jesuits church; 1s. 8d. Piazza del Populo; 1s. 3d. chiesa di St. Maria della pace; 1s. 3d. two prospa of the Louvre; 2s. 3d. Bernini's St Pieter; 5sh. Merchants Hall at Paris; 5sh. St Peters Chair; 6s. 3d. Forneseys Jesuit church at Rome; 3s. 4d. Scavanas large sheets of the Jesuit church at Paris 10sh. fifteen of Perills prospects 3s. 1½d. 200 view of Israells 22s. 8½d.

August 8th. Knox told way of cleansing pictures by scraping 1 ounce of castle sope in a pint of water and mixing it with flower long enough to make a batter, whych laid on a dirty old picture, and let lye for ¼ of an hour till dry, when washt would fetch off with water and a fine soft brush all the dirt stains and varnish and leave the picture as fair as if new.

6.15 Painterly sensibilities

By the seventeenth century the concept of the artist as a person with his own sensibilities and *amour propre* had begun to emerge. Vertue (*Notebooks*, vol. 4) recounted these anecdotes about the portrait painter John Riley (1646–1691).

Mr Roilly, who was a person well-skilld in the Art of face painting, especially colouring (not so solid in that part of drawing the lines) was a very modest man and knew his own foible, but conceald it as much as he could. When he drew King Charles the Second's picture, when it was done his Majesty lookd at it, and said, 'Is this like me? Well odds fish I'm an ugly fellow.' This so much dampt Mr Roilly's spirit that he could never endure to look on the picture, though a Noble man bought it & payd well for it, but the King would not . . .

Many times when persons were settinng to Mr Roilly for their pictures, or came to see them, they would find faults, and direct the amendments, often this would mortify him to such a degree that he would go out of the room and go into another where his scolars were, & vent his passion or uneasiness till he had eased himself, and then return to the company, express himself with an agreeable air, and with the countenance of satisfaction wait their pleasure and censures till they pleased to retire.

6.16 A fine house

That assiduous traveller and commentator on stately homes Celia Fiennes visited Broadlands near Romsey *c.* 1680, and her description of it in her *Journeys* gives a clear idea of the average country house of the period.

The road runns by a fine house of one of my relations John St Barbe, the rows of trees in the avenues runns just from the road to the front of the house; you enter a court that's walled in, and blew iron gates, the court has a round in the middle rail'd in, designed for a Bowling Green, and the Coaches drive round it to come to the entrance which is severall stone steps to a broad space

that is railed with balls and banisters, the space is paved with broad
free stone, the stepps the same 8 or 10; the house is a half
Roman H, the hall is in the middle with double doors, its very
lofty and large. There's a Chimney just against the Entrance, on
the right hand runns in an entry through the house to the backyard
where are the offices, Stillhouse and Barnes and Coachouse, and
a very fine stable built of brick, there are large partitions. In this
entry you have the pantry and Cellars and on the other side the
Kittchin Larders and Pastry which is one wing of the house, and
just behind the hall is the servants' hall, and a little parlour just by
the Pantry and backstairs, then the Great Hall is divided in halfe
by the Staircase, which hangs on its own worke, not supported on
either side to the first half pace [landing] and all the way up without
support on one side; they are of oake the railes and banisters are
varnished; the half paces are inlaid with yew wood, which lookes
a yellowish red, in squaires; they land on the next story with a
space of this Inlaid worke of a good bigness, the whole compass
of the Staircase. The roof of the staires is even with the roofe of
the next story. On the other side of the stairs are severall pillars
of wood, painted like marble for to walk between, and you pass
quite under the staires into a little Closet and a little further back
into a back yard, where is a Bathing House and other necessarys;
there is a screen stands on the side of the stairs next the Chimney,
to make that part more private. The hall runns quite through to
the garden where there is a door with steppes down, and so at this
door you see thro the house to that backyard I mentioned at the
end of the entry. The other wing of the house is a large Parlour
and drawing roome, this is out of the hall by the Garden. The Hall
is well painted and a carved Cornish [cornice] round and pillars on
the wanscoate round the room. The parlour is wanscoated and
painted a cedar colour. The next story you enter off this large half
pace on the right hand into a door which leads fore right to a
Balcony and on the left hand into a passage which leads to the
Chamber over the Drawing Room, and by it is a Servant's room
even with the passage. On the right hand is a passage which leads
to another roome just over-against; open the doors and there is a
perfect visto, so there is the other way and a servants; roome even
with the passage; beyond this room is a backstair leads to the Bath,
and by the Servant's roome is a large back stair that leads to the
next story, the Great Stairs ending here; and on the left they lead
into a large dineing roome and then a drawing roome, and next
a bedchamber which has a back doore to the back stairs by the

kitchin. These doores open through to the end one way, the best bed chamber and quite to the balcony, the other side a visto.

Within the dineing room on the left hand is a very large bedchamber which indeed is the best good tapistry hanging. Here is designed a velvet bed; its painted white, there are very good Pictures. Here is a little backstairs to the Servants' Hall. The dineing roome is wanscoated and varnished – the other roomes nothing done to, that is the drawing roome and chamber; within there is damask and camelet beds in the other rooms, and off these backstairs by the kitchin is a chamber anty-roome dressing roome two closets. These back stairs go up to the next story that leads to the roomes over this and to a long Gallery that is window all to the front and leads to all the chambers. Betweene are Servants' roomes and closets thence a little pair of staires leads up to the Gallery and tence up to the little Cupilow [cupola] which is in the middle of the house all Windowes round, and on the top has a golden Ball that holds severall galons. On each Wing there are little towers one has the clock, the other a Sun-dial and on top two gold balls of a lesser size.

The gardens are walled in, some with brest walls, some higher with flower pots upon them, severall places with open Grates to look through with stone balls or figures on the pillars each side the gates every way. There is a waterhouse thab by a Wheele casts up the water out of the River just by and fills the pipes to serve all the house and to fill the Bason designed in the middle of the Garden with a Spout in the middle. The Gardens are not finished, but will be very fine with large Gates open to the Grounds beyond, some of which are planted with trees. It's a fine thing, but doubt its no very good aire. It stands in a low place neare the river, the hills all round on that side, and the Mole and Soyle is black and such as they cut up for Peate.

6.17 Oriental textiles

Textiles from the east had been a regular feature of life since the Middle Ages, and had been increasing in quantity, brought back by diplomats and merchants, as well as being imported commercially. Sir John Finch who was British ambassador to Turkey from 1672 till 1680, included the following items in an inventory of his goods made up for returning to England in that year.

10 Indian, 6 Persian and 3 other table cloths.

7 Indian and 7 other coverlids or conterpanes.

4 Persian and 2 Indian carpets for tables.

The above are mostly of cloth of gold or satin, embroidered with flowers in gold and silver thread and coloured flowers worked with syrma [a kind of silk]. Amongst them are:

An Indian covert, white, small with lace flowers, yellow and blue for women to pray on.

An Indian coverlid of needleworke, yellow silk with a hunting scene of animals, men or horseback, women and houses, yellow fringe.

An Aboi of syrma and crimson velvet flowers, yellow satin, silver and gold fringe.

A Persian broad table cloth, the middle of cloth of gold, ground red with green flowers, the borders cloth of silver with flowers green and red, encompassed with crimson and white, the lining green and yellow satin, fringe white, red, green.

A very large tablecloth of Persia cloth of gold, ground red with green flowers, border green and red flowers between purple and white, lining yellow satin bordered with white and gudeline [a scarlet dye], fringe at the end white, green and purple.

A half moon coverlid, vastly large of 24 pykes, flowers of syrma upon red and blew, the whole ground crimson sattin.

A Persian large table carpett, the middle rose-colour with flowers of sirma gilt; within the first square blue, red and white flowers with sirma guilt a less border green and red with fringe green and yellow.

A Persian small table carpett with animals. Two serpents in the middle and great Persian writing about the borders.

An Indian table cloth, middle eight squares flowers, most outward, syrma and red silk and eight striscie [bands] of colour, the rest red and syrma flowers, fringe purple, red, green yellow, lining white with edging of striped silk.

Two cushions cloth of gold.

A narrow sideboard Indian cloth, lined with green bugbasin [bombazine?] fringe white, green, long flowers.

A portiere worked with syrma upon scarlet cloth in flowers.

A Scio quilt lined with green.

One sable typpett and two typpetts of sables' tayles.

Two silk smocks and a shirt of silk.

Of sandals pieces 125.

Bridle for a horse enamelled with gilt.

Five sable skins and sable tayles.

A target jewelled with massy gold, lined with crimson velvet and rings of massy gold.

A looking glass with rubys and emeralds, and a combe case of the same.

A mantle for a child, formerly for a chimney, of scarlet Londrino, with flowers of syrma, number 28, lined with blew bugbasin.

Two black fanns, three white and red.

A portiere of scarlet Londrino, with guilt sirma, yellow satin lining, flowers of sirma number 29 beside the middle.

A chimney piece of sirma large flowers, number 20.

Five pieces of diarberker red linnen, in each piece ten pike.

(*Historical Mss Commission Reports*: Finch)

6.18 Keeping control

The relationship between an architect and the masons or builders who carried his designs into actuality was a complex and varying one. Wren was most meticulous, in this respect. In 1675 Isaac Barrow, the Master of Trinity College, Cambridge decided to build a new library, and approached Wren – who gave his services gratuitously. The College records show that the Master Mason went to London to consult with Sir Christopher once in 1676; twice in 1680; three times in 1683 and twice in 1685, and Cornelius Austion, who made the woodwork went twice in 1690. In his correspondence with the Master, Wren explained his working methods with the workmen. (Robert Willis and John Willis Clark *The Architectural History of the University of Cambridge*, 1882, vol. 2).

A building of that consideration you goe about deserves a good care in the designe, and able workmen to perform it, and that he who takes the general management upon him may have a prospect of the whole and make all parts inside and outside corresponde together. I suppose you have good masons, how ever I would willingly take further paines to give all the mouldings in great, wee are scrupulous in small matters and you must pardon us; the Architects are as great pedants as Criticks or Heralds. And therefore if you approve the designes, let the mason take his measures as much as is necessary for the present setting out of the worke, and be pleased to transmit them to mee again, and I shall copie out partes of them at large, more proper for the use of workmen, and give you a carefull estimate of the charge, and return you again the originall designs, for in the hands of the workmen they will soon be defaced that they will not be able from them to pursue the work to a conclusion. I have made a Cursory estimate and it is not that at which you will stumble as not exceeding the charge proposed.

6.19 A printer's feast

Printing – like many other crafts – was still dominated by Guild rules and customs of medieval origin. 'Ancient Customs used in a Printing House' first appeared in 'Mechanick Exercises on the Whole Art of Printing' by Joseph Moxon (1677). After detailing a whole range of intricate customs it concludes with the following account of the banquet at Stationers' Hall.

The Printers of London, Masters and Journey-men have every Year a general Feast, which since the re-building of Stationers Hall is commonly kept there. This Feast is made by four Stewards, viz. two Masters and two Journey-men, which Stewards, with the Collection of half-a-Crown apiece of every Guest, defray the Charges of the whole Feast; And as they Collect the Half-Crowns, they deliver every Guest a Ticket, wherein is specified the Time and Place they are to meet at, and the Church they are to go to: To which Ticket is affixed the Names and Seals of each Steward.

It is commonly kept on or about May-day: When, about ten a Clock in the Morning they meet at Stationers Hall, and from thence go to some Church thereabouts; Four Whifflers (as Servitures) by two and two walking before with White Staves in their Hands, and Red and Blew Ribbons hung Belt-wise upon their left shoulders. These go before to make way for the Company. Then walks the Beadle of the Company of Stationers, with the Company's Staff in his Hand, and Ribbons as the Whifflers, and after him the Divine (whom the Stewards before engaged to Preach them a sermon) and his Reader. Then the Stewards walk by two and two, with long White Wands in their Hands, and all the rest of the Company follows, till they enter the Church.

Then Divine Service begins, Anthems are Sung, and a Sermon Preached to suit the Solemnity: Which ended, they in the same order walk back again to Stationers Hall; where they are immediately entertained with the City Weights and other Musick: And as every Guest enters, he delivers his Ticket (which gives him Admittance) to a Person appointed by the Stewards to receive it.

The Master, Wardens and other Grandees of the Company
(although perhaps no Printers) are yet commonly invited, and take
their Seats at the upper Table, and the rest of the Company where
it pleases them best. The Tables being furnished with variety of
Dishes of the best Cheer: And to make the entertainment more
splendid is ushered in with Loud Musick. And after Grace is said
(commonly by the Minister that preached the Sermon) everyone
Feasts himself with what he likes Best; whiles the Whifflers and
other Officers Wait with Napkins, Plates, Beer, Ale and Wine, of
all sorts, to accommodate each Guest according to his desire. And
to make their Cheer go cheerfuller down, are entertained with
Musick and Songs all Dinner time.

Dinner being near ended, the Kings and the Dukes Healths is
begun, by the several Stewards at the several Tables, and goes
orderly round to all the Guests.

And whiles these Healths are Drinking, each Steward sets a Plate
on each Table, beginning at the upper end, and conveying it downwards, to Collect the Benevolence of Charitable minds towards the
relief of Printers' Poor Widows. And at the same time each Steward
distributes a Catalogue of such Printers as have held Stewards ever
since the Feast was first kept, viz. from the Year of Christ 1621.

After Dinner, and Grace said, the Ceremony of Electing new
Stewards for the next Year begins: Therefore the present Stewards
withdraw into another Room: And put Garlands of Green Laurel,
or of Box on their Heads, and White-wands in their Hands, and
are again ushered out of the withdrawing Room by the Beadle of
the Company, with the Company's Staff in his Hand, and with
Musick sounding before them: Then follows one of the Whifflers
with a great Bowl of White wine and Sugar in his Right Hand, and
his Whifflers Staff in his Left: Then follows the Eldest Steward, and
then another Whiffler, as the first, with a Bowl of White wine and
Sugar before the second Steward, and in like manner another Whiffler before the Third, and another before the Fourth. And thus they
walk with Musick sounding before them three times round the
Hall: And in a fourth round the first Steward takes the Bowl of
his Whiffler and Drinks to one (whom before he resolved on) by
the Title of Mr Steward Elect: And taking the Garland off his own
Head puts it upon the Steward Elects Head. At which Ceremony
the Spectators clap their Hands, and such as stand on the Tables
or Benches, so Drum with their Feet that the whole Hall is filled
with Noise, as applauding the Choice. Then the present Steward
takes out the Steward Elect, giving him the Right Hand, and walks

with him Hand in Hand, behind the three present Stewards another Round about the Hall: And in the next Round, as aforesaid, the second Steward Drinks to another with the same Ceremony as the first did; and so the Third Steward, and so the Fourth and then all walk one Round more Hand in Hand about the Hall, that the Company may take notice of the Stewards Elect. And so ends the Ceremony of the Day.

This Ceremony being over, such as will go their ways; but others that stay, are Diverted with Musick, Songs, Dancing, Farcing, etc. till at last they all find it time to depart.

6.20 Evelyn and Gibbons

Though possibly slightly exaggerated, Evelyn's account of how he promoted the career of Grinling Gibbons suggests the patterns of patronage which operated at the time.

January 18th 1671. This day I first acquainted His Majesty with that incomparable young man Gibbons, whom I lately met with in an obscure place by mere accident, as I was walking near a poor, solitary thatched house, in a field in our parish [Deptford] near Sayes Court. I found him shut in, but looking through the window, I perceived him carving that large cartoon, or crucifix, of Tintoretto, a copy of which I myself had brought from Venice, where the original painting remains. I asked if I might enter; he opened the door civilly to me, and I saw him about such a work for curiosity of handling, drawing, and studious exactness, I have never before seen in all my travels. I questioned him why he worked in such an obscure and lonesome place; he told me that it was so he might apply himself to his profession without interruption, and wondered not a little how I had found him out. I asked if he was unwilling to be made known to some great man, for that I believed it might turn to his profit; he answered he was yet but a beginner, but would not be sorry to sell off that piece; on demanding the price, he said £100. In good earnest the very frame was worth the money, there being nothing in nature so tender and delicate as the flowers and festoons about it, and yet the work was very strong; in the piece were more than 100 figures of men etc. I found he was likewise musical, and very sober, civil and discreet in his discourse. There was only an old woman in his house. So, desiring leave to visit him sometimes I went away.

Of this young artist and my manner of finding him out I

acquainted the King, and begged that he would give me leave to bring him and his work to Whitehall, for that I would venture my reputation with His Majesty that he had never seen anything approach it, and that he would be exceeedingly pleased and employ him. The King said he would go himself and see him. This was the first notice His Majesty ever had of Mr Gibbons.

March 1st. I caused Mr Gibbons to bring to Whitehall his excellent piece of carving, where being come I advertised His Majesty, who asked me where it was; I told him in Sir Richard Browne's (my father-in-law) chamber, and that if it pleased His Majesty to appoint whither it should be brought, being large, and though of wood, heavy, I would take care for it. 'No' says the King 'show me the way, I'll go to Sir Richard's chamber' which he immediately did, walking along the entries after me, as far as the ewrie, till he came up into the room where I also lay. No sooner was he entered and cast his eye on the work, but he was astonished at the curiosity of it, and having considered it a long time, and discoursed with Mr Gibbon, whom I brought to kiss his hand. He commanded that it should be brought immediately to the Queen to show her. It was carried up into her bedchamber, where she and the King looked on it and admired it again; the King being called away, left us with the Queen, believing she would have bought it, being a crucifix, but when his Majesty was gone, a French peddling woman, one Mad. de Boord, who used to bring petticoats, and fans and baubles out of France to the Ladys began to find fault with several things in the work, which she understood no more than an ass or monkey, so as in a kind of indignation, I caused the person who brought it to carry it back to the chamber, finding the Queen so much governed by an ignorant French woman, and this incomparable artist had his labour only for his pains, which not a little displeased me, and he was fain to send it down to his cottage again. He not long after sold it for £80, though well worth £100, without the frame to Sir George Viner.

His Majesty's surveyor Mr Wren faithfully promised me to employ him [Gibbons actually did the choir stalls and other work in St Paul's]. I have also bespoke His Majesty for his work at Windsor, which my friend the architect Mr May was going to alter and repair universally, for on the next day I had a fair opportunity of talking to His Majesty about it.

August 8th. I went this morning to show my Lord Chamberlain, his lady and the Duchess of Grafton the incomparable work of Mr Gibbons, the carver, whom I first recommended to His Majesty, his house being furnished like a cabinet, not only with his own work, but divers excellent paintings of the best hands.

6.21 A great house, 1677

The acutely observant John Evelyn spent 3 weeks at Euston, in 1677.

Since first I was at this place I found things exceedingly improved. It is seated in a bottome between two gracefull swellings, the main building now being in the shape of a Greek pie [letter] with foure pavilions, two at each corner and a break in the front, railed and balustred at the top, where I caused huge jarrs to be placed full of earth to keepe them steady on their pedestalls between the statues, which make as good a shew as if they were of stone, and tho' the building be of brick, and but two stories besides cellars and garretts covered with blue slate, yet there is roome enough for a full court, the offices and out houses being so ample and well disposed. The King's apartment is painted *a fresca* and magnificently furnished. There are many excellent pictures of the greate masters. The gallery is a pleasant, noble room, in the breake or middle is a billiard-table, but the wainscot being of firr and painted does not please me as much as Spanish oak without paint. The chapel is pretty, the porch descending to the gardens. The orange garden is very fine, and leads into the greenhouse, at the end of which is a hall to eate in, and the conservatory some hundred feet long, adorned with maps, as the other side is with heads of the Caesars, ill cut in alabaster; over head are several apartments for my Lord, Lady and Dutchesse [his daughter the Duchess of Grafton] with kitchens and other offices below in lesser form, with lodgings for servants, all distinct, for them to retire to when they please and would be in private, and have no communication with the palace which he tells me he will wholly resign to his son-in-law and daughter, that charming young creature. The canall running under my lady's dressing-room chamber window is full of carps and foule, which come and are fed there. The cascade at the end of the canall turnes a corne-mill, which provides the family and raises water for the fountaines and offices. To pass this canal into the opposite meadows Sir Sam. Moreland has invented a screw-bridge, which being turned with a key landes you fifty foote distant at the entrance of an ascending walke of trees, a mile in length, as tis also on the front into the park, of 4 rows of ash trees, and reaches to the park-pale which is nine miles in compass, and the best for riding and meeting the game that I ever saw. There were now of red and fallow deer almost a thousand, with good covert, but the soile barren, and flying sand in which nothing will grow kindly. The tufts of firr and much of the other wood were planted by my direction some yeares before. The seate is admirably placed for field sports, hawking, hunting or racing. The mutton is small but sweete. The stables hold thirty horses and four coaches. The out-offices make two large quadrangles, so as servants never lived with more ease, never master more civill. Strangers are attended and accomodated as at their home, in pretty apartments furnished with all manner of conveniences and privacy. There is a library full of excellent books. There are bathing-rooms, elabatorie, dispensatorie, a decoy and places to keep fat fowl in. He has now in his new church (neere the garden) built a dormitory or vault with several repositories in which to bury his family. In the expence of this pious structure, the church is most laudable, most of the Houses of God in this country resembling rather stables and thatched cottages than temples in which to serve the most high. He has built a lodge in the park for the keeper, which is a neate building and might become any gentleman. The same he has done for the parson, little deserving it, for murmuring that my Lord put him some time out of his wretched hovel, whilst it was building. He has also erected a fair inn at some distance from his palace, with a bridge of stone over a river neere it, and repaired all the tenants' houses, so that there is nothing but neatness and accomodation about his estate, which I yet think is not above £1,500 a yeare. I believe he now has in his family 100 domestic servants.

6.22 Convenient offices

In November 1660 Sir Roger Pratt compiled in his notebooks (edited by R. T. Gunther, Oxford 1928), 'Certain Short Notes Concerning Architecture', which expressed with great clarity the kind of considerations which affected architects both professional and amateur in the designing of houses. This is what he has to say about the nature and disposition of the various rooms.

It will be convenient if no place at all is lost, and that all the rooms be so ordered that they may be most of service, but not the least kind of incumbrance to each other, viz; the kitchen and all its offices to lie together, and the buttery and cellar with theirs etc.

and all these to be disposed of in a half-ground storey, with their back-courts convenient to them; in that no dirty servants may be seen passing to and fro by those who are above, no noises heard, nor ill scents smelt; which to prevent good plenty of water to be brought by pipes into everyone of these offices, and a large common suer, made of about 3 feet in breadth, and four or five in height, laid sloping for the better current, and so placed that not only do all the scourings of them commodiously fall into it, but all the water from the roof, court etc. which will thoroughly clean it; at the outfall whereof, at a good distance from the house, the private ones may be built. In the other storeys, the common rooms of entertainment must have their withdrawing ones adjoining to them, and the whole be so ordered that upon any inconvenience of weather upon one side of the house, there may be a fit retirement to that of the other, which can only be done in a double pile; but the troublesomeness of the sun will be best avoided if the fronts be placed towards the North and the South. The bed chambers should all have a fit place for the standing of their beds, remote from the blowing of doors or windows, and not far from the fire. They must likewise have conveniences for the laying of woods and other privacies, which will easily be made by the projecture of the chimney, and so be made up afterwards again to range upon a straight line, the place for the chimney is to be chosen with like caution as that for a bed. Besides they must each of them have a closet, and a servant's lodging, with chimney both which will easily be made by dividing the breadth of one end of the room into two such parts as shall be convenient, and to the servants' room a pair of backstairs ought to be adjoining, which ought fitly to serve for all of that kind at the end of the building, and should be very private, and near a backyard. The floors ought all to be most equal, and without any thresholds. But above all the whole is not to be bigger for the purse or family of him for whom it is designed, whose rooms of ordinary use ought so to be placed as not to give the least disturbance to those of his strangers, nor theirs to each other. The offices of one kind should have doors out of one into the other, and also particular ones that they may on occasion be severally used; the garrets should be parted, the men's quarter from the women's, with particular stairs to them. Closets, servants rooms and stairs will be best placed at the ends of a building, the others in front of it etc. Beautiful it will be, if all the great rooms be placed just in the middle, and afterwards that those on each hand of them have alike positions, and also dimensions, as we find it to be in our own bodies, so that you will see nothing on the one side which you shall not find to be answered by its like on the other; but as great a care is to be had to proportionate them aright, which indeed is that which giveth them their principal grace and life. But above all to design nothing little or dark, so that each room according to its bigness may have light sufficient, and a door big enough, and not only so, but all the windows on one side of the house etc, to range exactly with those on the other, and the doors likewise, according to their various locations, but especially that there be a clear vista through the very middle of the building, where the principal entrances ought always to be placed. The chimneys likewise should even be made in the very middle of the length of some walling; and the rooms of better note to lie to the grand court or gardens, but especially of a graceful ascent with steps is to be made to the garden.

6.23 The beautifying of ceilings

The example of the Rubens' ceiling in the Banqueting House at Whitehall, and the examples to be found in France and Italy, had given mural painting a new impetus, and no newly built great house could be without a painted ceiling in one or more of its main rooms. In his *Notebooks* Sir Roger Pratt addressed himself to the problem in the latter half of the seventeenth century.

As to the beautifying of these [ceiling] panels, it is either done by painting or some bas-relief, if the ceiling be all of plaster.

Painting is either in fresco, which I take to be painting upon a new wet fresh wall with water-colours, and is much the cheaper, but the colours seem faint, and to want their vigour; or in oil, and that either upon the bare wall or ceiling, or upon linen cloth. If it be upon the former, great care that it be very well primed, the ceiling first being perfectly dry, and cracks mended, for so it will make it so exceedingly hard, that it cannot be so much as stained, though any reasonable quantity of wet should fall on the other side of it, so as it do not do so continually; and in this painting, and in fresco, you may, if you please, imitate all the seeming beams aforesaid, picture-frames etc, and so almost quite save the expense of them, if the rooms where you do it be not less than fifteen feet in height at the least, for otherwise though they be never so artificially done, yet never will they look so graceful, nor in the least manner deceive the sight, as in doing this, it seems to be intended.

An example of this there is in a withdrawing room at Wilde-house in the backside of Lincoln's Inn Fields, though the painting of it is not to be commended.

As to the painting on cloth, you must take great care that that for ceilings be exceedingly strong, and tightly strained, for otherwise, it is observed, in time that they will usually sag.

As to the figures to be placed in them, I take that those which are in a flying posture and of an airial nature, to be of all the most proper for them, as birds, cupidons, fairies etc. both in regard to the place which is supposed to be the sky, and likewise for that they are so represented to us in their natural positions, and the like may be said of figures descending or looking through the clouds. But for those which are ascending, or sitting as it were there, they cannot but be represented to us with much shortening and distortion, and so have something of harsh and monstrous in them, though performed by the most experienced masters in that curious art of perspective as will most evidently appear to all men upon the least observation.

There is in this painting, as in all others, two things chiefly to be remarked by us viz.; one the design, next the colouring.

Design

In a good design, which proceeds from the like invention, there is this, the most apt position of one figure or more to the most natural expression of what is intended by us, now in this we are to take heed that no one figure be placed in a ceiling as it were by chance, and without any dependence uppon anything else there, but that each one may do its part in its proper place towards the completing of some general storey wherewith the whole superficies of it is to be embellished, which will yet do much the better if it can be well made to have reference to anything of that family in whose house it is painted. In the designing upon which ceilings, there is yet this not be erred in, the placing of the most noble figure in the very middle of them, and if there chance to have been any oversight in the fashioning of them, such as are to be made in those faulty parts which may most aptly hide the imperfections of them, to perform all the which, it being most clear that it will be no less than a task to a most judicious workman; such only are to be employed, and mean ones not to be thought upon, but only that we may the more earnestly avoid them, for should we make use of them, their work would make us seem to have introduced deformity instead of ornament, to have made a description of the inhabitants of a hospital, and at our great charges to have erected a monument of our ignorance to be the sport and derision of all times till the first judicious of our posterity shall, out of his piety deface it for us.

It is likewise to be observed in this designing that the figures be made all of that bigness as to appear as great as the life at the least to those who view them from below, and as for minute painting, grotesque work etc., though there may appear much neatness in it, as in the pavilion roof at the Queen's new house at Greenwich, and in that of the Earl of Pembroke's at Wilton, yet when all is done, it appeared to be very graceless; the evidence whereof I conceive was the cause, that when the Long Gallery at Whitehall which is over the stone one, began so to be painted, that there was very little done of it before it was quitted.

Colouring

As to the colours; care is to be taken that they will be of the best; for there are those which, for the time being will look well, but will suddenly tarnish, viz. white, which is not flake ground in Nutt Oil will turn yellowish, blue green and so the rest. Now though it is not to be supposed that any such fault will be wilfully commited by any skillfull artists, though it were for nothing else but the credit of their work; yet we daily find amongst them those who regard money more than their reputations, such faults being committed especially who paint upon the bare ceiling, as the most mechanical, for there being a considerable difference in the price between the best and others, they make choice of such for the most part, by which they may be the greatest gainers. Though some pieces upon cloth of the best masters have not been faultless in this particular, as we see many of Sir Anthony Vandyke's to be in several places, for instead of ultramarine and other blueing, that blue is turned of an illfavoured green, to the great disgrace of his work which otherwise in itself is much to be esteemed, so that an honest man is to be looked for as well as a good workman. But we may in a great measure avoid this deceit if we make use of that painting which by the Italians is called *Chiaro Oscuero*, and was, with so high commendation, practised by Polydon and his companion Maturino, but in this we must be most sure that the design be perfect, there being very little else to hide any defect of the work. But I have observed that these painted ceilings do generally cast a gloominess upon the rooms where they are, except they be quicken by the gilding of the soffits and cornices etc.

6.24 Laying out the grounds for a house

Already by the seventeenth century there had become apparent that concern with landscaping which was to become such a passion with the architects and country-house owners of the following century. In his *Notebooks* under the section 'Notes as to the Building of Country Houses' Pratt gave the following advice *c.* 1670.

Let the house be placed, if not in a park, yet at the least in some large pasture, with grounds of that nature round about, for so, the surface of the earth being always green, will accordingly be pleasant, whereas arable is never so, but whilst the corn is upon it.

Let it stand at the least a furlong distant from the common way out of which you turn up to it, the ground gently rising all along and the level of it, both on the one hand and the other, if not equal, yet at least not remarkably otherwise; the height of the situation will not only render it very pleasant when you come towards it, and are afterwards at it, but will likewise occasion it to stand dry, by the fall of all wet from it, and also give you a great convenience for to drain all sinks and the like from it.

If the way to the house be not already bounded either with trees or hedges (for he who considers well before he builds, will be sure if any advantage may be had, to make use of it, if it consists with the former considerations, by reason of the slow and hazardous growth of those which are to be planted) let one be laid out by the line, equal at least to the whole front of the house, if not somewhat more, as to that of the court, and so let elms, fir-trees, or rather lime-trees, because of the sweetness and beauty of their flowers and broad leaves, if they can be had, and the ground be fit, be set at twenty foot distance from each other, on both sides of it, from one end to the other, and the like again crossways in a direct line with the front of the court, but that is intended not for a way, but a walk, and so the breadth of that is sufficient, if it exceed not between 20 and 30 foot; and so, if you please, you may plant the ground on either side of the great walk into squares alike, and place something in the middle of them for ornament, as statues, trees, little houses or the like, all of which cannot but add an exceeding grace to your seat, and will almost with pleasure ravish the beholder. For things being thus ordered, when you first come to the house, they will represent as it were a most beautiful scene to you, and when you are there, besides the content which may be had by viewing your own plantation and grounds, you may likewise enjoy a most pleasant prospect of the country round about, as it will chiefly be, when pleasantly varied, as here pasture, there arable, here wood, there water, here high ground, there lower, the view yet clear and uninterrupted, the horizon made by some pleasant hills, not so near as to stop the eye half-way in its course, nor yet so far distant as to be almost tired before it can reach it.

6.25 Of glass and casements

Glass had become of prime importance in domestic architecture, and in his *Notebooks* Pratt made some comments about both glass and casements.

The best glass that we have here of our own is that of Newcastle, but from abroad that of Normandy. The former cut into squares and leaded, will cost about 7d. a foot, but the latter, which is more beautiful 17d.

The most excellent qualities of glass are these; first that it be strong, secondly that it be purely crystalline, and not greenish, thirdly not sandy, fourthly not blistered.

Let the glass in your windows be so ordered, that all the panes be of equal dimensions, so will the leads fall perpendicular from the upper lights down to the bottom of the lower ones, besides the beauty which will arise from the quality of the transverse ones, against which let small iron bars be put in fit places on the outside whereby to uphold it, and that so exactly that those that are within shall very hardly, if at all, discern that there is any such matter.

The chiefest matter which is to be looked to in the ordering of your glass is; First that the panes be beautifully proportioned, which will be either about one square and a quarter, or which is yet better one and a half. The square in great windows is best to be about 4 or 5 inches etc. Secondly that the glass be very closely leaded and well soldered, and lastly that it be most closely tacked on to all parts of the window frame, to keep out the weather, which will otherwise break in.

The best material to make great folding casements is that of iron, for there is no sort of timber that can be so well seasoned, but that it will be altered by the weather either as to warping, swelling, cracking, swagging etc. or at the least to some one of them, for

I have most certainly informed by workmen at the Lord Duke's in Kent, [the Duke of Dorset's house at Knole] that oak was there made use of for that purpose, which, having been part of an old house, was at the least of 100 years' seasoning, and yet was found very much to deceive them, though quartered to prevent it.

These casements are to hang each of them upon 3 hooks, or hinges, if they be anything heavy, and are to have so many thwart bars, rivetted in them, as there are panes of glass in their height, to which each rank of them is to be fastened, but in the upper lights a bar for every other pane is sufficient, the thickness of them to be only such as that they may seem no broader than their leading, though their breadth may be such as shall be thought most convenient for the strengthening of them, they must be placed withinside, for otherwise the rain falling from them will irrevocably rust all Normandy glass, though ours of Newcastle does never receive the like prejudice from it, the reason they say is by reason of the salt which is used in making the other. The pinholes in the borders are everywhere so to be made as to be at the end of the ranges of lead, which may be done by giving the dimensions of the panes.

As to their outside they are to have two little buttons at the bottom to support the glass, and a kind of T placed so aptly upon some place both above and below of the frame, that in case of the casements blowing wildly open, neither the glass may be broken being driven upon the side architrave of the windows, nor yet the coins of that be defaced by the impulse of the iron frame upon it, but to prevent this yet more, there are certain strong iron springs, to be fastened to the wooden frame of the windows, which are called catches, and are of excellent use in case they be set, and will so hold, exactly level, otherwise they are of no use, and hooks are better.

As to the shutting of them, at the bottom of each, about the midst of their breadth, is to be placed some graceful handle over against some perpendicular lead of the glass, for pulling them to when they stand wide open; they will close much the better if they fall one into the other, in a kind of rabbet, and nothing can shut them either so tightly, or so gracefully, as a strong iron rod well fastened in three places at least on the frame, and turning about some iron pins strongly fastened both above and below in the wooden transoms of the windows, and so locking one into the other about the midst of their height, having a true lock only on the one side for use, but an apparent one opposed to it on the other to preserve uniformity. Now if these locks stand so high (as they will in great windows) so that women, and those who are low cannot well make use of them, there may be made an addition to them, with some handle bending directly downwards so low as shall remedy all inconveniences.

As a general rule, let your iron work and glass range with each other as much as maybe, and a uniformity be preserved in all. Lay the ironwork in oil with the purest white lead to preserve it from rust, as soon as maybe.

6.26 Wallpaper appears

Although John Houghton's *A Collection of Letters for the Improvement of Husbandry and Trade* first appeared in 1689 it clearly described things which had been prevalent since at least several decades earlier, and shows the extent to which the painted hangings on cloth which had covered domestic walls for the preceding centuries were being supplanted by paper, which was available in rolls.

A great deal of Paper is nowadays printed to be pasted on Walls to serve instead of Hangings, and truly if all parts of the Sheet be well and Close pasted on, it is very pritty, clean and will last with tolerable Care a great while. But there are some other done in Rolls in long sheets of a thick paper made for the Purpose whose sheets are pasted together to be so long as the Height of a Room, and they are managed like Woolen Hangings, and there is a great Variety, with curious Cuts, which are Cheap, and if kept from Wet, very lasting.

6.27 Garden design: walls, grottos, fountains

Although primarily known as an agriculturalist, whose *Systema Agricultura* of 1669 was the first large and comprehensive treatment of the subject, John Woolridge (or Worlidge) produced in 1681 a highly successful book *The Art of Gardening*, replete with information such as the following.

Of Walls

Next unto the Brick, Stone Walls are preferred, the Square-hewn Stone out of the Quarry, especially Sand or Free-Stone is the best, the cold white Stone, like unto Chalk or Lime-stone is not so good. The Rough Heath-stone, or Burre, is very dry and warm, but by its unevenness is unconvenient to tack Trees against, unless you disperse here and there in the Building some small squares of Timber or Brickbats, in the joints whereof Nails will enter and take. Flints are very cold and uneven jointed, and therefore the worst of all Stone for a Garden Fence.

In may places where Stone is dear, and Brick scarce, and Lime and Sand not near, Walls are often made by a Compost of Earth and Straw tempered with it. This Earth must be either of a clayish nature, or have a little mixture of Clay in it. It must be well wrought, and mixed long with Dung or Straw, which serves to hold it together until it be thoroughly dry; and then, according to the skill of the Workman, wrought up into a Wall and covered with Thatch, being not able to bear a more weighty Coping.

Of Grottos

It is a place that is capable of giving you so much pleasure and delight that you may bestow not undeservedly what cost you please on it, by paving it with Marble or immuring it with Stone or Rockwork, either naturally or artificially resembling the Excellencies of Nature. The Roof may be made of the same supprted with Pillars of Marble, and the Partitions made of Tables of the same.

Here follows a Description of Several Fountains

1. The Ball raised by a Sprout of Water.
2. The Water representing a double Glass, the one over the other.
3. A Dragon, or like, casting Water out of its mouth, as it runs round on the Spindle.
4. A Crown casting Water out of several Pipes as it runs around.
5. A statue of a Woman, that at the turning of a private Cock, shall cast Water out of her Nipples into the Spectators' Faces.
6. The Royal Oak with Leaves, Acorns and Crowns dropping, and several small spouts round the top.

6.28 Sash windows

The introduction of the sash window, as opposed to the casement, was stimulated by the fact that the proportions of the Wren type of window openings were admirably suited for such a type of window, which rapidly became as prestige-conferring as double-glazing is today. They were however often introduced injudiciously.

The glazier's work before substantial was
I must confess, thrice as much lead, as glass,
Which in the sun's meridian, cast a light,
As it had been within an hour of night.
The windows now look like so many suns,
Illustrating the noble room at once:
The primitive casements modell'd were no doubt
By that through which the pigeon was thrust out,
Where now whole sashes are but one great eye,
T'examine, and admire thy beauties by.
(Charles Cotton, *The Wonders of the Peake*, 1681)

6.29 The life of an apprentice

Some idea of the life of an apprentice to a craft can be obtained from this account written by John Fryer, son of a modest Buckinghamshire farmer, who was to become Lord Mayor of London and a baronet, of his experience as an apprentice to a Master Pewterer (Guildhall Ms.12017; reproduced in John Hatcher, *A History of British Pewter*, Longman 1974, pp. 191–92).

[I was brought to London in 1685, at the age of fourteen] to be improved in writeing and accompts that I might be fitted to go Apprentice to some trade. I haveing continued at writing Schoole till the Christmas, and my relations having heard of one Mr Harford, a Peuterer in Bishopsgate Street (the next house to the corner house of Cornhill) who wanted an Aprentice, it was soon agreed I should go on trial to him, which I did about the 16th of January, and on the first day of March I was bound to him for seven years according to the Custom of the citty of London; my honoured Uncle Edmund Boulter discharged what was necessary on my account: £10 in money and a new suit of Clothes was the condition on which I was bound. I must observe that he [Harford] had not been long sett up for himself, so that his Trade was but small, and that not being suficient to keep him and me in full work, he contrived to take in work from other men, which in that business is called Trucking, but properly it is working of Journy work. When I had been with him some time and was capable of finishing work, he began to get tired of working so hard, as we generaly did (and most young beginners do at first) so the work fell the heavier on me; and which added to my labour, the goods which I finished, I carryed on my back into Southwark where the owner dwelt, this was my custom 2 or 3 times a week, if not ofter. I had just reason to be very uneasy under this servitude for I was naturaly of a Weak constitution, and being the only surviving child, my Dear Mother had not inured me to any Hard labour, and which was worse, in my infancy I had been cured of a Rupture, and I found such carrying of burthens strained that part, and did me much hurt; my Master being of a very near temper in his house, and put me upon doing the servile part of the trade, such as turning the Wheel, Oileing and cleaning the Ware when finishd, carrying of Basketts of goods to the Inns and other things not commonly done by other aprentices, and some other things which I forbear to relate. These things, as well as my severe confinement were irksome to me, especially when I observed the pleasant and easie Trades that most of my Schoolfellows were put to, it did oft make me repine, butt under all these things the goodness of my god supported me. I had some thoughts of quitting such servitude, but then I considered my Mother haveing onlie me should I ruine myself, it would be a sore affliction to her. I had other trialls and tribulations dureing that seven yeares' servitude, such as the loose character of my Master, who when he found himself to prosper in the World, took more liberty to keep company and led a more dissolute life then when I first went to him. His company keeping brought him to such a sottish temper that his chief delight was in Alehouses and Taverns, and by furnishing of them he seems to get his chief buisness to this day, and by this sottish way he supprts himself, making of them pay an extravagant rate for goods, and by this way of life gained the name of Drunken Harry. But to return to this account of myself, when my time was expired, 1st March 1692/3 I workt a little while with him, was made free of the Company of Peuterers about the 21st of this month, and soon after of the Citty of London, and one of the Trade being ill, and desirous of leaving his buisness I waited on my Honoured Uncle Edmund Boulter and desired him to assist me to take the said shop etc., which request of mine he considered of and granted, he lent me the money that the goods came to, which I think was about £300, I gave him Bond and paid him intrest.

Biographical index

Ailred, Saint (1109?–1166) Abbot of Rievaux, and much involved in international politics, he also went as a missionary to the Galloway Picts, whose chief he persuaded to become a monk. Above all else, however, he was a prolific writer and historian, producing lives of St Cuthbert and Edward the Confessor, as well as a chronicle of Britain 'from the time of Adam to that of Henry I'.

Alan of Walsingham (d. 1364) Monk at Ely; became sub-prior and sacristan in 1321. Designed St Mary's chapel, and then the unique lantern of the cathedral. He was chosen as Bishop of Ely, but the election was not confirmed by the Pope.

Aldhelm (640–709) Bishop of Sherbourne. Educated under Theodore (q.v.) Archbishop of Canterbury, and became one of his group of reforming prelates. Built churches at Malmesbury, Bruton and Wareham, and monasteries at Frome and Bradford. He wrote several works in prose and verse.

Alfred the Glossater (c. 950) The author of the glosses in the Northumbrian dialect inserted in the Lindisfarne Gospels.

Alfred (849–901) King of the West Saxons, who defeated the Danes, united England, promulgated a coherent legal system, established schools, and was himself a writer and translator.

Anglesey, Countess of (c. 1600–1650) Wife of Christopher Villiers, first Earl of Anglesey, and younger brother of George, Duke of Buckingham (qv).

Anne of Denmark (1574–1619) Wife of James I. Daughter of Frederick II King of Denmark and Norway. She took a great interest in masques and other forms of entertainment, in which she frequently took part. As a result of her building activities she became involved in heavy debts.

Arundel, Thomas (1353–1414) Bishop of Ely 1374; Chancellor of England 1386–89, Archbishop of York 1388, and of Canterbury 1396; Chancellor again in 1399 and 1412.

Arundel, Thomas Howard, Earl of Arundel (1586–1646) Only son of 1st Earl, who died in the Tower in 1595. Soldier and politician, who never realised his ambitions in these fields but became instead one of England's leading art collectors, influencing by his tastes both Henry and Charles, the sons of James I. He spent most of the latter part of his life in Italy.

Ashton, Hugh (d. 1522) Archdeacon of York, and cofounder of St John's College, Cambridge.

Athelstan (895–940) King of West Saxons and Mercians who imposed a kind of suzerainty over all England, and inflicted many defeats on the Danish invaders.

Atkyns, Richard (1655–1677) Soldier, politician and writer. Very interested in typography, he tried to get a patent for printing law books, but failed and died in a debtors' prison.

Aubigny, Lady (1602–1683) Sister of James Stuart, fourth Earl of Lennox and ninth Seigneur of Aubigny, Lady Aubigny was a loyal, but unenthusiastic, supporter of the royalist cause.

Bacon, Francis, 1st Baron Verulam and Viscount St Albans (1561–1626) Lawyer, civil servant, politician, and a writer on many subjects.

Baines, Sir Thomas (1622–1680) Physician, Gresham Professor of Music, he accompanied his intimate friend Sir John Finch on embassies to Florence and Constantinople.

Baldock, Ralph (d. 1313) Dean of St Paul's; Bishop of London 1304; Lord Chancellor 1307. The author of a history of England.

Barrow, Isaac (1630–1677) Cambridge mathematician and classical scholar; the teacher of Isaac Newton, in whose favour he resigned the Lucasian professorship. He became Master of Trinity College, where he founded the new library in 1672.

Bathurst, Ralph (1620–1704) Scholar, divine and doctor. He abandoned medicine in 1660 and became a chaplain to Charles II. One of the founders of the Royal Society, he became Dean of Wells and left a large body of writings in both English and Latin. He was a munificent benefactor of Trinity College, Oxford, where he had graduated in 1638, became President and was largely responsible for its rebuilding.

Beale, Charles (*c.* 1620–1700) Deputy Clerk of the Patents 1660–65, and a chemist, specialising in artists' colours, which he made up for his wife Mary, Lely and others.

Beale, Mary (1632–97) A portrait painter, who was probably a pupil of Robert Walker, and had a degree of popular success. She copied many works by Lely, and herself produced portraits of Milton, Cowley, Charles II and other notabilities.

Becket, Thomas (1118–70) Of Norman extraction, Becket commenced his career in the household of Theobald, archbishop of Canterbury, studying canon law at Bologna and Auxerre. Like many ambitious ecclesiastics, however, he joined the king's household, and became an intimate of Henry II. In 1162 he was appointed archbishop of Canterbury, and, with that sense of the histrionic which was an integral part of his character, embarked on a course which brought him into direct conflict with the king over the rights of the church. As the result of an injudicious remark of Henry's he was murdered in the cathedral at Canterbury on December 29th 1170, and almost immediately became one of the major cult figures of Christendom.

Beckington, Thomas (1350–1465) Bishop of Bath and Wells 1445. In 1420 he had entered the service of the humanist Humphrey, Duke of Gloucester. He was an active diplomat, and *c.* 1443 became Lord Privy Seal. He adorned Wells with many fine buildings.

Bede, The Venerable (673–735) Historian and scholar, who was a monk at Jarrow. He not only wrote several historical works, but *De Natura Rerum*, one of the first books produced in England on the natural sciences.

Bellasses, Lord (actually Balasyse, Baron John) (1614–89) A leading royalist during the Civil War, who after the Restoration was a appointed Governor of Tangier, and then first Lord Commissioner of the Treasury.

Benedict Biscop (628–690) A monk of Lerrins, who came to Canterbury with Theodore of Tarsus, and formed part of that prelate's intellectual circle. First becoming abbot of St Peter's, he moved to the North East, founding monasteries on the Wear and in Jarrow. He collected an extensive library.

Benedict of Nursia (Saint) (*c.* 480–*c.* 547) The so-called 'Father of Western Monasticism', he almost inadvertently created what was to be one of the dominant cultural forces in the Middle Ages. Commencing his career as a hermit at Subiaco, he gradually accumulated around him a body of like-mindeed celibates at Monte Cassino, near Naples, and there he drew up in 515 a 'Rule' which, by virtue of its simplicity, its good sense and its well-ordered regulation of a community life, became the basis for the growth of the Benedictine order, the prototype of all monastic institutions.

Bess of Hardwick, Elizabeth Talbot, Countess of Shrewsbury (1518–1608) A domineering woman who made widowhood into a lucrative profession, amassing from a series of defunct spouses an income of £6,000 a year, much of which she spent on her magnificent houses at Hardwick, Chatsworth and elsewhere.

Bilfrith (*c.* 750) A monk of Lindisfarne, who adorned with gems and gold ornaments *The Durham Book*, an illuminated version of the gospels now in the Cottonian Library.

Blois, Henry of (*c.* 1110–1170) Bishop of Winchester, son of Stephen, Count of Blois, and younger brother of King Stephen. Greatly involved in political and ecclesiastical affairs, but also a considerable scholar and collector of works of art and antiquities.

Boorde, Andrew (1490–1549) Physician and traveller. Became a Carthusian monk, and then Bishop of Chichester. He then took up the study of medicine at Glasgow and wrote extensively on the subject.

Bradshaw, Henry (d. 1513) A Benedictine monk at Chester, of which he wrote a history. He also wrote a life of St Werburgh (q.v.) in English verse, which was first published in 1521.

Buckingham, 1st Duke of; George Villiers (1592–28) Collector and connoisseur who owed his great, but short-lived success to the fact that he was the 'favourite' of the predominantly homosexual James I.

Burghley, Lord (1520–1598) William Cecil, the outstanding Elizabethan civil servant and politician, was one of the dominant figures of his age. Far-sighted, secretive and pragmatic, he built up a large personal fortune, which found expression in the great house at Hatfield.

Carleton, Sir Dudley (1573–1632) Later 1st Viscount Dorchester. Diplomat, ambassador to The Hague, Venice and Paris.

Very active in collecting paintings for those whose favour he wished to curry.

Castelmaine, Countess of; Barbara Palmer (1641–1709) The daughter of the second Viscount Grandison, she bore five children to Charles II, all surnamed Fitzroy, one becoming the Duke of Grafton. Her lovers also included the Duke of Marlborough, Wycherley, and Jacob Hall, the rope-dancer. Pepys thought her the most beautiful of all the court ladies.

Cavendish, George (1500–1561) At the age of 26 he became usher to Cardinal Wolsey, and remained in his service till 1530. In 1557 he wrote a life of the Cardinal, which was first published in 1815.

Chamberlain, John (1553–1627) Born in London, where he spent most of his life, after graduating from Trinity College, Cambridge. Between 1598 and 1625 he wrote a series of letters which throw much light on the life of the times.

Chaucer, Geoffrey (*c.* 1345–1400) Son of a tavern keeper, he was an important figure in the civil service of his time and an outstanding poet, whose *Canterbury Tales* (*c.* 1387) are one of the masterpieces of English literature. He was buried in Westminster Abbey, as the first occupant of what came to be known as 'Poet's Corner'.

Chiffinch, Thomas (1600–1666) **and William** (1602–1688) Pages and closet-keepers to Charles II, with responsibilities for looking after the king's jewels etc. They were employed in multifarious secret transactions.

Cibber, Caius Gabriel (1630–1700) A sculptor of German origin, trained in Rome and brought to England by John Stone. He worked for Robert Hooke (q.v.) and amongst his other works is the phoenix over the south door of St Paul's cathedral.

Clovio, Julio (1498–1578) Croation-born painter and illuminator, who became a monk in Rome and was famous for the pictures he incorporated in his manuscripts.

Cogan, Henry (*c.* 1580–1660) A civil servant who in 1640 became Comptroller of the Mint. He looked after Sir Henry Wotton's (q.v.) affairs when he was abroad, and he himself translated several works from Italian.

Collins, Martin (*c.* 1460–1508) Treasurer of York Minster

1503–08. In his will he left many objects to the Minster, as well as the not inconsiderable sum of £100.

Cooper, Samuel (1609–1672) A leading miniaturist and also one of the best lutanists of his day. He visited France and Holland.

Cotton, Charles (1630–1687) Poet, traveller, translator of Montaigne and other writers. Published a book on agriculture, and in 1681 his *Wonders of the Peak*.

Crane, Sir Francis (*c.* 1580–1636) Of Flemish origin he became Director of the tapestry works first established by James I at Mortlake, and under Charles I built up a considerable fortune. MP for Launceston and Penry. He died in Paris.

Cromwell, Thomas, Earl of Essex (1485–1540) Statesman, banker and one of the architects of the Henrician reformation. Executed in 1540.

Cuthbert, Saint (d. 687) A shepherd, who became bishop of Lindisfarne, and spread the influence of the Roman church in the north of England. After his death his corpse was transferred eventually to Durham, where it became the centre of a cult.

Dallam, Thomas (*c.* 1580–1620) An organ builder and member of the Blacksmiths' Company, who built organs for King's College, Cambridge and the cathedrals of Worcester and York.

Dancres or Danckerts, Henry (*c.* 1620–*c.* 1680) Landscape painter, born at The Hague, who painted works for Charles II and Pepys. Eventually had to leave the country as a consequence of being involved in the Popish Plot.

De Critz, John (d. 1642) Sergeant-Painter to Elizabeth, James I, and Charles I. Painted portraits of Elizabeth, Walsingham, Cecil and Sir Philip Sidney.

Denny, Sir Anthony (1501–49) Privy Councillor and intimate of Henry VIII, who gave him extensive grants of land from dissolved monasteries, he was a typical Tudor civil servant. Appointed counsellor to the king's son Edward, he played an important part in the suppression of Kett's rebellion in 1549.

Dole, Wat (actually Dolle) (*fl.* 1670–1690) An engraver much employed by booksellers in engraving portraits and frontispieces.

Donne, John (1573–1631) Ordained in 1615 after a colourful youth. Dean of St Paul's 1621. A famous preacher, his poems were first published in 1632.

Dowsing, William (1596–1679) An enthusiastic destroyer of religious works of art, a foible he was able to indulge to the hilt as Parliamentary Visitor of the churches of Suffolk and Cambridgeshire. He kept a journal in which he enthusiastically recorded his iconoclastic experiences.

Dudley, or Grey, Lady Jane (1537–1554) Claimant to the throne, scholar and humanist. Proclaimed queen 1553; executed 1554.

Dwight, John (*c.* 1650–1710) A potter, who patented a porcelain similar to that produced in China, and established a factory at Fulham. He also specialised in the production of statuettes of contemporary celebrities, and mythological subjects.

Dyck, Sir Anthony van (1599–1641) A dominant figure in the history of Flemish painting, who perfected a style of portraiture which dominated western art for more than a century. It is especially evident in his portraits of the Stuart court, painted during his stay here which lasted from 1632 till his death.

Eadfrith (d. 721) A monk and later Bishop of Lindisfarne, who promoted the cult of St Cuthbert, and initiated the compilation of the Lindisfarne Gospels.

Ethilwald (*c.* 750) Bishop of Lindisfarne. Embellished the Lindisfarne Gospels, and added richly adorned covers.

Evelyn, John (1620–1706) Diarist, virtuoso, traveller; a foundation member of the Royal Society, for the initiation of which he was largely responsible. He wrote extensively on gardening, arboriculture and other matters.

Everelst (actually Verelst) Simon (1644–1721). A painter of flowers and occasional portraits. Born in The Hague, he came to London in 1669, and stayed there for the rest of his life, achieving a good deal of popularity.

Faithorne, William (1619–1691) Engraver, portrait painter and print-seller. His son William (1656–1701) also pursued the same activities.

Fanelli, Francesco (*c.* 1600–1665) Born in Florence he spent most of his working life as a sculptor in England, specialising in small-scale works. He described himself as *Scultore de Re della Gran Bretagna*. He published a number of engravings in 1642.

Fanshawe, Lady (*c.* 1570–1620) Wife of Sir Henry Fanshawe, Remembrancer of the Exchequer, scholar and translator of various works from the Italian. He was a close friend of Henry, Prince of Wales.

Fiennes, Celia (1622–1741) Daughter of Colonel Nathaniel Fiennes, second son of William, Viscount Saye and Sele, a zealous Puritan. Her engaging *Travels* are a prime source of information about life in late seventeenth-century England.

Finch, Sir John (1626–1682) Physician; British Consul at Padua, and Professor of Medecine at Pisa. Ambassador to Florence and then to Constantinople, where he died in the company of his intimate friend Sir Thomas Baines (q.v.). A founder member of the Royal Society.

Gage, Sir John (1479–1556) An important figure in Henrician England, he was successively governor of Calais, vice-chamberlain to the king, a commissioner for the surrender of religious houses, governor of the Tower, comptroller of the household and chancellor of the Duchy of Lancaster. On the accession of Mary he was created Lord Chamberlain, and given the custody of the Princess Elizabeth.

Gerbier, Sir Balthazar (1591–1667) Painter, art dealer, adventurer, diplomat and dabbler in many ventures, some more reputable than others. There is a miniature of Charles I by him in the Victoria and Albert Museum.

Gervase of Canterbury (*c.* 1140–1200) A monk of Christchurch, Canterbury, and a prolific and entertaining historian whose *Gesta Regum* and chronicle of Canterbury were edited in 1879 and 1880 by the redoubtable Bishop Stubbs.

Gibbons, Grinling (1648–1720) Probably the most famous wood-carver in the history of English art. Discovered by Evelyn (q.v.). He did much work for Wren, notably the choir stalls at St Paul's and for the royal family at Windsor, Whitehall and Kensington. A gifted sculptor he was responsible for the statue of Charles II at the Royal Exchange and of James II at Whitehall. He is buried in St Paul's, Covent Garden.

Gibson, Richard (1615–1690) A dwarf, who was miniature painter to Charles I and Henrietta Maria. He married Anne Shepherd, another dwarf, and Lely painted their joint portrait. Waller also commemorated their union in verse.

Giraldus Cambrensis (1146?–1220) Born in Pembroke, the son of a Welsh princess, he had an active ecclesiastical and teaching career at Paris and elsewhere. His extensive, and highly opinionated works, including books on history, topography and an autobiography were edited by J. S. Brewer and J. F. Dimock between 1861 and 1877.

Glanville, Bartholemew de (fl. *c.* 1230–*c.* 1250) An English-born professor of Theology at the University of Paris. He was the author of an early 'scientific' encyclopaedia, *De Proprietatibus rerum*, which was printed by Wynkyn de Worde in 1495.

Godcliff, Hugh (*c.* 1150–*c.* 1220) An architect employed by Abbot John of St Albans in the rebuilding of the abbey church between 1195 and 1214.

Goltzius, Henry (1588–1617) Predominantly an engraver, he became the leading spirit in the Mannerist school which dominated Haarlem in the early seventeenth century. His landscapes are remarkable for their sense of fantasy.

Gower, George (*c.* 1500–1585) Sergeant-Painter to Queen Elizabeth from 1581 till 1596. A fashionable portrait painter, he was a descendant of the Gower family of Stettenham, Yorkshire.

Guiscard, Robert (*c.* 1015–85) A Norman who conquered large sections of Southern Italy, establishing a kingdom there. He defended the papacy against the Greeks, who were trying to assert the primacy of the Byzantine Emperor, and against marauding Saracens. He died on the verge of besieging Constantinople.

Guthfrith (*c.* 830–895). King of the Danish kingdom centred in York, where he died on August 24th 895, and was buried in the Minster. He seems to have been a friend of St Cuthbert.

Hales, Johnson (d. 1679) Portrait painter and miniaturist. A rival of Lely and Cooper, he painted portraits of Pepys, his wife and his father. He had a considerable practice amongst the aristocracy.

Harrison, William (1534–1593) Topographer and chronologist, he was a canon of Windsor. His *Description of England* was printed with Holinshed's (q.v.) *Chronicles* in 1577.

Henry, Prince of Wales (1594–1612) The eldest son of James I, he studied at Oxford, was deeply interested in the arts, an interest which he transferred to his younger brother Charles, and he himself built up a considerable collection of paintings and antiquities.

Heynes, Simon (*c.* 1480–1552) President of Queen's College, Cambridge, 1528; Vice-Chancellor 1553–54; Vicar of Stepney 1534; ambassador to France 1535; Dean of Exeter 1537; envoy to Spain 1538; prebendary of Westminster 1540; assisted in the compilation of the Anglican liturgy.

Higdon, Henry (*c.* 1480–1539) Dean of York, and a great benefactor to Brasenose College, Oxford. He had a large house near York, 'with a goodly garden, and walks of topiary work'.

Hilliard, Nicholas (1537–1619) The most famous miniaturist of the Elizabethan age, he was also a goldsmith, and carver. He was granted the exclusive rights to produce images of James I.

Hobyill, William (fl. *c.* 1530) Canon of York and prebendary of Southcave. He became Archdeacon of Carlisle and Master of the Savoy.

Holinshed, Raphael (*c.* 1510–1580) A historian, who was first employed as a translator. His *Chronicles* which were first published in 1578 were very popular, and were much used by Shakespeare and other writers.

Hooke, Robert (1635–1703) Chemist, architect and astronomer. The first Secretary of the Royal Society, he designed Bethlehem Hospital, Montague House and the College of Physicians. A man of multifarious interests and undeniable gifts, he worked closely with Wren in the rebuilding of the City of London.

Hopton, Sir Arthur (1588–1650) Diplomat and man of affairs, who was secretary to Lord Cottington's embassy to Spain in 1639, and became ambassador in the following year, retaining the post till his death.

Houghton, John (*c.* 1640–1705) A fellow of the Royal Society who wrote about agriculture and related subjects. His popular *A Collection of Letters for the Improvement of Husbandry and Trade* was published in 1689. He first drew attention to the importance of the potato as an agricultural vegetable.

Howard, William, 1st Viscount Stafford (1614–1680) Fifth son of the 2nd Earl of Arundel (q.v.), to whom Peacham dedicated *The Compleat Gentleman*. He was executed on the false charge of being implicated in the Popish Plot.

Ine (d. 726) A West Saxon king, who founded the see of Sherborne in 705, and promulgated a series of laws in 690. He died on a pilgrimage to Rome.

John of Trevisa (1326–1412) Fellow of Exeter and Queen's College, Oxford and vicar of Berkeley, he translated several works including Higden's *Polychronicon* from Latin into English.

Jones, Inigo (1573–1652) The son of a Catholic cloth worker of London, he became a protégé of the third Earl of Pembroke, who recognised his talents as an architect and sent him to Rome to study. He designed scenery and costumes for court masques in collaboration with Ben Jonson, and became Surveyor of Works to Henry, Prince of Wales between 1610 and 1612. Amongst his many architectural works of importance are the Queen's House, Greenwich, the Banqueting House, Whitehall, Wilton and the piazza of Covent Garden.

Jonson, Ben (1572–1637) Poet and dramatist, he produced a number of brilliant masques for the court of James I, though he was not patronised by his successor. He was also an astute critic, and anticipated in his verse the kind of classicism which was developed by Dryden and Cowley.

Kempe, Margery (*c.* 1373–*c.* 1440) Daughter of the mayor of King's Lynn, and married to a wealthy burgher of the town, Margery Kempe had fourteen children, but she abandoned her family in middle age to undertake a pilgrimage to the Holy Land. Towards the end of her life she dictated her autobiography to a priest. (*The Book of Margery Kempe*, ed. S. B. Meech and C. H. Allen, Early English Text Society, 1940). It is one of the most remarkable documents of the English Middle Ages.

Kirke, Mistress (*c.* 1600–1660) One of Henrietta Maria's dressers, and the wife of George Kirke, Gentleman of the Robes to Charles I, and Keeper of the Palace at Whitehall to Charles II.

Knipe, Thomas (1638–1711) Writer and scholar, who became the headmaster of Westminster School.

Knollys, Lady (*c.* 1520–1600) The wife of Sir Francis Knollys the Puritan-inclined statesman and civil servant who was put in charge of Mary, Queen of Scots, 1568–69.

Lanfranc (1005–1089) Born at Pavia where he learnt Greek and became a monk. In 1070 he became Archbishop of Canterbury and, as one of the architects of the Norman conquest, reorganised the English church. He started the rebuilding of Canterbury cathedral, and wrote many works, which were first published in 1648.

Lanier, Nicholas (1588–1666) Musician and art dealer, who played an important part in the creation of the collection of Charles I, especially in relation to the Mantua purchase. He became Master of the King's Musick in 1625. He was largely responsible for introducing recitative into English opera.

Layton, Richard (c. 1480–1544) One of Henry VIII's chief agents in the suppression of the monasteries. Chaplain to the King; Clerk of the Privy Council. In 1539 he became Dean of York, and in 1543 was sent on an embassy to Brussels.

Lely, Sir Peter (1618–1680) Born in Holland, he spent his working life in London, where he built up a large and lucrative practice as a portrait-painter during the Commonwealth and under Charles II. He painted a portrait of Pepys, which is now in the National Maritime Museum.

Lilly, Edmond (d. 1716). A portrait painter, who specialised in works of enormous dimensions.

Long, Sir James Arthur (1617–1692) 2nd Baronet; served with distinction in the Civil War.

Loten/Looten, Jan (1618–1681) A landscape painter, born in Amsterdam, who came to England early in the reign of Charles II, and became very successful here.

Lydgate, John (1370?–1451?) Describing himself as Chaucer's pupil, he was a priest who celebrated civic ceremonies in verse for the City of London, and between 1412 and 1420 wrote *The Troy Book* for Henry, Prince of Wales (later Henry V). He was patronised by Humphrey, Duke of Gloucester.

Magnus, Thomas (d. 1559) Leaving York Minster for the service of Henry VIII, he became involved in diplomacy, and was present at the Field of the Cloth of Gold. He became a canon of Windsor, and Paymaster for the King's Forces in the North. For the last thirty years of his life he was Custodian of St Leonard's Hospital, York.

Manchester, 2nd Earl of (1602–71) Edward Montagu, who succeeded to his father's title in 1642, was one of the leading generals on the Parliamentary side in the Civil War, until, largely because of his incompetence at the Battle of Newbury, he was supplanted by Cromwell. He opposed the King's trial, and retired from public life during the Commonwealth. Restored to public favour at the Restoration, he became Chancellor of the University of Cambridge (from 1649 to 1651) and Lord Chamberlain.

Mansart/Mansard There were two architects of this name. François (1598–66) who introduced into France a simplified version of the baroque, exemplified for instance in the Château de Blois. He died a few months after Wren's arrival in Paris, and it is likely that the reference is to his great-nephew Jules Hardouin Mansart (1645–1708) who became chief architect to Louis XIV, and was largely responsible for the design of Versailles and the Grand Trianon.

Mercer, Mary (1647–1673) Companion to Mrs Pepys.

Morrison, Sir Charles (1587–1628) Became a Baronet and Knight of the Bath in 1611, probably as a result of the wealth he acquired by marrying Mary, heiress of Sir Baptist Hicks, 1st Viscount Campden, through whom he also acquired the Cassiobury estates.

Moxon, Joseph (1627–1700) Mathematician, astronomer and hydrographer, who also wrote about architecture and typography.

Nabbes, Thomas (*c.* 1591–*c.* 1638) A dramatist, who specialised in satirising the middle classes. His works were published in two volumes by A. H. Bullen in 1887.

Newcastle, Duke of (1592–1676) William Cavendish, first Duke of Newcastle, was an ardent royalist who spent some £1,000,000 on the cause. Previously governor of Charles, Prince of Wales (later Charles II), he was forced into exile in considerable poverty after his active part in the conflict, and was not fully reimbursed at the Restoration, despite the Dukedom conferred on him in 1665. A patron of Ben Jonson and Dryden he wrote plays and poetry as well as a book on horsemanship.

Neville, John de, 5th Baron Neville of Raby (d. 1388). A renowned soldier and sailor, who fought in France and Scotland. An enthusiastic builder, he was mainly responsible for Raby Castle, and founded a chantry in the Charterhouse at Coventry.

Norgate, Edward (d. 1650) An illuminator and herald-painter. In 1616 he became Blue-mantle Pursuivant, and was also employed in buying paintings for Charles I. He wrote *The Art of Limning c.* 1648.

Northumberland, 9th Earl of; Sir Henry Percy (1564–1632)
Served in numerous campaigns, and though a Protestant, was dissatisfied
by James I's treatment of Catholics, as a consequence of which he spent
some time in the Tower. He was known as 'The Wizard Earl' because
of his interests in science.

Nys, Daniel (*c.* 1580–*c.* 1650) An art dealer of dubious
reputation, who was involved in practically every important art sale of
the first half of the century. French by birth, he settled in Venice and
acquired the reputation of purloining the choicest items from the
collections which he sold to others. He eventually bankrupted himself
by overselling to Charles I, but re-established himself by selling, at an
inflated price, a great collection of gems and intaglios to Thomas
Howard, Earl of Arundel.

Olivier, Isaac (1556?–1617) A miniature painter of French
extraction, who was the pupil of Nicholas Hilliard (q.v.). Amongst his
better-known works are portraits of Sir Philip Sidney, James I, and the
family of Kenelm Digby.

Oxford, first Earl of (1661–1724) Robert Harley, first Earl of
Oxford. An unscrupulous and basically unsuccessful politician, he was
involved in the South Sea Bubble and intrigues with the Jacobites.
Responsible for developing the west end of London, he collected an
impressive library, and was on intimate terms with many literary figures
including Pope and Swift.

Palmer, Sir James (*c.* 1580–1657) Chancellor of the Order of
the Garter, and a close friend of Charles I for whom he undertook a
wide variety of missions.

Paul, Abbot of St Albans (*c.* 1030–1093) Reputed to be the son
of Lanfranc, he was appointed Abbot in 1077 and started the building of
the abbey, very much as it exists today. He despised the Anglo-Saxon
members of his community, and destroyed the tombs of his
predecessors.

Peacham, Thomas (1576–1643?) Artist, schoolteacher and
writer, he was also a composer and an expert on heraldry – in fact a
complete Renaissance man. In 1606 he published *Graphice*, a practical
treatise on art, which, under its amended title of *The Gentleman's
Exercise*, went through several editions. He became tutor to the sons of
Thomas Howard, Earl of Arundel (q.v.) and dedicated to them his most
successful publication *The Compleat Gentleman*, the first edition of which
came out in 1621, the last in 1666.

Pinkny, George (*c.* 1620–1681) A friend of Pepys and Warden of the Parish Clerks' Company. Warden also of the Goldsmiths' Company, he founded a banking firm which later became Barclays.

Petty, William (*c.* 1586–1654) Born in Soulby, Northumberland, where he became interested in antiquities through contact with Lord William Howard of Naworth. Graduating at Cambridge, he became a schoolmaster for a while, and then tutor to Howard of Arundel's son, but soon went on to become an art agent for the Earl, collecting pictures and antiquities from all over Europe and Asia Minor. The real creator of the Arundel collection, his energy was boundless, his archaeological discoveries remarkable.

Porter, Endymion (1587–1649) Educated in Spain, most of his life was deeply involved in political and diplomatic matters. He was a patron of several poets, and was one of the agents used by Charles I in amassing his collection of paintings.

Povey, Thomas (1615–1702) A colleague of Samuel Pepys and John Evelyn. Sat in the Long Parliament and was much favoured at court after the Restoration.

Pratt, Sir Roger (1620–1684) Belonging to a landed family of Norfolk, he graduated at Magdalen College, Oxford and then travelled in Italy. On his return he worked with Inigo Jones, and though retaining something of his amateur status became virtually a professional architect. He played an important part in rebuilding the city of London after the fire of 1666, and was knighted two years later. His *Notebooks* were edited by R. T. Gunther in 1928 (Oxford University Press).

Pultney, John de (*c.* 1285–1349) Mayor of London 1331, 1332, 1334 and 1337. A member of the Drapers' Company he lent large sums to Edward III.

Radcliffe, Sir George (1593–1657) Politician and lawyer, he was an enthusiastic supporter of the Royalist cause, and was adviser to the Duke of York.

Raleigh, Carew (1605–1666) The only son of Sir Walter, he was MP for Haslemere from 1648 till 1653, and in 1659. A year later he became Governor of Jersey.

Reginald of Durham (*c.* 1100–1173) A monk of Durham and an industrious hagiographer, who wrote lives of St Cuthbert, St Godric and St Ebba.

Reresby, Sir John (1634–1689) Baronet of Thybergh Hall in the West Riding. During the Commonwealth, like Evelyn, he travelled abroad, and his *Travels and Memoirs* were first published in 1675.

Richmond, Duke of; James Stuart (1612–1655) Fourth Duke of Lennox, created Duke of Richmond in 1641. He was a staunch supporter of Charles I.

Riley, John (1646–1691) A portrait painter, who was a pupil of Gerard Soest, and did many portraits of the royal family, becoming portrait-painter to William and Mary.

Riley, H. T. (1816–1878) Translator and antiquary. One of the first members of the Historical Manuscripts' Commission.

Ripa, Cesare (*c.* 1580–1620) Italian philosopher and antiquary.

Robert of Normandy (mid-thirteenth century) An English scribe commissioned by the Archbishop of Orleans to transcribe the commentary of Pope Innocent on the Decretals in 1260.

Roe, Sir Thomas (1581–1644) After Magdalen College, Oxford he entered the Queen's service, and was knighted in 1605. Sent by Prince Henry to discover gold in the West Indies, and became an MP in 1614. From 1615–18 he led a successful embassy to the court of Jehangir, Emperor of Hindustan, and other diplomatic missions. In 1640 he became MP for the University of Oxford. He left voluminous dispatches and diplomatic memoirs, containing much material about the purchase and shipping of works of art.

Roger, Bishop of Winchester (*c.* 1120–1174) Son of Robert, Earl of Gloucester, he followed Thomas à Becket into exile, and after the latter's death was sent to intercede for Henry II with the Pope.

Rubens, Sir Peter Paul (1577–1640) Painter, diplomat and art dealer, he was both prolific and versatile. Working in his native Flanders, he travelled extensively, and was patronised and befriended by most of the royal families of Europe. In 1629 he came to England to arrange a treaty between Charles I and Philip IV of Spain, and was commissioned by the king, to paint *War and Peace, St George*, designs for the Banqueting Hall in Whitehall, and portraits of the king and queen. He was knighted, and involved in various art dealing activities both with the king and various members of the court.

Rupert, Prince (1619–1682) Third son of Elizabeth, Queen of

Bohemia and daughter of James I. He played an important part in the Civil War, and was an accomplished soldier and sailor. Interested in science, he was a considerable artist, who was at least partly responsible for the introduction of mezzotint into England. Examples of his work are to be found in the British Museum and elsewhere. He also invented an alloy of brass, much used for door furniture in the eighteenth century.

Salisbury, Robert Cecil, 1st Earl of (1563–1612) Politician, diplomat and builder of Hatfield House. He was mainly responsible for engineering the trouble-free accession of James I.

Scrope, Lord John of Massingham (15th century) One of the Scropes of Bolton and a patron of York Minster. On his death many of his belongings were bought by John Barningham, treasurer of the Minster.

Smith, William (*c*. 1600–1665) An English painter living in Rome, who became attached to the circle of the Earl of Arundel, purchased many things for him, and accompanied him on his journeys.

St Albans, 1st Earl of; Henry Jermyn, (*c*. 1630–1684) Courtier, diplomat and politician he was an enlightened architectural patron, who planned St James's Square, and gave his name to Jermyn Street. A patron of Cowley he was ambassador to Paris in 1667.

'Stannop' Stanhope, Lady (*c*. 1600–1670) Wife of Philip, 1st Earl of Chesterfield, an ardent royalist who surrendered at Lichfield.

St Barbe, Sir John (1655–1723) Made a baronet at the age of eight, he married Alice, daughter of Celia Fiennes' (q.v.) uncle, John. He was largely responsible for building Broadlands in Hampshire, later the home of Palmerston and the Mountbattens.

Stone, Nicholas (1586–1647) Mason, sculptor and architect. He started his career in Amsterdam under Peter de Kayser, and was extensively employed by James I. Famous for his sepulchres, his major architectural works include the porch of the church of St Mary the Virgin at Oxford, and the gateway to the Botanical Gardens in the same university.

Streeter (Streater) Roberty (1624–1680)A mainly decorative painter, greatly extolled by Pepys and Evelyn. He was made Sergeant-Painter to Charles II in 1661.

Strype, John (1643–1737) Historian and biographer, who wrote extensively about the Elizabethans, His complete works were published in 19 volumes, and he had a great collection of manuscripts, some more than dubiously acquired.

Theodore of Tarsus (602–690) Of Greek birth he became a monk at Rome where he was consecrated Archbishop of Canterbury in 668. On arriving in England he reorganised church government. He was a considerable scholar and author.

Tillotson, John (1630–1694) He became Archbishop of Canterbury in 1691, and was a redoubtable preacher as well as a copious author.

Tooker, John (1601–1667) An excise officer who was a colleague of Pepys.

Toto, Anthony/Toto del Nunziato (*c.* 1480–*c.* 1550) He accompanied Pietro Torrigiano to England and worked for Henry VIII as an architect and a painter. According to Vasari, he had been a pupil of Ghirlandaio. In 1540 he was granted a licence to export 600 tuns of beer to Flushing, and in 1542 was granted a salary of £10 a year as Sergeant-Painter.

Ulfer/Wulfhere (d. 765) King of Mercia. He became a Christian and spread the creed wherever his dominion spread.

Vertue, George (1684–1756) A prolific engraver of portraits and subjects of antiquarian interest, he may be regarded as the father of English art history. In the course of his life he accumulated a vast amount of material about the history of art in England, disseminated rather haphazardly through a large number of notebooks. These were acquired by Horace Walpole who used them as the basis of his *Anecdotes of Painting in England* (1762–71). The original Notebooks have been published in their entirety by the Walpole Society between 1929 and 1952.

Walles, Steven (mid-sixteenth century) A successful joiner and Burgess of Cambridge, who was commissioned to do the woodwork in the new chapel at Trinity College.

Walter of Chichester A Benedictine monk, painter and sculptor who was employed on the decorative work at St Albans.

Walter (and William) of Colchester (*c.* 1180–1230) Two

brothers and monks at the abbey of St Albans who were involved in the sculpture and painting there during the time of Abbot John (1195–1214).

Walton, Izaak (1593–1683) An ironmonger in London, and one of the most delightful of English writers. Author of *The Compleat Angler*, his life of Donne was first published in 1648.

Webb, John (1611–1672) Architect who was a pupil of Inigo Jones (q.v.) and supervised the building of Greenwich Palace. He also edited Jones' strange tract about Stonehenge.

Werburgh, Saint (d. 700) Daughter of Ulfer (q.v.) King of Mercia. She became Abbess of Ely, and on the advent of the Danes her remains were moved to Chester, where they became the centre of a cult.

Whaley, Edward (*c.* 1600–1675) A woollen draper, who became a Major-General in Cromwell's army, and custodian of Charles I at Hampton Court. A regicide, he escaped to New England, and was still alive there in 1674.

Wilfrid, Saint (634–709) A monk who became bishop of York, and was involved in constant travels and quarrels with other ecclesiastics. He taught the Saxons to fish, according to one questionable legend. He was an active builder.

William of Malmesbury (d. 1143) A Benedictine monk, who was educated at Malmesbury, but spent most of his life at Glastonbury. Historian and chronicler, his main works were the *Gesta Regum Anglorum* and the *Gesta Pontificum Anglorum* both written in the 1120s, and a history of the abbey of Glastonbury which he finished in 1139.

William of Sens, (*fl.* 1180–1230) 'A man of great abilities and a most ingenious workman in wood and stone', according to the chronicler of Canterbury cathedral, he was summoned there from his native city, where he had been involved in the building of the cathedral, to create a new choir, to replace the one which had been burnt down in 1174. In doing so, he introduced into England the new style of architecture which had already appeared in the Ile de France. As a result of falling off a scaffolding, however, he was forced to return to France before the completion of the work, which was completed by an Englishman.

Willis, Dr Thomas (1621–1675) A physician who made important discoveries about the nature of diabetes.

Winwood, Agnes (*c.* 1570–1620) Wife of the diplomat and Secretary of State, Sir Ralph Winwood (1563–1617) a close friend of James I.

Wither, John (*c.* 1470–1534) Prebendary of Knaresborough and Canon of York.

Wolsey, Thomas, Cardinal (*c.* 1475–1530) Statesman and politician, who achieved great power under Henry VIII, accumulated great wealth, and came to sudden ruin. A patron of the arts and a lavish builder, his main monuments are Hampton Court and Christ Church, Oxford.

Woolridge/Worlidge, John (*c.* 1651–1698) An agricultural writer, whose *Systema Agriculturae* was published in 1669.

Worde, Wynkyn de (d. 1534) Printer and stationer, who was born in Alsace, moved to England and became an apprentice to William Caxton, who had introduced the process of printing into his London workshop. De Worde himself printed a large number of books, the most famous of which was the *Morte d'Arthur* of 1498.

Wotton, Sir Henry (1568–1639) Poet, writer, diplomat and scholar. He was English Ambassador to Venice from 1604–12, 1616–19 and 1621–24. In addition to his dispatches and letters, some of which describe his activities as a purveyor of paintings and other works of art to English patrons, he wrote, amongst other things, the very successful *Elements of Architecture*, 1634.

Wren, Sir Christopher (1632–1723) Architect, astronomer, mathematician, who was also interested in medical and scientific subjects generally. Prolific and remarkably inventive, he transformed English architecture.

Wykeham, William of (1324–1404) Bishop of Winchester, founder of New College, Oxford. King's chaplain and Surveyor of the Royal Castles, he was a superb administrator whose architectural undertakings were based on first-hand experience, and whose patronage of the arts stemmed from a passionate interest in them.

Index

Index